# Educational Equity in a Global Context

**ALSO AVAILABLE FROM BLOOMSBURY**

*Civic Contestation in Global Education*, edited by Meira Levinson, Ellis Reid, Sara O'Brien, and Tatiana Geron

*Pedagogy of Hope for Global Social Justice: Sustainable Futures for People and the Planet*, edited by Douglas Bourn and Massimiliano Tarozzi

*Comparative and International Education*, David Phillips and Michele Schweisfurth

*Education and International Development*, edited by Tristan McCowan and Elaine Unterhalter

*Peace Education*, edited by Maria Hantzopoulos and Monisha Bajaj

*Schooling for Social Change*, Monisha Bajaj

*Transnational Perspectives on Democracy, Citizenship, Human Rights and Peace Education*, edited by Mary Drinkwater, Fazal Rizvi, and Karen Edge

# Educational Equity in a Global Context

## Cases and Conversations in Educational Ethics

Edited by
Meira Levinson, Tatiana Geron, Sara O'Brien, and Ellis Reid

BLOOMSBURY ACADEMIC
LONDON • NEW YORK • OXFORD • NEW DELHI • SYDNEY

BLOOMSBURY ACADEMIC
Bloomsbury Publishing Plc
50 Bedford Square, London, WC1B 3DP, UK
1385 Broadway, New York, NY 10018, USA
29 Earlsfort Terrace, Dublin 2, Ireland

BLOOMSBURY, BLOOMSBURY ACADEMIC and the Diana logo are trademarks of Bloomsbury Publishing Plc

First published in Great Britain 2025

Copyright © Meira Levinson, Tatiana Geron, Sara O'Brien and Ellis Reid, 2025

Meira Levinson, Tatiana Geron, Sara O'Brien and Ellis Reid have asserted their right under the Copyright, Designs and Patents Act, 1988, to be identified as Editors of this work.

For legal purposes the Acknowledgments on p. xii constitute an extension of this copyright page.

Cover design by Grace Ridge
Cover image © Witthaya Prasongsin / Getty Images

All rights reserved. No part of this publication may be reproduced or transmitted in any form or by any means, electronic or mechanical, including photocopying, recording, or any information storage or retrieval system, without prior permission in writing from the publishers.

Bloomsbury Publishing Plc does not have any control over, or responsibility for, any third-party websites referred to or in this book. All internet addresses given in this book were correct at the time of going to press. The author and publisher regret any inconvenience caused if addresses have changed or sites have ceased to exist, but can accept no responsibility for any such changes.

A catalogue record for this book is available from the British Library.

A catalog record for this book is available from the Library of Congress.

Library of Congress Control Number: 2024943555

| ISBN: | HB: | 978-1-3503-9961-7 |
| | PB: | 978-1-3503-9960-0 |
| | ePDF: | 978-1-3503-9962-4 |
| | eBook: | 978-1-3503-9963-1 |

Typeset by Integra Software Services Pvt. Ltd.
Printed and bound in Great Britain

To find out more about our authors and books visit www.bloomsbury.com and sign up for our newsletters.

# Contents

*List of Figure* viii
*List of Contributors* ix
*Acknowledgments* xii

1  **Introduction: Conceptions of Equity in a Global Context**  1
   Author: Tatiana Geron, Meira Levinson, Ellis Reid, and Sara O'Brien

2  **Basic Education for All: The Politics of Implementing 100 Percent Transition from Primary School to Secondary School in Kenya**  13
   Case author: Wambura Kimunyu
   Conversation facilitator: Ellis Reid
   Conversation participants: Pierre Germain Belinga, Robert Jenkins, Asyia Kazmi, Isaac Nyangolo

3  **Private Equity: Are Governments Responsible for Private Schools in Times of Crisis?**  35
   Case author: Juan Espíndola, Sara O'Brien, and Leonel Pérez Expósito
   Conversation facilitator: Liz Block
   Conversation participants: María de Ibarrola, Sebastián Plá, Blanca Heredia, Irma Villalpando

4  **A Qualified Disaster: Allocating Student Grades during Covid-19**  57
   Case author: Hester Burn
   Conversation facilitator: Hester Burn
   Conversation participants: Diana Beech, Josiah Isles, Tom Richmond, Dylan Wiliam

## 5  Remaking the Grade: A District's Quest for Equitable Homework Policy   79
Case author: Janine Bempechat and Sara O'Brien
Conversation facilitator: Janine Bempechat and Sara O'Brien
Conversation participants: Colin Rose, Amanda Churchill Jimerson, Karen L. Mapp, Natasha Warikoo

## 6  Caught in the Web: Educational Risks and Rewards of Online Learning   103
Case author: Douglas Yacek
Conversation facilitator: Douglas Yacek
Conversation participants: Nicholas C. Burbules, Johannes Giesinger, Drew Chambers, Eva Simon

## 7  Remote Control: Blurred Boundaries in the Zoom Classroom   123
Case author: Alysha Banerji and Winston Thompson
Conversation facilitator: Alysha Banerji and Winston Thompson
Conversation participants: William Kuehnle, Benjamin G.S. Paxton, Alexander G-J Pittman, Laura Oxley, Ivelisse Ramos Brannon

## 8  School Choice in Hong Kong: Peking Ducks or Rich Expats?   143
Case author: Liz Jackson
Conversation facilitator: Liz Jackson
Conversation participants: Chi-Ming Lam, Eric W. Layman, Jan Gube, Emma E. Buchtel

## 9  A Uniform Decision: Commemoration and Community in Public School   163
Case author: Daniella J. Forster, Samuel Douglas, and Scott Imig
Conversation facilitator: Daniella J. Forster
Conversation participants: Maura Sellars, Heather Sharp, Maryam Popal Zahid, Matthew Bradley

**10 Conclusion: Structuring Equitable Discussion** 185
Author: Sara O'Brien, Meira Levinson, Tatiana Geron, and Ellis Reid

*Appendix* 199
*Index* 203

# Figure

1   Glenn Singleton's Courageous Conversations Compass   190

# Contributors

**Alysha Banerji** is a PhD student in Education at Harvard University, USA. Her research examines the role of post-secondary institutions in refugee resettlement and support. She is currently a Senior Ethics Pedagogy Fellow at the Edmond and Lily Safra Center for Ethics at Harvard University and has previously served on the Editorial Board of the Harvard Educational Review.

**Janine Bempechat** is a developmental psychologist with a deep interest in the socialization of achievement. As a Clinical Professor at Boston University, USA, she studies family, cultural, and school influences in the development of student motivation and academic achievement in low-income children and youth, both nationally and internationally.

**Hester Burn** is a PhD candidate in Economics at the Institute for Social and Economic Research, University of Essex, UK. Her research focuses on evaluations of education policy in England and Wales. Prior to her doctoral studies, she taught in UK state schools for five years.

**Samuel Douglas** (PhD) is a casual academic at the University of Newcastle, Australia. He has over fifteen years of teaching and research experience across a range of philosophical areas, particularly philosophy of language and professional ethics. Outside of academia, he works as a specialist advisor in the emerging areas of psychedelic ethics and education.

**Juan Espindola** is Associate Professor at the Institute for Philosophical Research at the National Autonomous University of Mexico. He was trained as a political theorist at the University of Michigan. His research focuses on transitional justice, education, and artificial intelligence.

**Leonel Pérez Expósito** is Professor of Sociology and Education at the Universidad Autónoma Metropolitana Unidad Xochimilco, Mexico. His research focuses on civic and political education, educational assessment, and equity in education.

**Daniella J. Forster** (PhD) is an educational ethicist with expertise in codes of conduct and ethics and a background in philosophy. Her research interests include school moral culture, moral development, and teacher professional identity, and she has published on controversial issues of policy use in schools, the use of codes of conduct and normative case studies in teacher education, and other ethical dimensions of schooling. She taught secondary school philosophy and English prior to becoming an educational researcher and teacher educator.

**Tatiana Geron** is the Design Studio Research & Evaluation Postdoctoral Fellow at the Edmond & Lily Safra Center for Ethics, Harvard University. Tatiana holds a PhD in Education from Harvard University, USA, and studies the ethical complexity of teacher decision-making and how teachers interpret their core values in relation to unjust social contexts. She has taught educational policy and philosophy at Colby College. Prior to entering academia, Tatiana taught middle school English Language Arts in Boston and Brooklyn.

**Scott Imig** is an Associate Professor of Education at the University of Newcastle, Australia, where he directs the leadership program in education. He has spent much of his university career studying the qualities of effective and engaging classrooms. His current research focuses on understanding and helping school communities support the integration of families with refugee and asylum-seeker backgrounds.

**Liz Jackson** is Professor of Education at the University of Hong Kong. She is also a Fellow and the Immediate Past President of the Philosophy of Education Society of Australasia and Former Director of the Comparative Education Research Centre at the University of Hong Kong. Her most recent books include *Beyond Virtue: The Politics of Educating Emotions*, *Contesting Education and Identity in Hong Kong*, and *Questioning Allegiance: Resituating Civic Education*.

**Wambura Kimunyu** is the CEO of Eneza Education, an Edtech company that provides hardware-agnostic, low-tech first, digital education curricula to K-12 students in Africa.

**Meira Levinson** is the Juliana W. and William Foss Thompson Professor of Education and Society at Harvard University, USA. She has written, co-authored, and co-edited seven books, including *Dilemmas of Educational Ethics*, *Democratic Discord in Schools*, and *No Citizen Left Behind*, and is currently working to start a field of educational ethics.

**Sara O'Brien** is the Director of Curriculum and Pedagogy for the EdEthics initiative, which is housed at the Harvard Graduate School of Education, USA, and the Edmond & Lily Safra Center for Ethics. In this role, she creates pedagogical tools that help educators, school and district leaders, and policymakers think through challenging ethical questions in education. Prior to her work with EdEthics, Sara taught in public and independent secondary schools in Massachusetts and California.

**Ellis Reid** holds a PhD in Education from Harvard University, USA, and is currently an Associate Program Officer at The Spencer Foundation. His primary areas of scholarship lie in democratic theory, practical ethics, and education policy. In particular, his work focuses on the normative dimensions of school governance. Ellis has served as an Ethics Pedagogy Fellow at the Edmond and Lily Safra Center for Ethics and as the Co-Chair for the Editorial Board of the Harvard Educational Review. Before coming to Harvard, Ellis was the Associate Director for Next Generation Scholars, a college-access program in Northern California.

**Winston C. Thompson** is Associate Professor of Educational Studies and Philosophy at The Ohio State University, USA. His scholarship explores ethical/political dimensions of educational policy and practice. His work on race, justice, and the role of education in a pluralistic, democratic society has appeared in internationally published journals and books.

**Douglas W. Yacek** (PhD) is a research fellow in educational foundations at the TU Dortmund University, Germany. His research interests include educational ethics, moral and democratic education, and the history of educational thought. His most recent book is entitled *The Transformative Classroom: Philosophical Foundations and Practical Applications* (2021).

# Acknowledgments

This volume was made possible by the work of numerous authors, contributors, and supporting individuals and organizations. We'd like to begin by thanking Jacob Fay for his invaluable insight in helping to develop the NCS method, co-leading the Harvard Radcliffe workshop "Ethical Dilemmas of Educating during the COVID Crisis: An International Workshop on Normative Case Study Development," and conceiving of this resulting case collection. We are likewise grateful to the Harvard Radcliffe Institute for their financial and operational support for the workshop, especially Amy Montilli, Maura Madden, and Sean O'Donnell. We'd also like to thank Alysha Banerji and MG Prezioso, who served as Writing Fellows for the workshop and whose knowledge, encouragement, and editing skill improved the cases in this volume immensely.

We are grateful to have found a home for these two international case collections at Bloomsbury Publishing, and would like to thank Michael Hand for his support, as well as Mark Richardson and Elissa Burns for their editorial knowledge. We are also grateful to Maricruz Vargas Ramirez for her masterful translations and Katherine Lee for her editing work. Russ Cox contributed conversation transcripts at record speed, for which we are immensely grateful! Liz Block also provided countless acts of administrative and moral support across this and the host of EdEthics projects.

The global EdEthics community has been a motivating force, a sounding board, and an enthusiastic cheerleading squad throughout the writing and publication process. We are especially grateful to participants at the 2023 Educational Ethics Field-Launching Conference in Cambridge, Massachusetts, and the 2022 Association for Moral Education conference in Manchester, UK, for piloting discussion of these cases prior to publication. Many of these cases were also field tested by regular participants in our monthly NCS discussion workshops, as well as students in Jacob Fay's Educational Justice course at Harvard University. Finally, we wish to extend our gratitude once again to the discussion participants who brought their perspectives and insight to the case conversations in this volume. Thank you for helping tease out the many ethical dimensions of these equity dilemmas in education—readers have a much richer understanding of them thanks to you.

# 1

# Introduction: Conceptions of Equity in a Global Context

*Tatiana Geron, Meira Levinson,
Ellis Reid, and Sara O'Brien*

---

Across the globe, "educational equity" has captured the attention of teachers, scholars, policymakers, and families. Equity is a driving value behind a host of education policy initiatives and urgent conversations all over the world: college access and supporting students with disabilities in the United States; gender and caste parity in elementary education access in India; grading and test performance in Germany; infrastructure improvement for rural, migrant, and indigenous students in Mexico; school funding in Australia; and equal preschool access and primary school readiness for girls and boys in South Africa, among many other issues.[1] Yet even as educational equity has emerged as a shared global value, it has also been recognized as a shared global struggle. Debates about how to define, measure, and achieve educational equity in policy and practice are hashed out behind the scenes by policymakers, in full public view by the media, and around seminar and dinner tables in classrooms and homes worldwide.

These debates raise hard normative questions about the meaning of educational equity broadly, in addition to more specific questions about what it means to realize equity within particular contexts. As part of a larger effort to help citizens across borders reason with one another about the meaning and implications of educational equity, this volume presents eight pairs of normative case studies and normative case study discussions centered on dilemmas of educational equity across seven different countries.

By elevating the variation of equity dilemmas in all their complexity across borders, and inviting in nearly forty educators, philosophers, students, policymakers, scholars, and other people with diverse forms of expertise to share their wisdom and struggles in collective conversation about the cases, we hope to strengthen discussions of educational equity within and across contexts.

# Normative Case Studies and Conceptualizing Educational Equity

Defining educational equity is a fraught endeavor. Educational equity is a term "all too replete with meaning," containing multiple understandings of access, opportunity, and justice.[2] This ability to take many different forms and definitions can be challenging for actors trying to make educational equity a reality in their communities: if educational equity can mean everything, it can easily come to mean nothing. Clarifying what we mean when we talk about "equity"—even if we disagree—can help facilitate better discussion, goal-setting, and policy.

As Levinson, Geron, and Brighouse (2023) explain, the term "educational equity" has a number of different popular usages. It can be used to mean:

- *equality of outcomes* (as when policies focus on achieving equal graduation rates in rural, suburban, and urban districts)
- *equality of resources* (as when all students in a district receive the same amount of per-pupil funding)
- *equality of opportunity* (as when refugee and native-born students are offered the same opportunities for school involvement)
- *equality of access* (e.g., students across a multicultural city have the same access to quality schooling regardless of differences between their home language and the school language of instruction)
- *benefiting the less advantaged* (e.g., sending school-issued laptops home with students who do not have a computer at home)
- *providing an adequate* education (e.g., ensuring literacy and basic numeracy, even in a very crowded school environment)
- *liberation* (e.g., fully reimagining contemporary schooling and usually other sociopolitical structures in order to ensure educational justice).

These conceptions of equity assume different ideas about what young people deserve and have very different implications for specific questions of educational policy and practice. Indeed, when we get precise about the different working conceptions of equity, we can see that some conceptions don't even directly relate to *equality* at all. Benefiting the less advantaged, for instance, insists that some young people deserve *more* resources precisely because they are at a disadvantage compared to others. Providing an adequate education, on the other hand, has nothing to say about inequalities above a certain threshold of educational provision. Different disagreements over how equity is *conceptualized*, therefore, often lead to larger dilemmas about what equity *demands*.

Contestation over the meaning of educational equity is not a problem per se, as long as educational stakeholders are clear with themselves and others about what they mean when they use the term. However, the multitude of definitions creates problems when we assume that those with whom we are discussing "equity" have the same beliefs and working definitions that we do. When we use the term to assume a shared value or gloss over the complexities and difficulties of putting educational equity into practice in very different contexts, we often end up talking past one another or creating conflict rather than finding solutions to shared problems.

Normative case study discussions are one venue for articulating and clarifying what we mean when we talk about equity in education. Normative case studies (NCS) are *"richly described, realistic accounts of complex ethical dilemmas that arise within practice or policy contexts, in which protagonists must decide among courses of action, none of which is self-evident as the right one to take."*[3] Written to make the specific realities of complex theoretical problems and concepts visible (and vice versa), NCS provide tangible real-world examples of the many ways issues of "equity" can manifest. They are designed to spark dialogue and discussion, to have more than one avenue for resolution, and to draw connections between values and practices, creating room for nuanced thinking and even disagreement. The philosophy behind the NCS method is that ethical dilemmas are complex and context-sensitive, and that addressing them requires collaborative, grounded praxis rather than simply a top-down application of principles derived from abstract, decontextualized theorizing. Normative case study discussions (described in detail in the conclusion to this book) focus as much on supporting participants in thinking through the values, assumptions, and concepts present in the dilemma and its potential resolutions as on helping participants make a final ethical choice. In this process, discussion participants can develop new conceptual and practical understandings about the values that matter to them.[4]

Equity represents one important recurring theme, showing up in different ways in different cases. We invite readers to consider what conceptions of equity are arising in the background of these cases and conversations, and how those conceptions are shaped by the contexts—regional, national, and local—in which they occur. For those reading the collection as a whole, we invite you to consider how the different conceptions of equity in these cases and conversations relate to one another, and create a global mosaic of a complex value.

# Cases and Conversations: Equity in Many Forms

The eight normative case studies and conversations presented in this book explore dilemmas of educational equity in-depth across seven different countries. Together, they offer a global picture of equity challenges in their many forms. The perspectives developed through the cases and accompanying conversations also demonstrate that there are many different potential compelling ways to understand educational equity, and that discussing these varying perspectives in light of specific, tangible issues can help move us forward in the global goal of providing all young people the education they deserve.

This common focus arose out of a workshop on international normative case study development that we led (along with Jacob Fay, Alysha Banerji, and MG Prezioso) at the Harvard Radcliffe Institute in 2021. The past several years have seen an explosion of global interest in the NCS approach, as educators around the world have been downloading, discussing, and teaching cases from our website justiceinschools.org and prior case books. However, until 2021, the vast majority of case development had taken place in and about educational institutions in the United States. This workshop aimed to broaden the NCS scope by supporting international scholars to explore and write cases about ethical educational dilemmas that are grounded in and relevant to their own contexts. The fifteen scholars who participated in the workshop each partnered with a mentor from the EdEthics initiative at Harvard University who used their genre writing expertise to help them develop their chosen dilemma into a case set in their national context. Expanding case authorship was itself a goal rooted in equity, and as we convened the workshop in the middle of the Covid-19 pandemic, issues of educational equity in the face of disrupted schooling worldwide loomed large in workshop conversations about ethical dilemmas in education. The workshop cases eventually coalesced around two main themes—civic education and equity—each of which grew into its own volume. We invite you to explore the companion to this collection, *Civic Contestation in Global Education: Cases and Conversations in Educational Ethics*, for a full picture of the dilemmas raised in our workshop.

## Normative Case Studies

The first three cases in the collection, from Kenya, Mexico, and the UK, respectively, prompt readers to consider equity concerns in designing, maintaining, and navigating school systems. The first case, "Basic Education for All: The Politics of Implementing 100 Percent Transition from Primary School to Secondary School in Kenya" (Ch. 2), imagines a fictional conversation among school leaders that grapples with the very real challenges that educators have had to navigate after the Kenyan government introduced mandatory secondary school. This new law swiftly and significantly expanded secondary school enrollment among young people in a nation still developing the capacity for universal education access. As three heads of school debate the moral imperative of offering secondary education to marginalized families versus the logistical impossibility of funding and resourcing schools to handle increased capacity, a portrait emerges of dilemmas of educational ethics in developing school systems. These include trade-offs between pursuing radical change versus gradual implementation, the relationship between justice and pragmatism, and conceptions of equity as equal access to schools versus educational adequacy.

"Private Equity: Are Governments Responsible for Private Schools in Times of Crisis?" (Ch. 3) is a nonfiction case about the challenges faced by private schools in Mexico in the wake of government-mandated school closures during the Covid-19 pandemic. This case asks whether the Mexican government's refusal of financial support for private schools during the Covid-19 crisis was ethical educational policy since these schools tend to serve more privileged families and students, or whether the government should bear more responsibility for supporting the educational opportunities that private schools provide, particularly in light of public schools' lack of capacity to serve all students in Mexico. Like "Basic Education for All," "Private Equity" prompts discussion about how to develop equitable, inclusive, and just national systems of education, but it does so by raising questions about how private providers should be incorporated into "universal" provision models and what obligations, if any, this relationship imposes on government entities to support private schools.

"A Qualified Disaster: Allocating Student Grades during Covid-19" (Ch. 4) is also a nonfiction case about governmental responses to Covid-19 based educational disruptions. The case reviews the British government's cancellation of national GCSE and A-Level examinations in England, Wales, and Northern Ireland during the Covid-19 pandemic in 2020 and 2021 and the subsequent grading crises that resulted. By highlighting inequities in the exam process and the fragility of high-stakes accountability measures, the changes to exam policy during the pandemic ushered in talk of larger reform. However, the messy rollout, including significant discrepancies between algorithmically assigned and teacher-assessed grades that were each offered as candidate exam replacements, created more ethical questions than answers. This case asks what current and future ethical and equitable assessment and accountability could look like as part of a national system, in the UK and beyond.

The following three cases in the collection surface equity issues in school and district decision-making. "Remaking the Grade: A District's Quest for Equitable Homework Policy" (Ch. 5) is a nonfiction case based in the United States that dives into Arlington (Virginia) Public Schools' decision to revamp their homework policy in the name of educational equity. By eliminating penalties for late and missing homework assignments—as well as eliminating grades for homework altogether—a district working group hoped to ameliorate differences in educational outcomes for the district's students of color. However, the policy's critics have argued that it actually works against equity goals by removing teacher autonomy in handling individual cases as well as structure and practice for students who need it. As the debate moves through the Arlington Public School district in real time, what can districts and schools globally learn about how to speak across conceptions of equity to devise fair grading and homework policies?

"Caught in the Web: Educational Risks and Rewards of Online Learning" (Ch. 6) also raises questions about how school policy reform can impact students differently. This fictional case focuses on a German high school whose principal is deciding whether to transition the school to hybrid instruction amid a regional push for expanded online education. As she explores the possibilities, she is forced to confront the trade-offs between the special benefits that online learning can provide to some students and the educational goods that may be lost in the transition away from traditional classrooms. This case prompts readers to consider the equity issues that arise in reforming school policies and practices in the digital age. What risks and rewards are at stake for students participating in online instruction? What aims of education do different teaching models serve? What should the relationship be between school and district or regional policy?

"Remote Control: Blurred Boundaries in the Zoom Classroom" (Ch.7) also explores potential inequitable impacts of remote learning policies, but from the perspective of primary school teachers in the United States. This fictional case follows a fourth-grade teaching team as they discuss their camera policy for "Virtual Fridays"—their district's new one-day-a-week practice of online instruction. Their discussion about this micro, grade-level policy issue quickly raises ethical dilemmas around competing aims of education, the right to privacy, and the relationship between home and school, as well as questions about the difference between equity and equality. This case also models the kind of discourse and disagreement that equity questions can raise between colleagues, particularly in today's fraught political environment.

The final two cases focus on the role schools play in providing equitable access to *cultural* and *community* goods as well as academic skills and learning. Each addresses the important role that schools play globally in creating shared national identity, often for groups with very different cultural backgrounds and with very different schooling needs and desires.

"School Choice in Hong Kong: Peking Ducks or Rich Expats?" (Ch. 8) transports readers to an open-air food market in Hong Kong, where they experience a heated dinner discussion among a group of friends reflecting on their own educational experiences and their schooling decisions for their children within the array of choices in their city. This fictional case is both broadly recognizable in its portrayal of parental care for their children's futures and vivid in its specifics of a school system where cost, location, language of instruction, and teaching and learning approaches frequently create dilemmas for parents. This chapter brings home a crucial question for issues of educational equity worldwide: How do families make ethical choices for their children within the educational structures they live in?

The final case in the collection, "A Uniform Decision: Commemoration and Community in Public School" (Ch. 9), is a moving portrait of a school trying to make equitable decisions around care, community, and culture in the midst of a changing student population. Set in an Australian primary school serving both a local low-income, Aussie-born community and a recent arrival of Afghani and Syrian refugee children, this fictional case follows a school principal trying to figure out whether and how to commemorate Anzac Day, a holiday of military remembrance that, for many, serves as a cornerstone of Australian national identity. As the principal weighs the competing and mutual needs of two vulnerable populations, he wrestles with the meaning of educational equity in complex, changing circumstances. This case raises dilemmas of the school as a cultural force with the power to hand down national tradition and determine access to cultural memory, community, and nationhood.

## Model Conversations

Each case in this collection is accompanied by a transcribed and edited conversation about the case among three to five diverse interlocutors: philosophers, teachers and teacher educators, school leaders, parents, equity specialists, international NGO leaders, psychologists, students, and others. The conversations are designed both to add new analytical dimensions to the case and to provide a pedagogical example for how cases can be used. The conversations model the kind of reflection we, the editors, have come to expect from the NCS discussions we frequently lead: reflection that encompasses scholarship, professional expertise, and personal experience, facilitates both consensus and disagreement, and leads to nuanced thinking and novel avenues for resolution. In a commitment to the ideals of equitable participation that underlie many of the collection's cases, our participants are diverse along multiple lines of identity, including race and ethnicity, occupation, age, and national identity.

Unsurprisingly but importantly, their conversations reflect the many different ways those working toward equity define the concept and think about its implications. For example, in the discussion of "Basic Education for All" (Ch. 2), Asyia Kazmi, Robert Jenkins, Isaac Nyangolo, and Pierre Germain Belinga debate the aims of an equitable national education policy: if education is a right, is that right related to *outcomes* (such as receiving a diploma), *access* (the possibility of attending secondary school in the first place), *quality* (students achieving learning outcomes and having positive experiences), or something else? How do these conceptualizations change when the most impacted students are those who have been historically marginalized by their gender, migration status, or rural geography?

The discussions also expand conceptions of equity. In the discussion about "Remaking the Grade" (Ch. 5), participants grapple with the school district working group's unilateral decision to prohibit homework grading and penalties in the name of equity. Their dissatisfaction with the district's decision—and their deep-dive into its conceptualization and enactment of equity—leads Colin Rose to the conclusion that equity is "not just an outcome, [but] also a process." This understanding of equity as a matter of deliberation and community involvement breaks open new possibilities for resolving the case and enacting equity in practice. As Rose summarizes at the close of the conversation, "You can't speak to equity unless you have an intentional process that is engaging folks, especially folks that are most affected by whatever you're trying to make a decision around. It's important to be very intentional around your planning, embedding equity within each step of that planning." Rather than focusing their frustration at the dilemma on the working group that crafted the policy, Rose and his colleagues Amanda Churchill Jimerson, Karen L. Mapp, and Natasha Warikoo expand their discussion to think about whose voices were left out of the decision. Together, they build an understanding that discussion itself is a core part of making equity a reality—so long as the discussion centers the opinions of those whose need to be treated equitably is most at stake.

All of these conversations model ethical deliberation and reflection using normative case studies. Each looks a little different, representing the many possibilities for a successful case discussion. For example, some follow our discussion protocol (described in the Appendix) quite closely (see Ch. 7) while others diverge with case and context-specific discussion prompts (see Ch. 6), and some invoke personal experiences (see Ch. 8 and Ch. 4), while others dive deep into policy details (see Ch. 3). These conversations recognize that ethical judgment can come from many different sources. NCS are premised on the idea that sound ethical judgment in matters of education requires practical wisdom developed through the interplay of experience and reflection. NCS discussions allow participants the space to reflect on the ethical dimensions of educational practice—space that is hard to come by in most of the settings where educational practice occurs. Through bringing together diverse perspectives, making time and space for ethical deliberation, and providing skillful facilitation, these conversations provide an example of how the NCS method can support ethical development in educational decision-making.

For those interested in teaching with NCS or learning more about the practicalities behind the NCS method, the conclusion to this volume includes pedagogical strategies for setting up and facilitating NCS discussions. In particular, the conclusion focuses on practical techniques for establishing accessible and inclusive discussions that embody equity as well as explore it conceptually. For easy reference, the discussion facilitation guide developed by the EdEthics initiative at the Harvard Graduate School of Education can be found in the Appendix. Additionally, the conclusion includes many suggestions for tailoring the facilitation guide to your group size, schedule, and context, as well as for using the conversations as a pedagogical tool to explore the case dilemmas from new perspectives. Equity is a value that requires continual reflection and revision to clarify, work towards, and achieve, and the pedagogies modeled and shared in the conversations and conclusion are designed to help work toward equitable discussion in form and substance.

# Conclusion

Dilemmas of educational equity around the globe require intentional, collaborative deliberation to ameliorate. We hope that these cases and conversations can offer a venue for thoughtful consideration and an example of meaningful conversation about educational equity, one grounded in the particularities of place and circumstance. Moreover, we hope these cases can support readers in defining and clarifying their own definitions of educational equity so that they can have clear-eyed conversations with others about how to approach these issues.

# Notes

1. "Department of Education Equity Action Plan | U.S. Department of Education," Accessed August 14, 2023, https://www.ed.gov/equity; "Education for All 2015 National Review Report: India," Accessed September 22, 2023, https://unesdoc.unesco.org/ark:/48223/pf0000229873; "Equal Educational Opportunities for All—Wellbeing in Germany,"

Accessed August 14, 2023, https://www.gut-leben-in-deutschland.de/report/education/; "Mexico | INCLUSION | Education Profiles," Accessed August 14, 2023, https://education-profiles.org/latin-america-and-the-caribbean/mexico/~inclusion; "Equity in Australian Education | Gonski Institute for Education—UNSW Sydney," Accessed August 14, 2023, https://www.gie.unsw.edu.au/research/equity-in-Australian-education; "The Sustainable Development Goals in South Africa: Goal 4 Targets" (2023). United Nations South Africa. Accessed September 22, 2023, https://southafrica.un.org/en/sdgs/4.

2. Levinson, Meira, Geron, Tatiana, and Brighouse, Harry (2023). "Conceptions of Educational Equity." *AERA Open, 8.*

3. Levinson, Meira and Fay, Jacob (2016). "Introduction," in *Dilemmas of Educational Ethics: Cases and Commentaries.* Harvard Education Press. pp. 3–4.

4. Geron, Tatiana (2023). *Opening the Black Box of Teachers' Ethical Decision-Making: Context and Complexity in Educational Justice.* Doctoral dissertation, Harvard Graduate School of Education.

# 2

# Basic Education for All: The Politics of Implementing 100 Percent Transition from Primary School to Secondary School in Kenya

*Wambura Kimunyu*

---

*The Public Policy and Basic Education Act of 2013 rendered basic education in Kenya both compulsory and a right, but the secondary school Net Enrollment Rate (NER) still sat at only 53.2 percent by 2018.*

The Kenyan public school system is nationally governed and in January 2020, the Government decreed that it would be enforcing 100 percent transition from primary school to secondary school with immediate effect without exemption, requiring government officials to comply and threatening to penalize parents who did not. By this policy the government was newly determined to ensure that every child received twelve years of basic education which entailed ensuring that all learners transitioned from their eight-year stint in primary school into secondary school.

This would be no mean feat. The rollout of Free Primary Education in 2003 had succeeded in increasing primary school enrollment so that the NER had risen to 92.4 percent by 2018. This in turn had led to an increase in the number of students ready to transition into high school. The problem was that there were not enough secondary school places for all those who completed primary school to be absorbed comfortably. For example, in 2016 there were 33,223 *primary schools with an average class size[1] of 309 and 9,966 secondary schools with an average class size of 273. School leaders found themselves grappling with the challenges of welcoming an influx of new students into their schools.*

--

Hearing laughter outside her office, Rayhab Kieti knew what it signified. Isaiah Koech, principal of Kilima Boy's Secondary School, was here. She rose to her feet as he pushed open her door, poked his torso in and announced: "We are here."

"Karibu[2]!" she chirped, to match his flamboyant personality. Then she craned her neck to peer beyond him, asking, "Who is 'we'?"

"The indomitable Mwalimu[3] Peter Makau, of course," Isaiah boomed, throwing the door open to reveal the stocky man behind him.

"Karibu," Rayhab said, to the head of Kilima Primary School, a school strategically situated between Kilima Girls' Secondary School, which she helmed, and Isaiah's school. "Please, take a seat," she invited, gesturing at the two seats arranged in front of her desk, "and tell me, to what do I owe this pleasure?"

Peter, already seated, chuckled. "This one," he said, pointing at Isaiah, who was squirming in his seat in search of the perfect position, "came and dragged me out of my office. I suspect he has something to get off his chest and he needs me here as referee." Rayhab shook her head, laughing. Everyone knew Peter was not easily derailed—if he was there, it was because he wanted to be.

They both turned to Isaiah expectantly.

"Referee?" Isaiah scoffed. "I do not need a referee. But we all know you have the ear of senior people at the Ministry. You are here because I want them to know what we really think, even though Rayhab and I might disagree."

Rayhab propped her elbows on the desk, perching her chin on her clasped hands.

"Disagree about what, Isaiah?" she asked, although she had a fairly good idea what he was animated about.

The previous day, in response to pushback at a press conference about the impracticality of enforcing the government's 100 percent transition rule, the Cabinet Secretary for Education had defiantly declared: "It is better to have a child in school under a tree than have him or her loitering at home." That juicy soundbite had played on the evening news across multiple TV and Radio channels.

"About what the Secretary said yesterday, of course," Isaiah confirmed. "Learning under trees? Is that what you people call access? Is this your equity?"[4]

"Well," Rayhab said, calmly. "Learning under a tree is the lesser of two evils—surely you must see that. If this is what it takes to achieve 100% transition today, then so be it. Leaving any child behind is a far worse proposition than teaching under trees, especially because, as you well know, it is the poorest and most marginalised children who are likely to be left behind."

Isaiah turned to Peter and sighed, as though to say "I told you." Peter shook his head and smiled, politely refusing to be reeled into the conversation until he was right and ready.

"Are you really surprised that I'm defending 100% transition?" Rayhab pressed. "Of course I am. The more pertinent question, Mwalimu Isaiah, is, why won't you?"

"This is not about not supporting 100% transition and you know it, Rayhab," Isaiah pushed back. "It is about *not* supporting this shoddy implementation. There are just not enough places to accommodate 100% transition, and it is extremely irresponsible of this government to attempt to push it through. You can't snap your fingers and manufacture almost 500,000 new secondary school places by the power of positive thinking. I hardly have room for the 320 students I have been forced to accommodate these past three years. Now the ministry has notified me that I must somehow accommodate 450. How?"

As a sign of his growing agitation, the pitch of Isaiah's voice rose as he spoke.

"My dormitories are already congested. I have to squeeze eight students into a space better suited for four. Now I'm somehow supposed to cram twelve students into the same space? Have we all forgotten the school safety guidelines imposed on us because of the fires? Do those building new safety codes no longer matter?"

Rayhab cocked her head slightly in surprise. Isaiah had been exasperated at the building safety codes imposed on boarding schools by the government after a series of fires had plagued them in 2016. He had dismissed the codes as superficial—a face-saving exercise. It was instructive that he was bringing them up now. She let it pass for the moment and listened to him rage on.

"Do we just take up these additional students when we know that it increases the safety risk for everyone? What about classrooms? Do they want me to squeeze seventy students into a classroom now? How do they imagine that my teachers will teach? Do you actually believe there will be any meaningful learning achieved at all?"

While he ranted, Rayhab had gradually leaned back, folding her arms across her chest, instinctively bracing herself against the onslaught. She understood that Isaiah was not attacking her personally—he just needed to vent—but his frustration was palpable.

They had met as bachelor of education students at Kenyatta University. Rayhab had always been passionate about teaching. Her mother was a teacher, and she had grown up hearing from strangers how much her mother had positively impacted their lives. Isaiah, on the other hand, had stumbled into education as a stopgap measure while he decided what to do with himself. After graduation they had been posted to schools in different parts of the country and had lost touch until six years previously when Rayhab had transferred to Kilima Girls as Deputy Principal and discovered that Isaiah was principal of Kilima Boys. She was surprised. He hadn't seemed the type who would last in the teaching profession and yet there he was, occupying a coveted perch in a national school.

They had rekindled their friendship easily and when Rayhab rose to the role of principal, he had taken to visiting her office regularly to debate matters of education. Sometimes, as today, he dragged along Peter Makau, Headmaster at Kilima Primary School. Isaiah was flamboyant and forceful and most people were intimidated by him, but Rayhab and Peter weren't. Rayhab was cool-headed and firm, and while Isaiah might consider her a tad naive for assuming that most people had the best intentions, he appreciated that she took his larger-than-life personality in stride.

"Look," Rayhab was saying now, "I get your frustration with all of this. You know I have room for only 60 incoming students and yet they're sending me 94. But tell me, what's the alternative? What happens if we don't find places for all these students? The lives of the half a million kids who didn't transition into secondary school last year are almost certainly irreparably compromised. They will only ever be qualified for lower order, lower paying jobs. We have condemned them to a life at the margins. Not just them but their children too, probably. These are the children of the poorest and most marginalised Kenyans among us. Where is our sense of justice? How can we not do everything we can to make room for them?"

"But how?" Isaiah countered. "Tell me how exactly I'm supposed to make room? I understand justice, but do you understand pragmatism?"

Rayhab glanced over at Peter, who had been sitting quietly, listening. She wondered what he was thinking. A few years older than Rayhab and Isaiah, he was usually content to serve as an audience of one as they volleyed arguments back and forth. He had led Kilima Primary School for twenty-six years, had a strong network nationally, and was well-respected within the local community.

"Mwalimu Peter, what do you think?" Rayhab prompted.

"It's difficult but not impossible," he began, attempting as he sometimes did to straddle the line between Isaiah and Rayhab.

"I know many parents at my school who would agree with you, Rayhab. They had despaired that they would not be able to afford their children's secondary school education—despite the fact that the government has committed to covering the cost of tuition through the Free Day Secondary Schools[5] policy, schools are still not free—many administrators are charging exorbitant fees for infrastructure projects which they cannot afford. Now that the government has announced that secondary school is compulsory and that parents cannot be forced to pay for these infrastructure projects, they are happy to send their children to school and their children are happy to have the opportunity to go. You have to give the government credit for trying to fulfil its obligation."

Rayhab's frame was angled toward Peter but through the corner of her eye she could see Isaiah crossing, uncrossing, and recrossing his legs, obviously itching to interject.

"The thing is, though," Peter continued, "where's the funding?"

At the mention of funding, Isaiah jumped in eagerly: "Yes, where's the funding? Have you received anywhere near enough funds to do even a fraction of what you need to do to prepare for the influx? To buy new beds, and new desks? To build new dormitories, new classrooms, new toilets, new labs? To hire new teachers? It's one thing for the Secretary to declare that they can learn under trees but who will teach them? And where will they sleep at night? The government is sending me 22,000 Ksh[6] per student for a whole year. How am I supposed to run an entire school on that?"

Peter chimed in: "The money is never enough. TSC[7] have asked for 15 billion shillings a year to train the additional 25,000 teachers they estimate will be required to support 100% transition. The government says it can only manage 2 billion shillings. The School Heads Association said they need 9 billion shillings a year in order to pull this off. The government says it can only give 1.5 billion shillings."

"Exactly!" exclaimed Isaiah, energized by the fact that Peter seemed to be fighting in his corner. "Plus: 100 transition means that everybody has a right to continue with their education no matter how poorly they performed in their exams.[8] That means teachers will not only have more students, but many of them will also be woefully unprepared for secondary school. Mwalimu Peter here says he knows parents and children who are happy that this new policy makes it possible for them to attend secondary school. Good for them. But what about those who qualified by working hard and passing their national exams? Those who earned their rightful place in a national school like Kilima Boys? Don't we care that this will compromise their learning? And this comes at a time when the World Bank is now breathing down our necks talking about a learning crisis and learning poverty and about how a majority of our students are not acquiring basic skills, and telling us to improve the quality of our education."

"Mwalimu Isaiah," Rayhab interjected, politely but firmly, leaning forward to make her point. "Unfortunately I do not have sway over the World Bank."

"They're right in one respect, though," Isaiah powered on, "being in school is not the same as learning, so 100% transition implemented in this rash way will not improve anybody's prospects. I'm sorry, but this is not what access for all should look like."

Then, as if he had suddenly run out of steam, he flopped back in his seat and said, "A gradual implementation I can deal with. This radical approach is untenable."

"So: just so I can make sure I understand, Mwalimu Isaiah," Rayhab challenged, "you're saying we should implement 100% transition slowly, over the next few years?"

"Absolutely. I don't see what the rush is."

This was just the kind of statement designed to get a rise out of Rayhab.

"The rush, Mwalimu, is the half a million students we are leaving behind every single year. The rush is the stunted productivity that that portends, the reduced income, the increased social inequality. The rush is that by denying these young people a basic education today we are adversely impacting the next eight decades of their lifetimes: socially, politically, and economically. The rush is that they have a constitutionally guaranteed right to an education and who are we to tell them to wait? That is the rush, Mwalimu."

Rayhab caught the quick look the men exchanged and brushed it aside. She understood that the circumstances were less than ideal. But whenever she considered the half a million children annually who would be left behind absent the implementation of 100% transition, she could not think of anything more unjust.

"I don't buy the argument that failing students being pushed through the system are going to unnecessarily burden it. If children are failing to learn in school, is it not the system that is failing them? Aren't we, as teachers and administrators, a critical cog in that system?

Besides, everyone knows just how constrained for resources the government is right now—we're spending above the OECD average of GDP on education. The truth is, as the ministry is always happy to remind us, 75% of that spending is on recurrent expenditure, most of it on teachers' salaries. What is left is hardly enough to fund the capital investment in infrastructure that we desperately need. But we also know that the government is not doing absolutely nothing. Has it not built those low-cost boarding schools in arid and semi-arid areas and even set up some mobile schools?"

Peter leaned back in his seat and contemplated his two colleagues, both of whom he respected. Isaiah was right to be piqued that the government had made this sweeping decree when it was administrators on the ground who would have to grapple with the breadth of consequences—from overcrowded dorms and classrooms to an overworked and irate teaching force. Isaiah's tenure at Kilima Boys had seen a marked improvement in the school's academic performance in national rankings. It was clear that Isaiah feared that 100 percent transition implementation would compromise his commitment to academic excellence. Rayhab had a valid point, though. The Constitution of Kenya had declared Basic Education a right—that had to mean something. She was also right to be concerned that anything less than an unequivocal implementation of 100 percent transition would exacerbate the marginalization of the most vulnerable communities.

His old friend Eliud Ndambuki who served as an Undersecretary in the Ministry of Education's Directorate of Secondary and Tertiary Education occasionally sought him out to get a sense of what was going on the ground. Peter was due to have lunch with Ndambuki in Nairobi that Friday, as a matter of fact. While he understood and sympathized with both Isaiah and Rayhab's positions, he wondered which side he would take when the topic came up with Ndambuki, as it likely would. Should he support prioritizing quality in order to stem the learning crisis, or prioritizing access for all? Was it pragmatic or unjust to limit secondary school admissions to only the spaces currently available? Did the situation demand radical change or call for a gradual implementation?

# Conversation

**Ellis Reid:** Let's jump right in here. What are the dilemmas in this case and for whom are they dilemmas?

**Isaac Nyangolo:** At first sight, it's tempting to say that the dilemma is between quality and access. Isaiah is for quality education, and Rayhab is for education to be as accessible as possible. But I think there's a bigger dilemma here: when you have limited resources, how are you going to ration? Will you provide a lot of access to an experience that is less than ideal, or provide an ideal experience to a small group of people? Framed that way, it's not easy to say Rayhab is right, or Isaiah is right. I love the framing of the case, which really draws you into each of the experiences of the two key protagonists, and enables you to see the stakes. There is no perfect solution.

**Asyia Kazmi:** I really appreciated the way the case brought the dilemma to life and it made it real, in contrast to the dry reports we quite often read. I think the dilemma is the head versus the heart, and the quality versus the quantity, and the urgency of learning poverty versus sensible programming. Essentially, it's learning versus schooling. But we should ask ourselves, what are we trying to grant access to if not a quality education? For example, there's some evidence that girls are dropping out because they're not actually learning. So this question—what are we getting the access to?—is perhaps the dilemma as opposed to these dichotomies—between quality and quantity, between learning and schooling—that might actually not be as distinct as we think they are.

**Robert Jenkins:** I think the only other dilemma to add would be time. How quick can you make a difference and enable all kids? There is a tension between speed and urgency versus taking time for systemic, longer-term change that's needed.

**Pierre Germain Belinga:** I'd also add that poverty is a menace to various education systems across the globe. It complicates issues of access in global public policy.

**Asyia Kazmi:** To Pierre's point, the case mentions funding for the tuition side or the teaching side, but not necessarily funding for the school infrastructure and the hidden costs of education that we know parents need help to cover in low- and middle-income countries. What is the full cost of education? How is that shared between private and public funds? There are other questions of infrastructure, too. The case references the idea of the boarding school versus teaching under a tree. What's the physicality of a school? Is it a boarding school? Is it a day school? Or just an amazing teacher under a tree? These questions point towards dilemmas about how we use school funding. Do we spend money on the school building? On teaching the teachers? And then what kinds of teacher training are required for what subjects, especially at the secondary education level? Who are those teachers preparing, and what are they preparing them for?

**Isaac Nyangolo:** I'd like to pick up on what Asyia said about the framing of the heart versus the head. In one way, the sense of right is defined in moral or idealistic ways: every child deserves to get education. On the other hand, there's a more practical or pragmatic framing: we want everybody to have a good quality of life. So if you're thinking about education as a basic human right, you can't put dollar signs next to it. However, if you're thinking about it with a pragmatic view, you may argue that we can provide people with out-of-school training, and they'll still have a good life without secondary education. In Rayhab's view, denying students access is unconscionable. But from the pragmatic side, it's difficult to understand why someone would insist on pushing people through a school system that's probably not providing any quality.

**Asyia Kazmi:** There are so many dilemmas and for so many people, including the students themselves. How will they benefit from going to this school versus what they could do alternatively? Their parents must also consider what they lose by having children in school, which is sometimes informed by gender. Then there are the benefits and costs for teachers. When I was a teacher, I used to think thirty-two children were too many to have in the classroom. So what if teachers suddenly have twice that or more? So there's the teacher angle, and there's the social justice lens, which came through so powerfully in the case. Rayhab asks, "If children are failing to learn in school, is it not the system that is failing them?" I would make that question even more important: is it not *we* who are failing them?

**Pierre Germain Belinga:** Education has long been considered an ideal of personal accomplishment and an ideal of accomplishment for a society, but we also identify education as a right, just as Isaac said. To use John Rawls's phrase, education is a primary good: it is a basic good every human being needs, regardless of their personal conception of what a good life looks like.

**Ellis Reid:** I'm curious. Say enrollment does go from about 53 percent to 70 percent or 80 percent in a few years, as I believe the government hopes it will. Do we think the education those students would get would improve their well-being, their future opportunities? Or are we worried about what the quality would be?

**Robert Jenkins:** I think all evidence would indicate we should be worried about the quality. Without some learning outcome measurements, you run the risk of kids going to school without any learning. Now, having said that, a piece of paper can be a useful thing. In many countries, students are finishing secondary school without achieving learning outcomes, but that piece of paper still has social capital associated with it. So going to secondary school, regardless of learning, could open up a different part of the labor market or help social standing. But obviously the key is for attendance to be associated with learning, which we obviously cannot assume is the case.

**Asyia Kazmi:** I think it's also interesting to look at studies on the impact of schooling for women and girls. Women who complete more schooling have fewer children, experience a small decrease in child mortality, and an increase in agency.[9] While we don't know what aspect of education contributes to its wider benefits for women (the act of attending school; the socializing aspect of schooling; the knowledge transferred to future mothers; or the acquisition of literacy and numeracy skills) we do know that advances in women's education have undoubtedly played a role in improving health outcomes, but the effects are not as strong as previously thought.[10]

Yet the impact of schooling combined with learning, on wider outcomes for girls such as health and agency, is likely to be at least three times higher than schooling alone.[11] But we don't know what aspect of increased schooling has that effect: just attending, socializing, the actual knowledge transferred, or the acquisition of skills? But we also have more recent research showing that the positive benefits are much greater when schooling results in actual learning. It is the wider skills that will allow students to have more meaningful engagement in higher education, in training, in employment, and entrepreneurship. We need more evidence on this.

**Pierre Germain Belinga:** This issue of quality is very important. If I am a pupil in a classroom with too many students, I fear I won't be able to prepare for my exams in that classroom. But in a classroom with fewer students, I can feel very sure that the teacher will be able to help me reach my objectives. But for the government, for policymakers, success may depend on having large numbers of pupils in school, not on the quality for individuals.

**Ellis Reid:** I want to keep diving a little bit into this question. There are two groups of students here: those who will already likely continue to secondary school, about 53 percent of the population, and those who won't, the other 47 percent. Who are these two broad groups of students? And how should that impact our thinking?

**Asyia Kazmi:** These students are the marginalized. They're the underserved. They're in rural areas and live in poverty. The relationship between opportunity and outcomes is so high. In a high-income country, nine out of ten children can read by the age of ten. In a low-income country, nine out of ten cannot.

That's on the global level. We see those statistics correlating closely with income and outcomes within countries as well. Those students from underserved populations who are already going to secondary school have been able to battle through many challenges. They have to be really, really lucky as well as talented. So how many of those children are we leaving behind by not giving them the opportunity to get to secondary school in the first place? To go back to the head and the heart, we need to get more children into and through secondary education, but if they are not going to receive a quality education, what is the point of having them sit for hours and hours learning absolutely nothing in the classroom?

**Pierre Germain Belinga:** There are also many groups that really need the opportunity to get an education: people with disabilities, women, migrants. The problem is that it's very challenging for sweeping government policies to identify the groups that have those specific needs. But it's an important challenge.

**Isaac Nyangolo:** When I think about it from the policy lens, a policy that excludes 47 percent of the population isn't really working. So from that perspective, it's pragmatic and not just moral to think about how to include everyone. For the policy to work in a pragmatic sense, you need to come up with a solution that brings everybody in. This is especially important because I suspect that if parents get an education, however ineffective, the next generation is more likely to be educated. Here, I'm thinking about what Asyia said about outcomes for girls who are able to attend school. Of course, if you're thinking about it from the perspective of the 53 percent, who were previously receiving great access to quality education, then they might have an axe to grind with expanding capacity. So questions remain, but from the policy side, it now just seems less of a dilemma.

**Ellis Reid:** Earlier, Asyia asked, "What is access, if not to quality?" And in some ways, Isaac, you're offering an answer to that. You're saying, "Well, there are so many students who are excluded–girls, rural students, other students from different groups that are unjustly marginalized for other reasons. If we can bring these students into the secondary school system, even very imperfectly, we may well actually realize some important benefits, maybe even longer term cultural and social changes." I'm curious what other people think about this tension.

**Asyia Kazmi:** There's also an assumption of the very traditional school model: if one teacher had X number of people, they're now going to have X+500 people. Perhaps innovation needs to happen. There's so much talent in Kenya, people doing incredible, innovative things, but in education, we seem to be not as innovative as we could be, even with technology. The pupil-teacher ratio is something that we hear again and again across the continent, but why not try older students teaching younger students so that you're breaking down that 40:1, 70:1, sometimes even 100:1 pupil-teacher ratio? What policy solutions could give everyone the right to education without compromising on quality?

**Isaac Nyangolo:** Maybe that's one of the weaker points of the case, the assumption that quality education is only measured in terms of whether you can read or write. There are other, wider goals like good citizenship and cultural awareness and understanding. These are skills you really have to learn in a school setting. Even when students may not read or write, they can still learn to be better citizens by going to school.

**Robert Jenkins:** What enables a secondary school student to have realized her potential, let's say, or have her needs met in her right to education? I think the conversation in this case study could be seen as a little narrow, as though there is one path through primary school and that a student must then continue their learning trajectory in secondary school. I think increasingly, as children age into the secondary education skill set, we need multiple learning pathways: learning online, learning offline, internships, externships, micro credentialing, etc. It's reasonable to ask a secondary aged child now, "What are you interested in?" And we need multiple potential pathways to realize that vision.

**Asyia Kazmi:** How do you get the balance right between what guidance a young adult needs and what path that they can forge their own way? What tools do they need to forge in their own way? It's also important to remember that you don't know what you don't know. Students in a rural area, who have never been exposed to technology, aren't going to ask to be trained on artificial intelligence. Somebody must provide input on the range of possibilities and the mechanisms to get students the knowledge they need. Students have the right to be educated as far as they want to be. How do we write policy that opens doors for them without tying ourselves to the traditional model?

**Pierre Germain Belinga:** We should also remember that every student needs basic skills. It's not a matter of wanting those skills, but rather needing those skills. I think that the reason why basic education is compulsory, in any education system, is just because at a certain age, every pupil needs basic skills.

**Isaac Nyangolo:** I'm thinking about the very definition of what an education is. How can we recognize education—or prior learning—even when it doesn't happen within a classroom setting? There are different ways that education could be delivered outside the traditional sense. For example, I visited my friend who lives in Paris. She attended Harvard; her credentials are fantastic. But she runs a family bakery that has been operating since 1932, and the secret sauce for making the bakery work is not really her classroom training. She got her knowledge through apprenticeship with her parents and grandparents. That too is education. We need to think about education in a broader way, beyond utilizing innovation to deliver learning in the traditional classroom or a slightly different classroom context. We must make sure that this apprenticeship doesn't get lost, or indigenous knowledge about medicine, as another example. When we talk about education in a very narrow sense—do you read English?—then we lose out on a lot of things.

**Asyia Kazmi:** Looking through this lens of equity and social justice, you continuously need to examine who is benefiting and who is not, especially when you are innovating and creating different opportunities and pathways. At the moment, we roughly have a 50 percent problem: 50 percent staying in secondary education, 50 percent not. But then within that 50 percent —and hopefully, as that becomes 80 percent and 90 percent and maybe 100 percent —we're examining which pathways are being taken by what groups of students. Are there some preferred pathways for students from different socio-economic classes, geographic locations, genders? We must examine the outcomes of the different models and who benefits. Otherwise, you'll have pathways set at birth, not because of students' talent and capabilities, but because of inequitable systems.

**Robert Jenkins:** I fully agree with that. But beyond who benefits, another tricky question is: who decides what is beneficial? What I feel is beneficial may not be what a fourteen-year-old feels when prioritizing the various benefits. Those assessments of what is beneficial aren't objective. If we want to make sure all doors are open to all students, what is the role and the obligations of the government and the providers, in secondary education and in other pathways? How does the system more effectively meet individual needs?

**Isaac Nyangolo:** I love Rob's question: who decides? If the student decides, how do we know they have enough competence to make that decision? For instance, in Kenya, we had a very academically oriented curriculum, where grades are all that matter, but we're moving to a competence-based curriculum, where the competencies are very broadly defined. Beyond the academic path, there's even a sports and art track, so I'm imagining that a student who hopes to become a soccer player will not need to go through calculus, though I don't know yet. But at fourteen, does the kid have the capability or enough context to be able to make that decision? At what point have they acquired the basic competencies they should get from the education system, before you narrow them down into one path?

**Pierre Germain Belinga:** Clearly we cannot ask a young boy of three years old what he needs, in terms of quality of education, just because he is not in the position to identify by himself what he really needs. I think that choice is an important dimension of justice in education. For very young people, that choice belongs to parents and others who are responsible for them. But once students reach university, they make the choices. Policy makers must provide many choices, so that students can have not only that traditional system of education, but also other pathways to accomplishment, according to their specific needs and their age.

**Asyia Kazmi:** For me, it isn't just about choice. It's the ability to make an *informed* choice based on an understanding of where those choices will take you, and the benefits and costs of certain choices. There's a Caribbean saying: "it takes a village to bring up a child." It might also take a "village" to support that child's choice making. As adults making choices, we consult a range of people and understand the consequences of those choices. The network around you helps you to make those informed choices. Thinking back to my own upbringing in London, I had a smaller network than my children have to make those choices. That network has a huge impact on their ability to benefit from the choices they make, partly because they help them know what they don't know. So we need innovation, wider opportunities, and a wider sense of choices, but let's make sure we apply an equity lens when helping students making those choices.

**Ellis Reid:** I also want to bring back Pierre's idea that there are certain basic things that we want all students to develop. We might think, for instance, that we want all students to develop those civic skills they need as adults to be full participants in a society, which might be a robust set of capacities and dispositions that require a fair bit of work to develop. How do we square that need for basic skills with this desire to personalize and to allow students to choose their pathways?

**Robert Jenkins:** I think a key dynamic is whose responsibility or obligation this is. If you use a human rights framework, you have rights-holders and duty-bearers, meaning people have rights, and others have corresponding duties to enable those rights to be realized. The current case study, I think, is overly focused on government. They're the only duty-bearer. I think that's increasingly not the case. And perhaps it never was. As per the discussion taking place in the case study, it's clear that the government does not have the capacity to realize its obligations, even if it wanted to. Hence, multiple duty-bearers must be responsible for realizing the right of this fourteen-year-old that we're talking about to successfully access the appropriate pathway for learning that enables them to realize their potential.

**Ellis Reid:** What should be done in this case? What duties need to be fulfilled? And who are the stakeholders who should be taking action?

**Pierre Germain Belinga:** When we are talking about choice, we must keep in mind the various levels of fair deliberation. I think that fair deliberation requires good public policy. You can't have a good educational system if you don't have a good democratic political system and a good economic system. The education system depends on the social vision of society. When we come together to deliberate, we must have a commitment to the common good. I agree with Amy Gutmann, who argues in *Democratic Education* that before you can deliberate about education, you need to deliberate about principles. Once we agree on the principles that will guide the society, we can come together for good deliberation. And good deliberation requires reciprocity. In some societies, mainly in African societies, the problem of reciprocity is not addressed enough, because there are many people who are able to deliberate and others who are not able to deliberate. So deliberation becomes something that belongs only to a specific group of people. When we apply that to education, we get the kind of educational system that results from the deliberation of a specific group. So the system works well for that group, but those who haven't taken part in the deliberation can't succeed as well in that system. That is why it is important to deliberate and to organize the principles for good and fair deliberation.

**Isaac Nyangolo:** What Pierre was saying just lit a bulb in my head. First, society needs to define the basic competencies of what comprises good education. Second, the deliberative process of defining these competencies must bring everybody in. And I think the government should be the custodian of this process. The tone of the case study suggests that the policy was made in the absence of this deliberation. And as a result, it was just working for one group of people, perhaps this 53 percent of people. But everybody should come together to decide what this basic competence entails, to bring everyone to a level where they can make informed choices. Then we should essentially come up with an education system that works not just for the 53 percent, but for everybody else, built around this idea of competent choice because not everyone will make the same choice. Maybe 40 percent will go for the traditional route, another 40 percent for a different route. And maybe if we build a system that works differently for different people, some of the resource constraints might dissipate.

**Asyia Kazmi:** I really like the framing of the duty-bearers and the rights-holders. Often when we talk about education, the discourse goes right to what we need to train the teachers to do and what we want the students to have. Many countries have a national curriculum, which is an articulation of what they want their citizens to know and be. But perhaps we need to go back and consider: what do citizens need to know to make informed policies, to enact those policies, to be able to understand how they benefit from those policies justly?

I also want to point out that we're assuming that the education that builds citizens comes through schooling. But if you visit many different countries in many different societies, you see that students have qualities that come from the culture that they're embedded in, even if they have only been to primary school. We need to recognize that education goes beyond formal schooling. How do you develop a system for young people that builds on the qualities that the country has embedded in them, and equips them to benefit from the wider culture as well? We need careful innovation.

**Robert Jenkins:** To keep following the duty-bearer/rights-holder framing, I think the challenge is that with more pathways available to students, more actors come into the space as duty-bearers. However, we need to make sure that having more duty bearers doesn't dilute the responsibilities of some of the key actors, meaning parents or children themselves and/or governments. In this case study, bringing in more actors—the private sector, the public, community-based organizations, technology companies—should by no means let the government of Kenya off the hook. Now, the government may do something different than what it did twenty years ago, or fifty years ago, when they were the sole provider of education. They may move into a regulatory role, a financing role, a networking role, a certification role, etc. Education can be the great equalizer, or the great enabler, but all need to realize their obligations to the maximum of their capacity. Everyone's role is changing and needs to change very, very quickly, given how quickly the world is changing, and how underperforming many current education systems are.

**Ellis Reid:** I'm hearing some tension among the recent responses being offered. Whereas I'm hearing Pierre and Isaac emphasize fair deliberation among different stakeholders in the society about what we mean when we talk about quality education or educational access, I'm hearing a different idea about government in some of the other answers. Rob, for instance, you suggested that systemic change needs to happen and that that might involve a total reorientation of the role of government, shifting from service provider to contractor responsible for managing a diverse array of state and private education providers, providing the flexibility needed to realize educational justice for young people in Kenya. These strike me as fairly different positions. Whereas one emphasizes the importance of talk among different stakeholders, facilitated by the government and guided by an ideal fair deliberation, the others put the emphasis elsewhere–on efficiency, flexibility, and choice perhaps. Is there some tension here? Or am I wrong, and, in fact, we can do both things simultaneously?

**Asyia Kazmi:** I'm not sure that's how I'm hearing it. I think there is a difference between the what and the how. Before the government can work with other actors, they must understand what they are trying to do. And the "what" has to come from deliberation, from some sort of consensus on what we want our children and our society to be. What kind of values do we want to prioritize? What is the role of formal and informal education in teaching those values? Once there's some consensus building on those questions, you have to think about how that's going to be done and then have a bit of experimentation to see what kinds of models will work, where, and for whom, so that you don't impose a policy that only benefits half the population.

**Isaac Nyangolo:** I agree: deliberation should precede action. In the case, the framing offered by the three protagonists makes it seem that there was no deliberation, just a mandate from the government. But I do think that once the deliberation has been done, the government is duty-bound to lead the implementation of whatever policy is created. Outside actors, like the World Bank, which is referenced in the case, can interfere with the conversations that happen in local communities and districts because they come in and say, "Do things in this particular way." Governments need to act as the conveners to collect views from everybody—including parents and communities—regardless of how much money or how many voices they bring into the conversation.

**Robert Jenkins:** Building on an earlier comment, to transform education, our learning opportunities need to be transformed. From Canada, my own country, to Kenya in this case, I think everyone agrees we need disruption, and we need new and different ways of learning. Can a bottom-up consultation process that gives everyone an equal voice enable such a massive transformation? Or do we actually need instead some powerful actor, whoever that may be, with ideally some progressive big play? I would argue that a consensus-building, bottom-up consultation process does not enable the needed transformative change. It's a bit controversial to say, but we've seen rapid change and amazing transformation in places like Singapore, South Korea, and Vietnam. That didn't happen from a bottom-up consultative process. That happened with a progressive prioritization by top leadership across public and private sectors, almost pushing change through, despite many opinions. Learning opportunities and education systems are actually based on social constructs that need to be broken open in order for every child to realize their full potential and vision. There's obviously a balance that needs to be struck here, but if we want transformation and disruption, we need disruptors and transformators to be empowered to make those changes.

**Asyia Kazmi:** It goes back to Pierre's really important point: what does fair deliberation mean? It isn't about everybody having a vote and going for the lowest common denominator. It is about the skill and the talent within the country having an informed discussion about where they want their country to go. It's not imposed by advisors. Isaac, you mentioned the World Bank. The World Bank's not an entity. It's made up of individuals. Should one or two individuals have the influence to decide what a country is doing? Absolutely not. I'd love to hear Pierre's view about fair deliberation that allows for action to be taken.

**Pierre Germain Belinga:** I think that as far as social transformation, it requires all the citizens of a country. It is the citizens that identify something as innovation. There are many innovations that are not good for society, or that may be good for one society but not for another. And there are innovations that are only innovative and good for their creator, or for a small number of people. So we need ways to evaluate innovation through social deliberation, which cannot just happen in a laboratory, in a classroom, or in an office by a small group of people. But I do agree that in any society, we need experts and specialists. If you don't have specialists in education who can create good proposals for those who are going to deliberate, you won't get good deliberation. And the citizens need to understand what they're discussing; an ignorant person cannot deliberate.

**Isaac Nyangolo:** Even when that expertise exists within the local communities, I think resources play an outsized role. So for instance, Kenya has one of the most dynamic educational technology sectors in Africa. But the policies that shape how that subsector within education operates are heavily influenced by outside groups like UK Aid or the World Bank because they have the money to get the attention of policymakers or education implementers. A fair deliberation requires bringing all the expertise to the same table. But in Kenya, and maybe a lot of the countries in Africa or the Global South, it's funding, not the quality of the ideas, that gets a very big seat at the table. So that fair deliberation that Pierre talks about generally does not happen.

**Pierre Germain Belinga:** It's so important to have more than one vision in deliberation. Everyone agrees that children deserve a good education, but different societies will have different definitions of what a good education means. We must hear all of those diverse visions with respect, and education in a multicultural setting, where we live together, can actually help us build that respect for one another.

*Pierre Germain Belinga is Research Officer at the National Center for Education—Ministry of Scientific Research and Innovation (Cameroon). He is also the Scientific Coordinator of the Ethics and Public Policies Laboratory (EthicsLab) of the Faculty of Philosophy of the Catholic University of Central Africa. His works are based on Public policies of Education, with a particular focus on global justice in education.*

**Robert Jenkins** *(EdD) is the Global Director of Education, UNICEF, with over twenty-five years of experience in international development and humanitarian programming in Africa, Asia, and the Middle East. Prior to his current appointment, Dr. Jenkins served as the UNICEF Representative, Jordan, from 2014 to 2019, and Deputy Director, Division of Policy and Strategy in UNICEF*

Headquarters from 2009 to 2014. From 1995 to 2009, Robert Jenkins served with UNICEF in program and management positions in Uganda (1995–7), Bangladesh (1997–2000), Myanmar (2000–3), India (2003–6), and Mozambique (2006–9).

***Asyia Kazmi*** OBE *is the Global Education Policy Lead at the Bill & Melinda Gates Foundation, with a focus on effective instructional practices, education advocacy and edtech, and India. Nearly half of Asyia's thirty-year career in education was spent as a mathematics teacher and teacher coach. Before joining the foundation, Asyia was a management consultant in PwC leading the Girls' Education Challenge. Her areas of expertise include teaching, learning and formative assessment; school improvement; and large-scale program management.*

***Isaac Nyangolo*** *is the Co-Founder & CEO of Zeraki, a Pan-African EdTech startup based out of Nairobi that provides parents, teachers, and students with innovative technology tools to make teaching and learning effective, engaging, and productive. With over 2.5m users, Zeraki is one of Africa's leading EdTech platforms. Isaac is the 2022 African Union Commission's Innovating Education in Africa Award winner.*

# Character Guide

| Setting |
|---|
| Kilima Boy's Secondary School, Kilima Girl's Secondary School, and Kilima Primary School in Kenya |

| Primary Characters | |
|---|---|
| **Isaiah Koech:** principal of Kilima Boy's Secondary School<br>**Rayhan Kiete:** principal of Kilima Girl's Secondary School | **Peter Makau:** principal of Kilima Primary School<br>**Eluid Ndambuki:** Undersecretary in Ministry of Education's Directorate of Secondary and Tertiary Education |

# Discussion Questions

1. One conception of equity that resonates in this case is the importance of benefitting the least advantaged. How does this conception shape

some of the arguments made for the government's policy? How much do you agree that this conception of educational equity should be prioritized in the case?
2. Isaiah expresses concerns about the challenges teachers will face under the new policy. How should the interests of teachers shape our thinking about the case?
3. Because Rayhab and Isaiah both lead boarding schools, they must accommodate any additional students they are assigned not only in classrooms but also in dormitories. How does the prevalence of secondary boarding schools in Kenya influence your thinking about the dilemmas in the case?
4. Isaiah brings up the question of merit when he argues that the new policy will negatively impact the learning of "those who qualified by working hard and passing their national exams." What role, if any, should merit play in allocating placement in secondary school? Do you agree that the government should consider educational quality for high-performing students as it writes policy to ensure universal access?
5. Rayhab and Isaiah took very different pathways into their roles as educational leaders. How might their personal backgrounds influence their values and beliefs, as well as their views on the new government policy? How might your own experiences influence your views about the dilemmas that arise in the case?
6. Isaiah briefly mentions the World Bank. What obligations, if any, do international non-governmental organizations (NGOs) like the World Bank, and the countries that fund them, have toward Kenyan young people?
7. How does this case help you think about which students have access to secondary (and post-secondary) education—and what those opportunities look like for different students—in your own context?

## Notes

1. Class size here is a reference to the total number of students in a particular grade or level, not the number of students in a classroom. A class in this respect might consist of anywhere between one and five different streams depending on the size of the school.

2. Karibu means Welcome in Kiswahili.
3. Mwalimu means Teacher in Kiswahili.
4. Kimatu, Sammy (2020). "Kenya: Form 1 Transition—10 Children Rescued from Mukuru-Kisii Slum." The Nation, February 18, 2020, sec. News. https://allafrica.com/stories/202002180116.html.
5. In 2008, former President Kibaki introduced a free [day] secondary school plan. Under it the government would only meet the cost of tuition, while parents footed the bill for boarding and uniform.
6. Approximately 200 US dollars.
7. Teachers Service Commission.
8. All Kenyan students sit for a national exam, the Kenya Certificate of Primary Education, at the end of Grade 8, which also marks the end of primary school. They are then posted to secondary schools based on their performance in these exams, with the best-performing students able to access the top-performing, best-resourced public secondary schools.
9. Psaki, Stephanie R., Chuang, Erica K., Melnikas Andrea J., Wilson, David B., and Mensch, Barbara S. (2019). "Causal Effects of Education on Sexual and Reproductive Health in Low and Middle-Income Countries: A Systematic Review and Meta-Analysis," *SSM—Population Health* 8: 100386. https://doi.org/10.1016/j.ssmph.2019.100386; Kaffenberger, Michelle, and Pritchett, Lant (2021). "Effective Investment in Women's Futures: Schooling with Learning," *International Journal of Educational Development* 86: 102464. https://doi.org/10.1016/j.ijedudev.2021.102464.
10. Mensch, Barbara S., Chuang, Erica K., Melnikas, Andrea J., and Psaki, Stephanie R. (2019) "Evidence for Causal Links between Education and Maternal and Child Health: Systematic Review," *Tropical Medicine & International Health* 24:5: 504–22. https://doi.org/10.1111/tmi.13218.
11. Kaffenberger, M., Pritchett, L., and Sandefur, J. (2018). "Estimating the Impact of Women's Education on Fertility, Child Mortality, and Empowerment When Schooling Ain't Learning." *https://www.hks.harvard.edu/publications/estimating-impact-womens-education-fertility-child-mortality-and-empowermentwhen, consultado el, 10.*

# 3

# Private Equity: Are Governments Responsible for Private Schools in Times of Crisis?

*Juan Espíndola, Sara O'Brien, and Leonel Pérez Expósito*

---

Escuelas particulares *(as private schools in Mexico are called) comprise a small fraction of the Mexican educational system. They serve between 10 and 20 percent of the student population, depending on the instructional level. Mexico's educational private sector pales in size in comparison to other nations in both the Global South and North that have entrenched voucher and charter school arrangements, both of which have not been introduced in Mexico. However, despite their modest size, private schools play a large role in the Mexican system. They contribute to the goal of full educational coverage, which the public sector has been unable to achieve, and they stand in for public schools where the latter fail to provide certain educational goods. Furthermore, the private sector is very diverse: it includes elite schools, middle-class schools, and low-fee schools; religious and secular schools; and schools serving ethnic Indigenous students. Private schools are also said to be valuable insofar as they enable social and cultural pluralism. But they are also charged with creating or exacerbating social stratification. Due to the diversity of these schools and the families who demand their services, their effect on educational justice is worth considering.*

--

On March 14, 2020, the Mexican government announced[1] that all schools—public and private, at every level from preschool through postsecondary education—would close for one month in response to Covid-19. They remained closed for seventeen months. After the initial shutdown, the government quickly implemented *Aprende en Casa* (Learning at Home), a distance learning program built on existing infrastructure for educational television.[2] This program allowed students without home computers or internet access to continue their education, which was particularly important for rural families who often lacked these resources. Teachers were expected to supplement this national system, assigning homework and communicating with their students via telephone, text messages, video calls, and social media.[3]

This disruption to education impacted all schools, including private schools. Before the pandemic struck, approximately 10 percent of Mexico's primary school students and 20 percent of secondary school students attended private schools. But with all students suddenly forced to learn from home, some private school parents questioned whether those school fees were now worth the cost.[4] Their concerns were compounded by the economic downturn that Mexico experienced during the pandemic. "Because we've seen so much unemployment," one business leader explained, "the first thing [families] take off the list is paying for a private school."[5]

With the future of their schools uncertain, panic set in for teachers, administrators, and families. "We are facing a tremendous crisis," lamented the president of the National Association of Private Schools. "Many schools are losing students and will certainly have to close."[6] For one principal of a middle-class private elementary school with fewer than eighty students pre-pandemic, losing more than five kids in three months started to feel like "the most severe crisis the school has ever faced [...] Many parents experienced a very difficult economic situation [...] We tried to support them, but that meant a significant reduction in our income while keeping our regular expenses [...] Even when we shifted online we still had to pay the rent, otherwise we would lose the building."[7] This school leader's experience was hardly unique. By the end of the 2021–2 school year, private schools had seen enrollment drop by 19.5 percent, from preschool through upper-secondary education. At the end of that same academic year, the Ministry of Education registered a drop of 3,038 private schools in the same education levels, compared to the academic year 2018–19.[8]

In the summer of 2020, private schools petitioned the government for assistance, requesting forgiveness for payroll and property taxes, and asking to reopen for in-person learning before the national shutdown was lifted. At first, it seemed that the government might provide some support to private schools. In early August 2020, President Andrés Manuel López Obrador stated: "No one will be left without the right to education and to the best of our ability we will also help these private schools. We have to do it because it is about education."[9] However, ultimately the government denied all petitions from private schools, with the Secretary of Education explaining that "our relationship with private schools is about study plans and programs," not finances.[10]

The situation in Mexico raises a question: during times of crisis, what do governments owe to the private schools that exist alongside their public system? This question is relevant not only to Mexico but to countries around the world where private schools educate significant numbers of students. And given the likelihood of future pandemics, climate disasters, and civic unrest, times of crisis will almost certainly come again. Was the Mexican government's refusal to support private schools an ethical policy choice? Were more ethical alternatives available?

## Prioritizing the Most Vulnerable or Creating New Vulnerability?

At first glance, the answer to these questions seems simple: In a time of crisis, the government should prioritize the most vulnerable. And the most vulnerable students were clearly not private school students. Even before the pandemic, the Mexican education system struggled to produce equitable results, with the richest 20 percent of students five times more likely than the poorest 20 percent of students to complete upper secondary school.[11] The pandemic only exacerbated this inequality, as students in rural areas struggled to access even the digital learning materials provided by *Aprende en Casa*.[12] In contrast, most private schools were located in less socially disadvantaged areas, where students had better access to the internet.[13] And students from private schools came from families who could afford school fees and were thus better resourced than the poorest students. What grounds could justify diverting government resources from schools that struggled to educate their students even before the pandemic hit to private schools that (on the whole) served a more affluent and advantaged population?

Moreover, private school students whose schools closed would not be denied an education; after all, schooling from preschool through upper secondary school is compulsory in Mexico. "Nobody's going to be left out. We're ready to receive this wave of migration from private schools," Deputy Education Minister Marcos Bucio announced at a press conference.[14] One could argue that, rather than divert funds to private schools, the government should reserve its funds to ensure that the public system was ready for those private school students whose schools closed. Students who didn't wish to attend public school could enroll in another private school. From this angle, the policy was clearly equitable.

However, it was unclear whether the public system could actually absorb large numbers of private school students. The Mexican education system frankly relies on private schools to cushion enrollment, especially at the preschool and upper-secondary education levels. For example, while preschool was declared compulsory by Congress in 2004, the public system has not kept pace with the demand for enrollment.[15] From 2010 to 2019, the number of private preschools grew at a higher rate than public ones,[16] and 15.7 percent of preschool students were enrolled in the private system in 2019–20.[17] Upper-secondary education, in turn, was declared compulsory by Congress in 2012. Representatives set a ten-year period to achieve 100 percent of enrollment at this level. However, by 2021, the gross rate of enrollment was only 77.2.[18] Though the number of public high schools grew faster than private ones in that decade, and though private high schools were more likely to exist in places with higher-income families, still 18.1 percent of upper-secondary students across the country were enrolled in a private school in 2021.[19] Without private schooling, the gross rate of enrollment in upper-secondary education would be only 63.2. It is difficult to deny, then, that private preschools and high schools in Mexico contribute to the public goal of expanding access to education.

Offering support to help private schools stay open potentially could have helped stem the flood of students who left the educational system during the worst years of the pandemic. In total, in the academic year 2021–2 there were 1,681,250 fewer enrolled students than there were in the school year 2019–20, a decrease of 5.5 percent.[20] Among the population between 3- and 29-year-olds who were not enrolled in school during the 2020–1 academic year, 400,000 reported that their main reason for non-enrollment was that "There was no school, it was far, or there were not enough spots."[21] The highest percentages of unenrolled students were found in preschool and upper-secondary education, exactly where private school enrollment is highest. These numbers suggest that the government's lack of support for private schools did in fact end up hurting Mexico's youth.

Furthermore, the government could have used the pandemic to nudge the private system toward more equitable and inclusive ends. To support vulnerable students and make private education more accessible, the government could have offered conditional support, requiring private schools to strengthen their impact on the public good. For instance, it could have made financial support contingent on private schools' providing scholarships based on socioeconomic need. Similarly, the government could have taken individual schools' needs and student populations into consideration—perhaps by giving support only to those private schools serving a higher percentage of middle-class and low-income families, or those located in areas where such families reside.

Direct financial support for private schools would have been unusual, but not entirely unprecedented. Two tax subsidies for families already existed: private school fees were not taxable, and parents with children in private schools could exclude part of the tuition from their taxable income. These forms of state support have become such a vital part of the educational system that when the federal administration proposed eliminating the tax exemption for school fees in 2013, arguing that it amounted to a regressive economic incentive, all parties in Congress (except the then-president's party) rejected the proposal. One representative in Congress declared, "Public education has not been able to meet the educational needs of the country. Many middle-class Mexican families make great efforts to invest in their children's education, making tuition payments in private schools […]." So perhaps the government already had more of a financial relationship with private schools than the Secretary of Education suggested when he denied their requests for assistance.

Furthermore, maybe there were good reasons for the government to support all private schools during Covid, regardless of the student population they served. School closures are difficult and disruptive for children, families, and communities under any circumstances,[22] and the Covid-19 pandemic was a particularly chaotic time for young people; one could argue that working to preserve stability for children in times of turmoil would in fact be a worthy ethical goal. One mother of a primary student diagnosed with special needs lamented the disruption the pandemic caused to her daughter: "She is just desperate! She misses her friends. She is constantly saying that she wants to see her friends, her teacher, be at school."[23] Students across the country faced the same disruption, which was compounded for students whose schools never reopened. Furthermore, private schools offer Mexican students communities that are difficult, if not impossible, to find in the public system. Among other things, they can provide alternative pedagogical philosophies and methods and offer religious education.[24] A principal of a Montessori elementary school said that multiple parents forced to leave the school shared with her "their frustration of taking their children out of a school community with the kind of Montessori pedagogy we practice [...] Which was the kind of education they wanted for their kids."[25] Private schools allow students and families to build community around shared values. Losing these unique environments and school communities could create new populations of vulnerable children.

## Reopening Early, Moving Ahead, Leveling Down

And what of the private schools' other request? Even if the government chose not to grant tax subsidies, they could have allowed these schools to open their doors to in-person instruction if they could do so safely. With their small size and strong infrastructure, many private schools were well-positioned to provide safe in-class learning opportunities. While there was little guidance from the federal government about the necessary conditions for reopening, the non-profit organization Mexicanos Primero created the Back to School Index, an analysis of the very different conditions across Mexican states and municipalities, which might have allowed some schools to return earlier than others. One of the two dimensions in the index was *Opportunity to Return*, which considered three main indicators: schools' characteristics, households' vulnerability, and epidemiological context (infection, hospitalization, and vaccination rates). According to the index, some schools across the country, both public and private, presented a high opportunity to return before the government finally reauthorized in-person classes in June 2021.

However, *Opportunity to Return* was not the only dimension on the Back to School index from Mexicanos Primero. The second was *Educational Urgency*—in fact, the initiative was created to "reverse a management of the opening and closing of schools based solely on epidemiological information,"²⁶ shifting the focus to educational equity instead. A school's urgency to return was based on family demographics that contributed to students' marginalization and prevented them from accessing remote learning. Many schools with high educational urgency were located in rural areas, which were far less likely to have private schools than the urban centers. So while granting private schools' requests for early reopening might have made sense from a health perspective, it might not from an ethical one.

Furthermore, if private schools had been authorized to open, the result would have been a deepening of the existing problem of inequality. While private schools are not a homogenous group, in many cases the students who attend them are socio-economically better off than those in public schools, particularly public schools in rural or low-income areas, which scored high in educational urgency. Authorization to reopen would have exacerbated already existing inequalities, giving private school students the social and pedagogical advantages that come with in-person instruction.²⁷

Indeed, the highest-profile case of a private school wishing to reopen early underscores these questions about equity. When Humanitree School, founded by Mexican billionaire Ricardo Salinas Pliego and located in a wealthy neighborhood of Mexico City, reopened its doors without government permission, they faced a scandal. One X (formerly known as Twitter) user vividly expressed their concern: "What privileges does @ricardobsalinas have that his Humanitree school in Lomas is open when @SEP_mx [the Federal Secretary of Education] has not given the green light?"²⁸ While Humanitree's average class size of twelve students²⁹ did make reopening safer than it would have been in more crowded classrooms, those small class sizes came at a big cost: 15,000–17,000 pesos per month, a prohibitive amount for all but the wealthiest families.³⁰ Why should such "privileged" children, in the words of the disgruntled X user, receive yet another advantage, in-person instruction, when so many across the country were denied it? At the same time, requiring private schools who requested to reopen to remain closed didn't actually provide any benefit to the most disadvantaged children. What far-reaching consequences would the rigid mandates that kept both private and public schools closed ultimately have? Would Mexico see a leveling down effect, sending a generation of students into the job market with diminished qualifications? Would the social-emotional challenges of remote learning have negative effects on their mental health for years to come?

## Looking Back and Looking Ahead

So was the Mexican government's response to private schools during the pandemic ethical educational policy? Recall that over 3,000 private schools closed in just three years, disrupting the lives of thousands of students and their families. Should the government have helped those schools stay open—even at the cost of diverting resources from other vulnerable populations during this time of unprecedented crisis?

While this case explores the ethics of the Mexican government's response to private schools during Covid, many countries around the world rely on private schools to educate students. What responsibility—if any—do governments have to help private schools remain open? What responsibility—if any—do governments have to the children and families who have come to rely on those school communities? How should these countries respond if their private schools ask for aid in the next time of crisis?

# Conversation

**Liz Block:** What are the dilemmas in this case and for whom are they dilemmas?

**María de Ibarrola:** First, there's the dilemma of whether the federal government should support private schools in either of two ways during the pandemic: through financial support and tax funding or authorizing them to restart activities before public schools. But private schools themselves are another complexity. There's great diversity among private schools. There are religious schools, schools that have some national commitment, schools that are indeed businesses, schools that are excessively expensive. There is no equitable geographic distribution of private schools in the country, either.

**Sebastián Plá:** The dilemma occurs in the context of profound inequality in general, and especially in terms of education. Plus, it occurs during a crisis in which there were, in my opinion, many deficiencies in the State's actions and policies, plus reduced or limited resources for programs like *Aprende en Casa* (Learning at Home). In Mexico, private education is mainly sustained by parents' tuition and fees payments, so it is, in a way, independent of the state, despite the fact that there are some relatively new tax exemptions for parents. So the problem has to do with specific equity policies and logics of social justice in contexts of deep inequality.

**Irma Villalpando:** I would follow Sebastián's line, acknowledging that in Mexico, private schools do not receive a subsidy, so they are selective in that parents who choose private school have a purchasing power that allows them to do so. In this sense, segregation and the effects of deep inequality definitely underlie the dilemma. And in the context of Covid, we need to consider the government's precarious response to the public schools' problems, where support was really needed, for example to help guarantee connectivity.

But we should talk about a policy to support the middle classes, which make up the largest proportion of families who choose private schools. The elite private schools, with high educational costs, are already very few. This middle-class sector sacrifices to pay for that education, and their enrollment decreased because of Covid.

So the dilemma is about social justice and the duty to the common good. The authorities' decision to not allow private schools to reopen early, applying the same rules for everyone, prevented us from making more ad hoc local decisions, considering ratios, structures, and levels of contagion and vaccination. Private schools' only possible response was survival. We had to do much more than *Aprende en Casa*, which was the only resource for public schools; otherwise, we wouldn't have survived.

**Blanca Heredia:** To me there's no dilemma. Inequality is, from my point of view, the country's central problem. Not just social inequality but the fact that social inequality has become increasingly rigid in the last forty years, especially at the extremes of income distribution and wealth. In this context, with a public system built on the taxes of all Mexicans, I don't see why, during the pandemic or at any other time, everyone's money should be used to support those who have better conditions. With this, I am not saying that all private school families are rich. Irma is right: a very significant number of private schools in the country serve the middle-low class. Still, I don't think it's unethical that the government has only supported public schools because private schools contribute to this rigid inequality, which is the main problem blocking the possibility of Mexico growing, developing, and moving towards being a more prosperous, inclusive, and just society.

**María de Ibarrola:** Well, private schools have also been described as public service, by the law and in Article 3, which simply states that every Mexican citizen has a right to education, and that the state must guarantee that right. Additionally, those who attend private schools and pay taxes also contribute to the government budget. In that sense, I don't think the dilemma is that private schools are supported at the expense of the public sector. I totally agree with the issues of inequality that have been raised, but I don't think all private schools have contributed to this inequality. There are actually schools in some places that may be helping to solve another problem—the problem of demand. Private schools contribute to national coverage.

I think the government could have differentiated between schools, but they either haven't wanted to or they don't have the capacity to. So instead they do "the same thing for everyone," as Irma said, "all equal." It seems to me that the government should know exactly which problems it faces and support those schools that effectively contribute to solving those problems. Private schools take advantage of the inequality in Mexico, but they do not create it.

**Blanca Heredia:** But private schools contribute to a structure of rigid inequality and an obvious social segmentation. These students have the opportunity to attend private school because of factors that they didn't choose: they were born into a family that can pay for it. They will live a very different life from those who didn't have that possibility, especially if that private school is good.

Full disclosure, I attended private school all my life until college, and my daughter did, too. Those with children in private schools also pay taxes and fees, but the taxes pay public services in general, including public educational services. I could have gone to public school, but because my family didn't want to use that service, they decided to pay for a private school. So that argument doesn't convince me. However, the argument about private schools helping to cover the demand seems worth considering. There are certain sectors, preschool, for instance, where private schools make an important contribution to this problem. But I insist that private schools have contributed to generating a society that's almost a caste system, where a small group lucky enough to be born in a home with resources stays like that forever.

**María de Ibarrola:** I think that society's division is not so sharp. We always go to extremes, and we forget the whole sector in the middle that is not part of the super-rich who go to schools that charge 18,000 pesos a month.

**Irma Villalpando:** But why do parents choose private school? One of the factors is dissatisfaction with public education and its deficits. A school with broader curricular components—English, extended schedules, perhaps more flexible learning environments, a smaller ratio—is better for families. It's reasonable for parents to want that, not just because of some desire for consumption. Particularly middle-class families with the aspiration to move up.

On the other hand, it seems to me that there is another component: a need for affiliation with well-off families, and therefore for class segregation. Parents hope that belonging to a specific school community will make a difference in their desire for their children to have better opportunities.

And there's another dilemma here, a tension, a strong paradox. We seem to be coming to a consensus that we must support an egalitarian vision of a good quality public school, a vision of equity. But personally, I also sent my children to a private school because I knew it could have other benefits. It's that idea of "Every man for himself" that Mariano Narodowski mentions when he talks about private education in Argentina, right? The middle class says, "Well, things aren't getting better here, so at least I'll make sure to secure my children's future." In the end, this is also an illusion; if we don't improve society as a whole and we don't question these views, we'll continue this class segregation.

**María de Ibarrola:** I'd like to bring up another topic that I think is very important to parents' decision to send their kids to private school. Public schools have reduced hours and it's an absolute mess. They only offer four hours of class per day, which determines many parents' decisions as they go crazy figuring out how to manage that school schedule. I'm also from a private school, but I don't feel like I had a choice. I think public schools could, and need to, do better.

**Sebastián Plá:** The argument that we're paying double doesn't convince me, as the father of children in private school. Even as a former principal of a private high school—one that could be considered elite in Mexico City—I believe that the government should not support private schools. In that sense, for me there is not much of a dilemma. However, the pandemic was a time of crisis, and there are nuanced differences between the different education levels in this dilemma. At the preschool level, for example, remote learning is just impossible.

**Blanca Heredia:** That brings up the dilemma about whether or not to allow private schools to stay open. Why should these institutions—which the government has authorized to offer their services—not be allowed to open and offer a service to those who paid for it? Why can't those who pay the school fees access this additional benefit that requires them to go beyond paying taxes so that their children need not suffer in confinement?

I think the dilemma is: to what extent should the government have respected the contractual freedom of the private school with the people who hired that service? After all, some exclusive schools had impressive virtual programs that widened the gap between public and elite private school students. In the public schools there were teachers delivering books to their students as they could, on a truck, on a ranch, while children in big cities had access to high-quality services even with all the pandemic restrictions. So yes, I see a dilemma in that aspect. However, I still agree with the decision to not support private schools.

**Irma Villalpando:** I see a duality in the government's relationship with private schools. On one hand, there's rigorous control in terms of certification and incorporation, and on the other hand, an indifference to what happens to those of us who work in that sector. The SEP (Secretariat of Public Education) has control over private schools; in interviews I've done, private school principals report a culture of subordination and surveillance coming from the authorities. This level of control made it impossible to open private schools before public ones. We suggested opening schools to offer academic tutoring, for example, and the answer was no, no, and no.

Yet when I participated in a big study at the national level, doing research about the pandemic, and suggested including the private school sector, the researchers weren't interested. In the public discourse, private schools are marginalized in development, research, and so on, which is a shame. Why don't we look for ways to communicate between the private and public schools in terms of methodology, teaching training, and initiatives?

I want to be clear that I'm talking specifically about dilemmas in times of crisis. In general, I would totally agree that there's no need for special support to private schools, and much less if this implies a detriment to public schools. Certainly, there is inequality in all areas: access, coverage, permanence, quality, resources, and time of instruction, which is critical. And, of course, during the pandemic, this inequality deepened. Still, it seems that the government missed an opportunity to provide differentiated support during the pandemic.

**Sebastián Plá:** That also has to do with the SEP's centralist tradition. It was much easier for them to make a single decision and have greater control of the population and its mobility during the pandemic, regardless of whether it was over the private or public sector.

During the pandemic, to be honest, I didn't ask myself much about private schools because I was living in a small town in the countryside, and I saw children in a really vulnerable situation, all by themselves, playing in the park, working in the *milpa* [cornfield], and not being able to go to school. This resulted from decisions that, as you mentioned in the text, were a single decision for all, even when there were a variety of situations.

Now, there were also instances of civil disobedience. I know two cases, one in Puebla, in a Waldorf school that never closed. And I know a secondary school that apparently received students every Friday in the Mountain Region of Guerrero. That is, they never closed. They designed their response based on the local conditions. As Maria said, there was enormous diversity in the issues of the different schools, and a variety in the decisions and actions of the different communities.

**Liz Block:** I'd like to shift the question toward the values and principles at stake in this dilemma. But I'd like us to specifically consider the possibility of a different ethical matrix for moments of crisis. I heard some of you mention at different points, "Well, I mean, I don't agree with this in normal times, but we're talking about Covid during the pandemic and school closures." So, to shift the conversation a little bit, in moments of crisis, when inequalities are magnified or deepened, in situations where the government doesn't have the capacity to give what it should, is there an ethical difference or different values that should be considered?

**María de Ibarrola:** This makes me think about the difference between equality and equity, where equality means that everyone is given the same, and equity means trying to find specific needs for each population group. Although people have fought for it, one of the things that hasn't yet happened in Mexico is the allocation of the best educational resources for the most vulnerable groups. This has been discussed a lot; we researchers have insisted that the country's schools are totally penetrated by inequality; poor schools are without water, bathrooms, and electricity. The diagnosis that the INEE (National Institute for the Evaluation of Education) made on school facilities is truly overwhelming. The way the public sector has treated education is terrible.

Now, in the private school sector, there has always been a very strong tension between the Mexican government and private schools. We need to remember socialist education, the Cristero War, the times of rural education … There is an ideology that doesn't allow for a good relationship between the public and private sectors in education. And by the way, about twenty-five articles in the General Law of Education talk about the supervision and control of private schools. It is not just an ethical question.

The other main factor is the lack of resources. And finally, the inefficiency and incapacity of the SEP means that they cannot make differentiated decisions and don't allow the states of the republic to make differentiated decisions.

**Sebastián Plá:** I'd like to look at some nuances. I think there is a different relationship between public policies and public and private schools. And I understand that there has been this dichotomy, which we see clearly today, but I think private schools also have had a comfortable life in general. Perhaps some smaller schools have had their survival threatened, but not the big, elite ones.

Of course, there have been tensions and inequalities. But I don't think that the relationship is tense in practice. I think there are negotiations, but what generally predominates is a certain authorization for private schools to have their own curriculums, their own practices, even their religious positions and teachings. Considering this, I think that, in reality, private schools survive pretty well.

**Irma Villalpando:** Yes, in the elite segment of private schools there's a kind of collusion. The government accommodates these schools and lets them be. But it's not like that with the middle- and lower-class schools. I've seen huge suffering of administrators in those schools to comply with authority, and the supervisor becomes a source of fear. The supervisor exercises the power of the governmental norm, and often with a very orthodox interpretation. I saw the files at the schools I advised, and the size of the problems they faced, and that doesn't happen in schools with high economic power.

There are two other central values that are in conflict here: equality and freedom. Deep down, I think the only legitimate justification for private education is freedom: freedom to choose what I want my children to study. For example, maybe I think it's important that my children maintain a certain identity—my identity—and I want them to follow it in confessional schools. Or maybe I want them to go to a nice school or to have access to a tennis court. Anyway, because I want it, I can pay for it. And this conflicts with the idea that the public education system has the fundamental goal of generating conditions to level the playing field. In that sense, the public system should, in principle, offer equal treatment for everyone. That might include the defense of freedom for everyone *within* the public system. Those are the two fundamental principles that I think could be in conflict, equality and freedom.

**Liz Block:** Would anyone like to comment on values or principles, not in the situation of elite schools, but in places where there is no public coverage, where there is an important lack of resources, and where institutions or private services are covering part of these needs? What are the tensions in these situations?

**María de Ibarrola:** In primary and secondary school, access is almost covered, so there's little need for private education to come to the rescue. What's changing a lot is what happens *inside* the different schools. Many upper-middle-class schools are created to respond to particular educational demands. Private schools are much more flexible than public schools in terms of schedules and allowing students to work, for example. There are private schools that, for a long time, insisted that both working and studying were important, which was not the case with public schools.

Private education is still private because here is no other way. Like Blanca, I believe that the issue is the defense of the right to freedom of education. Pablo Latapí fought for this right for years: the idea that you must have the freedom to choose what kind of education you want. The freedom to teach religion in schools appeared in 1993, with a very small change that Salinas de Gortari made. He said that private schools had to comply with section B of Article 2 of the law. They didn't have to be secular anymore, as private schools are and, in my opinion, should be. So I'd say that this tension goes beyond ethical values. What would be ethical? An ethical situation would be a quality education for everyone.

**Irma Villalpando:** And that's the point that makes me think about this issue of freedom. Sure this is an exercise of freedom of choice, but not for everyone— only for those who can pay. I've seen some studies, not in Mexico, but in other countries in the region, that ask parents of public school students: if you had the money, would you put your child in private education? And their answer is yes. But they don't *have* a choice, because they don't have the purchasing power.

I want to go back to the discussion about preschool. The data shows that the decrease in enrollment was higher in preschool than in primary and secondary school. The question is: where did those preschool children go? Either they transferred to public preschools, or they're being homeschooled, or their education is being postponed. The issue is that if we analyze the numbers, there's no correspondence between the decreased enrollment in private schools and the increase in public schools. So, we have a disaffiliation problem.

If we look at the primary or secondary level, where the enrollment in private schools has decreased, it's interesting because the enrollment decreases but not the number of schools, which means that schools have the capacity to continue, although with fewer children, which is related to an issue of survival. But the question is, where are *those* children? If it's true that they transferred into the public system, then the public system lost more than they say because this exodus would have actually increased their numbers.

A considerable number of primary schools are also disincorporated because the mechanisms to obtain certification at the end of the year are known; even when adopting homeschooling. I have seen this phenomenon mostly at the preschool level, an impulse for disincorporation.

**María de Ibarrola:** The preschool problem has a very interesting origin. When compulsory preschool was being discussed, a year of compulsory preschool was proposed, which was practically achieved already. But the union and the Congress wanted more, and they pushed for three years of preschool, which hasn't been achieved yet. There was an issue with the expectation that children would learn to read in preschool so they could start elementary school already knowing how to read, which is something that hasn't been achieved yet. And then you have the fact that the pandemic is a unique crisis. Schools had never been closed like that before. That's the moment we realized that school is crucial. The children who couldn't go to school were affected, and the parents who didn't have anyone to leave their children with were affected. It had a really negative impact; it was a unique crisis. And the solutions that were given for preschool weren't good. I was going to mention this joke when you asked, where are the children? Well, their grandparents are taking care of them, right? One of the ministers said that grandparents should take care of them when the children's care centers closed. They suggested giving money to mothers so they could pay the grandparents!

So the particular case of preschool makes me believe we should study government support for private schools—but according to the case, according to the crisis, according to the type of school, in order to take differentiated measures. And always with the principle of adequacy, which the Constitution states clearly, considering the best interests of all the children.

**Blanca Heredia:** I'm convinced that private school is one of the factors that contributes to rigid inequality in Mexico because as long as those with greater resources, who could be more interested in promoting educational quality, have the option of choosing a private school, the public system is deprived of those voices and their possible demand to improve the quality of the public system. So, if those better equipped to demand a better public education system have the option of leaving for private school, then we think about public school in our free time, but we don't do what we would do if the only option for our children was a public school. In that sense, private school is part of the problem. It is endogenous.

Having said that, we could also extend that argument to the case of the State, and the private schools that currently cover the part of the enrollment that the State *should* cover but doesn't. Like so many things in Mexico, it would be convenient for this to be transitory and for the State to give those schools support until it manages to cover demand. But instead, because private schools do that work, the State becomes lazier, and it is no longer interested in covering this demand because there are already some private schools covering it.

**María de Ibarrola:** I agree with Blanca that private schools are private because they deprive others of something. They are taking away those who could be more prepared to demand quality public education. But I think we can't imagine a utopian situation in Mexico where all the schools are public. We don't have that tradition and history. In Colonial times we had religious schools; in the nineteenth century, we had religious schools. Plus, this idea of freedom predominates, right? But we could improve the relationship between both sectors. And while I think that for this dilemma, the principle of not supporting private schools is evident, it was a very special case. I wonder: did someone fight the government's decision not to give them resources?

**Irma Villalpando:** When parents saw their children at home learning remotely, they said, "I'm not going to pay the same tuition." Some because they lost their jobs, but others simply because they knew that remote education was of lower quality than in-person instruction, and they demanded to pay less. I remember parents were outraged and they took this concern to the PROFECO (The Federal Consumer Attorney). And I remember that in the presidential morning conference, the representative of PROPECO said, "We will talk to the parents' association to see what we can do." They gave some hope; even the president, two or three times, said, "We will support you," and then they didn't. I also remember thinking, "Well, there are no resources for it." It's a problem in urban education, and there are more private schools in regions with higher socioeconomic levels. I knew there wasn't any financial support. And something I learned anecdotally is that many schools, during the school closure, didn't charge the same. They charged 50 percent, 30 percent, to sustain themselves, of course, with consequences for the teachers. We don't know if private schools in Mexico will recover their pre-pandemic numbers. But the truth is that the percentage of private schools in the education system in Mexico has remained very stable, even though the logic about private schools can be very naive. The State should at least recognize how much it saves thanks to enrollment in private schools and parents' tuition payments. As I've always said, this could be used to strengthen the public schools to achieve redistribution and equity.

**María de Ibarrola:** Sebastian and Blanca say there is no dilemma because private schools just shouldn't be supported by the state. My position is that it depends on the crisis, on the region, and on the types of schools. Since public and private education are public services, protected by the Constitution and the law, maintained with public resources, and since parents earn and contribute to public education with their taxes, and pay for the privilege they have, I think private schools could be supported in very special cases. It would have to be in exceptional crises like this one.

And the other thing is that public schools have to make a better effort. The demands on middle-class parents are unnecessary. Congress and the laws have made clear that education should be of adequate quality, they have reiterated it over and over again, and yet, they never provide the resources for it.

**Blanca Heredia:** I think that there is a previous dilemma that has nothing to do with Covid, but it does have to do with the fact that the public education system doesn't have the essential quality characteristics we would like, which leads many of us to opt for the private system. The precariousness of the public system puts everyone in a terrible position of having to choose something that maybe they didn't want, and that contributes to the inequality in Mexico and to the lack of attention to public education, which stops us from having the education system we really want.

**Irma Villalpando:** I'm leaving this conversation thinking about [philosopher John] Rawls' veil of ignorance. These educational decisions have to be made without us knowing where in the social strata we could end up, right? That's necessary to guarantee equity. I'm thinking about the relationship between the state authority and private schools. We also need sharp self-criticism in private schools. It seems to me that private education has its own problems, its own logic, that don't get reviewed, and nobody in government cares about, so there is no accountability for it. The SEP is focused on bureaucracy in completing forms, but not evaluation even though there are aspects of private education to analyze, in terms of errors, defects, and bad educational practices.

**Sebastián Plá:** I believe that in Mexico, whoever looks at this situation from the historical perspective, considering the relationship between public and private schools, will be convinced to lean towards what Blanca and I think. Not because we are right or wrong, but because the position has to be public education over private, in general. It is an element of the social imagination: education as social justice.

**Liz Block** *is the Director of Strategy, Partnerships, and Outreach for the EdEthics initiative at the Harvard Graduate School of Education and Edmond & Lily Safra Center for Ethics, USA. Prior to this, Liz was a teacher, head of school, and school developer for Early Childhood through secondary dual-language community schools. She graduated with a BA in Political Science and International Relations with a Minor in Latin American Studies from UCLA. She also holds an Ed.M. in Educational Theory and a Certification in School Management and Leadership from Harvard University.*

**Maria de Ibarrola** *is a Doctor of Education Research in the Departamento de Investigaciones Educativas Center for Advances Research Mexico. Her main line of research and teaching is in the politics and institutions of education and work. A member and ex-President of the International Academy of Education, she has served as a National Researcher since 1984 and emeritus since 2021.*

**Blanca Heredia** *is a political scientist by training. She writes and researches Mexican politics, educational policy, and the promotion of young intellectual talent. She is the founding Director of the Talentum MX Group, which specializes in the design and implementation of highly demanding programs for young people, especially those from socially disadvantaged backgrounds.*

**Sebastián Plá**, *PhD, is Professor of the Research Institute for University and Education at the National Autonomous University of Mexico. His main research interests are the political analysis of educational discourse, especially the curricular configuration of social knowledge and processes of exclusion that produce; theory and practice of teaching history in Mexico and Latin America; and different public and political uses of history.*

**Irma Villalpando** *has a doctorate in pedagogy from the National Autonomous University of Mexico. She teaches at the Acatlán Faculty of Higher Studies and works at a private educational institution.*

# Discussion Questions

1  To what extent do private schools in Mexico provide a public good— and what impact, if any, should that have on the government's funding choices?

2 The private school sector in Mexico is diverse, ranging from highly resourced, elite schools serving the wealthiest families to quite basic low-fee schools primarily serving students from low- and middle-income families. How, if at all, should this diversity have informed the government's response to pandemic-related requests for support from the private school sector?
3 School closures and remote schooling were challenging for all students, not just those enrolled in private school. During health crises like pandemics, how should governments balance students' physical health and their mental health as they consider school closures and other responses?
4 How do different stakeholders in the case conceptualize equity? What might an equitable response to the private schools' requests be?
5 Mexico's finance minister stated that the relationship between private schools and the government is based on "study plans and programs," not finances. What do you think that relationship should be based on?
6 What does the government's refusal to allow any schools, private or public, to reopen early reveal about its conception of educational equity? How closely do you agree with their decision?
7 While this case is set in Mexico, private schools serve students across the world. What forms and roles do private schools take on in your context? How does this case help you reflect on your government's policies toward private versus public schools, in general or specifically during a time of crisis?

# Notes

1. Secretaría de Educación Pública (2020). "Comunicado Conjunto No. 3 Presentan Salud y SEP Medidas de Prevención Para El Sector Educativo Nacional Por COVID-19," *gob.mx*. https://www.gob.mx/sep/es/articulos/comunicado-conjunto-no-3-presentan-salud-y-sep-medidas-de-prevencion-para-el-sector-educativo-nacional-por-covid-19?
2. Ripani, María and Alessia Zucchetti. 2020 "Education Continuity during the Coronavirus Crisis." https://oecdedutoday.com/wp-content/uploads/2020/07/Mexico-Aprende-en-casa.pdf.
3. Cárdenas, Sergio, Lomelí, Dulce, and Ruelas, Ignacio. (2022). "COVID-19 and Post-Pandemic Educational Policies in Mexico. What Is at Stake?," *Springer International Publishing*, January 1, 2022. https://link.springer.com/chapter/10.1007/978-3-030-81500-4_6.

4. Diaz, Lizbeth (2020). "In Mexico's Televised 'Return to Classes,' Parents Turn to State Schools," *Reuters*, August 24, 2020. https://www.reuters.com/article/mexico-education/in-mexicos-televised-return-to-classes-parents-turn-to-state-schools-idINL1N2FO09W.
5. García, Gabriela (2020). "Disminuyen Alumnos En Escuelas Privadas Por Crisis de COVID-19," *Tres PM | Noticias*, June 26, 2020. https://www.trespm.mx/edomex/disminuyen-alumnos-en-escuelas-privadas-por-crisis-de-covid-19.
6. Torres, Lizbeth and Diaz, Noe. (2020). "'Una Crisis Tremenda': Coronavirus Golpea Regreso de Estudiantes En México." *U.S.*, August 24, 2020. https://www.reuters.com/article/salud-coronavirus-mexico-clases-idLTAKBN25K1GV.
7. Personal interview.
8. This is our own calculation, based on SEP. (2019). *Principales Cifras del Sistema Educativo Nacional 2018–2019*. Ciudad de México: SEP; and SEP. (2022). *Principales Cifras del Sistema Educativo Nacional 2021–2022*. Ciudad de México: SEP.
9. Susy Buchanan (2020). "Private Schools May Get Help as Students Move to Public System," *Mexico News Daily*, August 6, 2020. https://mexiconewsdaily.com/coronavirus/private-schools-may-get-help/.
10. Martínez, Verónica (2020). "Maestros Sin Trabajo, El Problema Que Viene Tras El Cierre de Escuelas Privadas," *Cuestione*, August 12, 2020. https://cuestione.com/nacional/maestros-sin-trabajo-el-problema-que-viene-tras-el-cierre-de-escuelas-privadas/.
11. Global Education Monitoring Report Team [1022], Laboratory of Education Research and Innovation for Latin America and the Caribbean [6], UNESCO Office Santiago and Regional Bureau for Education in Latin America and the Caribbean [761] "*Global education monitoring report, 2020, Latin America and the Caribbean: inclusion and education: all means all*"(2020).
12. Pozas, Marcela, Letzel, Verena, and Schneider, Christoph (2021). "'Homeschooling in Times of Corona': Exploring Mexican and German Primary School Students' and Parents' Chances and Challenges during Homeschooling," *European Journal of Special Needs Education* 36:1: 35–50. https://doi.org/10.1080/08856257.2021.1874152.
13. Based on National Commission for the Improvement of Education (2021), which classified public and private schools under the degree of Social Backwardness of their location, according to the Index of Social Backwardness (Índice de Rezago Social), developed by the National Council for the Evaluation of Social Policy (Coneval).
14. Diaz, Lizbeth (2020). "In Mexico's Televised 'Return to Classes,' Parents Turn to State Schools," *Reuters*, August 24, 2020. https://www.reuters.com/

article/mexico-education/in-mexicos-televised-return-to-classes-parents-turn-to-state-schools-idINL1N2FO09W.
15. In 2021 the gross and net rate of enrollment in this level were 71.7 and 69.8, respectively. Gross enrollment counts the total number of students enrolled at that level, regardless of age. In contrast, net enrollment counts only those students in the ideal age range for that level; for upper-secondary schools, net enrollment would include students aged 15–17.
16. National Commission for the Improvement of Education (2021).
17. Own calculation, based on SEP. (2020). *Principales Cifras del Sistema Educativo Nacional 2021–2022*. Ciudad de México: SEP.
18. The net enrollment (the enrollment for students of the ideal age for that level of education) was even lower at 63.2. Source: National Commission for the Improvement of Education (2021).
19. National Commission for the Improvement of Education (2021).
20. The number of students in the private system (preschool to upper-secondary education) decreased from 3,755,809 to 3,025,091 (19.5 percent), from 2019–20 to 2021–2. The public system passed from 27,079,075 students to 26,128,543.00 (a drop of 3.5 percent). Source: SEP. (2019). *Principales Cifras del Sistema Educativo Nacional 2018–2019*. Ciudad de México: SEP; and SEP. (2022). *Principales Cifras del Sistema Educativo Nacional 2021–2022*. Ciudad de México: SEP.
21. According to "Encuesta Para La Medición Del Impacto COVID-19 En La Educación (ECOVID-ED) 2020," Accessed October 31, 2023. https://www.inegi.org.mx/investigacion/ecovided/2020/.
22. While there is little research about the impact of school closure in Mexico, research from other countries highlights the distress felt by students and families when their schools close. See Eve Ewing's *Ghosts in the Schoolyard* (2018), for example, for an account of the trauma of public school closures in Chicago.
23. https://www.tandfonline.com/doi/full/10.1080/08856257.2021.1874152. While this quote is attributed to an anonymous parent in the paper, the authors note that "most Mexican participants [in the study] attended inclusive private schools."
24. For instance, according to the mission statement of the Colegio Israelita, "The Hebrew and Judaic Studies Program is the essence of the institution. It gives students a sense of identity, belonging, responsibility and solidarity with the Jewish People at the individual, community level and with the State of Israel. It connects students with the origins, traditions, history and future of their people." See https://www.colegioisraelita.edu.mx/nuestra-escuela. Along similar lines, the mission statement of Colegio Maguén David states: "We work so that each of the students discovers their interests, develops their talents and manages to live a full and meaningful

life in community, contributing their knowledge, attitudes and values to Mexican society, the Jewish community and the world in general, in the social, cultural and labor spheres, with an ethical and moral commitment." See https://chmd.edu.mx/filosofia/. For more on religious education in Mexico, particularly Catholic education, see Torres Septién, Valentina (1997). *La Educación Privada En México (1903–1976)*. México, D. F.: El Colegio De México.

25. Personal interview.
26. "Evidence and Learning: Strengthening Crisis and Risk-Related Data and Institutional Education Information Systems." n.d. https://inee.org/sites/default/files/resources/Case%20Study%20-%20Mexicanos%20Primero_Back%20to%20School%20Index_BAT.pdf.
27. Fifty percent of the private academic offerings in Mexico cost, at most, MX$ 2,600 (US$ 135.13) and MX$ 3,700 (US$ 192.30) per month for the primary and secondary levels respectively. The academic offerings for the primary and high school levels are mostly low-cost, while secondary schools are mostly medium-cost. Families in Mexico City who enroll their children in private schools seem to prefer more expensive schools as their children's educational level progresses.
28. Martínez, Marco Antonio (2020). "Dan Clases Presenciales En Colegio Humanitree, Pese a Prohibición," *La Silla Rota*, Accessed October 31, 2023. https://lasillarota.com/metropoli/2020/10/27/dan-clases-presenciales-en-colegio-humanitree-pese-prohibicion-252181.html.
29. 177 students spread over fifteen groups averages to 11.8 students per group. Data retrieved from: Rodríguez, Darinka (2020). "El Colegio Del Empresario Salinas Pliego Imparte Clases Presenciales a Pesar Del Cierre Impuesto Por La Pandemia," *Ediciones EL PAÍS S.L.*, November 10, 2020. https://elpais.com/mexico/2020-11-10/el-colegio-del-empresario-salinas-pliego-imparte-clases-presenciales-a-pesar-del-cierre-impuesto-por-la-pandemia.html.
30. The cost is approximately $700–800 per month. Rodríguez, Darinka (2020). "El Colegio Del Empresario Salinas Pliego Imparte Clases Presenciales a Pesar Del Cierre Impuesto Por La Pandemia," *Ediciones EL PAÍS S.L.*, November 10, 2020. https://elpais.com/mexico/2020-11-10/el-colegio-del-empresario-salinas-pliego-imparte-clases-presenciales-a-pesar-del-cierre-impuesto-por-la-pandemia.html.

# 4

# A Qualified Disaster: Allocating Student Grades During Covid-19

*Hester Burn*

*Many students in England sit a set of national examinations at age sixteen and eighteen, called General Certificates of Secondary Education (GCSEs) and Advanced Level qualifications (A Levels) respectively. These examinations occur over a period of about four weeks toward the end of the academic year, and opportunities to re-sit after this time are rare. For each qualification, students usually sit the same examination paper at the same time across the country. The examination scripts are then marked externally, and a national regulatory body sets grade boundaries to ensure that the distribution of grades is comparable across years. At GCSE, grades range from one (low) to nine (high), with grades four or five being considered a pass and seven an indication of higher-level proficiency. At A Level, the grades range from "E" (low) to "A\*" (high). The average student will take eight or nine GCSE and three A Level, or equivalent, qualifications.[1] The grades that students receive have significant long-term consequences. Many schools and colleges admit students for A Levels and for skilled vocational training based on their GCSE grades, making this benchmark highly determinant of future educational prospects.[2] GCSE and predicted A Level (or equivalent) grades are also the primary means by which universities offer places to prospective undergraduates, and are often requested in job applications long after students have left school.[3] The grades achieved by a school cohort also determine that school's place in national league tables and their likely enrollment—and therefore funding—for the subsequent year.*

GCSE and A Level examinations were canceled in both 2020 and 2021 due to the Covid-19 pandemic. Policymakers were tasked with deciding how to assign grades in their place. In 2020, the Department for Education opted to use teacher predictions alongside a statistical moderation process to ensure that the grades that students received—both overall and within each school—were not considerably higher than those in previous years. However, this approach led to a public outcry of such magnitude that the policy was withdrawn the day after students received their grades, with the Prime Minister blaming a "mutant algorithm" for the U-turn and publicly dismissing a top civil servant.[4] In 2021, schools were instead asked to run their own examinations and then submit grades with evidence to back up each of their decisions. However, this approach did no better at commanding public trust, with some parents preparing formal appeals against their children's schools even before the 2021 grades had been released.[5] The challenge facing policymakers was that Covid-19 highlighted the fragility of the existing examinations, bringing to light both new and old issues embedded in long-established processes. If 2020 and 2021 grading needed to compensate for problems exacerbated by the pandemic then which, if any, should take precedence?

## Fairness Between Cohorts

For some, the most important consideration for grading processes in 2020 and 2021 was consistency. For a decade, the grade boundaries for these national examinations had been specifically set so that the proportion of students achieving each grade was similar to that in previous years.[6] This was primarily intended to allow future employers and advanced education providers, such as universities, to fairly compare applicants from different cohorts who apply for the same opportunity.[7] When examinations were canceled in 2020 and 2021, and teachers were tasked with assigning grades to their own students, it was considered likely that the grades would be higher than those in previous years. This was, in the words of one school leader, because "schools may, understandably, [give] some students the benefit of the doubt when they are on the borderline" between two grades.[8] However higher grades for the 2020 and 2021 cohorts would make life harder for many students in non-disrupted years who would end up competing with them for university places and entry-level jobs, especially given that a considerable number of the 2020 and 2021 cohorts were likely to defer applications until after the height of the pandemic had passed.[9] In addition, at least some students from these more and less generously graded cohorts were likely to apply for the same employment opportunities in the future, for which GCSE, A Level, and equivalent grades are often still requested. As another school leader commented, "when we're thinking about fairness and equality, of course, first and foremost, we think about this year's cohort. But we have to think about fairness and equality with previous cohorts and with future cohorts as well."[10]

In 2020, the Department for Education addressed concerns about consistency and fairness by deciding that students' examination grades would not be determined by teacher assessment alone. Instead, the Office of Qualifications and Examination Regulation (Ofqual) would determine the final grades received by students by applying an algorithm to those given by teachers. This would ensure that the proportions of each grade received at both the school level and the national level were consistent with previous years, informed by data on the historical results of each school and a ranking of students within them.[11] It also guaranteed that no school was raising their grades significantly more than another. The policy was welcomed by Universities UK, representing the UK higher education sector, who believed that the qualifications would therefore "hold their value" and that the processes would enable progression to further education or jobs without being at "the expense of academic standards."[12]

When the grades were released in August 2020, however, the public response was overwhelmingly negative. Many students felt as though they'd had little agency in determining the grades that they received. One reason for this was that much of the existing data that schools had on student attainment were through "mock" (practice) examinations collected months before schools had closed. Did these data not provide an outdated representation of students' full potential? As one young person noted, "when we took [the mock examinations], we were under the impression that they weren't really important, and now they are."[13]

A second reason was that, as the grades that students received were informed by the prior performance of their school, some students in previously low-attaining schools were unable to be assigned top grades even if they would have performed considerably better than their older peers, resulting in many missing the grades that they needed to meet their university offers.[14] Indeed students from disadvantaged backgrounds were found to have been more likely to be downgraded at A Level, impacting—

in the words of the president of the National Union of Students—"who's had to pick a different university, who's been forced to defer … [and] on the demographics of our universities" in a manner which was "completely unjust."[15] One student who was initially downgraded and therefore missed a conditional offer at her chosen university stated: "I just think it is very unfair that because of past performance in this area and particularly in my school that I haven't got in … that computer doesn't know that I got to school every single day at 7am revising … that computer doesn't even know who I am and that I exist."[16]

Was it defensible that these students' futures had been upended due to the decisions of a statistical model? Such outcomes were near-impossible for the government to justify.

In the end, the fiasco was instead blamed on a "mutant algorithm" and the higher, purely teacher-assessed grades were restored within a matter of days.[17]

## Fairness Between Schools

By 2021, although students had more or less returned to classrooms, new issues regarding the fairness of national examinations had risen to the surface. During school closures, the education that schools were able to provide at a distance had varied greatly, with some able to rely on their students each having a personal laptop while others had relied on packets of printed resources.[18] Moreover, many of the poorest areas of the country were the most heavily impacted by school absences and partial closures after the height of the pandemic, meaning that, even once schools reopened, their students missed out on a greater amount of face-to-face learning than those in more affluent regions.[19] The injustice that these circumstances unveiled was not new, but it was more blatant. The potential negative consequences for students in more economically marginalized schools if examinations went ahead "as normal" were palpable.

For policymakers deciding how grades should be assigned in 2021, one solution was to still allow students to sit examinations but to put contingencies in place which accounted for differences in learning opportunity during periods of school closure. Teachers were therefore instructed to disregard the full extent of the curriculum and to instead create examination papers which were customized to test their students only on topics about which they had actually been taught. Schools would then combine these results with other data at their disposal and use this evidence—which could be checked by an external adjudicator—to assign each student a grade. OCR, an exam-setting organization, stated that such a "strongly evidence-based approach" would "promote public confidence" in the examination results received.[20]

This compromise, however, was not wholly watertight. The flexibility granted to schools was incomparable to the strict processes of the pre-pandemic years, including allowing schools to distribute lists of the topics to be examined in advance and to hold the examinations in low-intensity classroom settings. Many felt that such flexibility was long overdue. However, when the proportion of top A Level grades in one fee-paying school soared from 34 percent in 2019 to 90 percent in 2021, and when this was found to be exemplary of a wider trend by which grade increases were a lot higher in fee-paying schools than those which were government-funded, concerns grew.[21] Was it fair to merely replace variation in how schools were impacted by Covid-19 with variation in how schools designed and marked their own assessments? Could it really be claimed that these results were as robust as those in non-disrupted years? And, even if this was possible in theory, did the importance of students' results to school league tables in England introduce incentives against which it was impossible to mitigate? Although, on release, the 2021 grades were not subjected to the overhaul experienced the previous year, students lodged four times as many appeals against their schools' decisions.[22] Students of teachers who had put faith into the system acting fairly were likely the ones who faced the greatest repercussions when it became apparent that it had not.

## Fairness Between Students

Finally, despite the 2020 and 2021 grading policies attempting to achieve a semblance of fairness *between* schools, it was impossible to ignore the fact that schools would be facing dilemmas about fairness *within* their own student bodies. How should the examination performance of a student who, during school closures, had had consistent internet access and a quiet room in which to work be compared to that of a student who shared a single device with their siblings? How should teachers judge the attainment of a student who had to take on extra paid work during the pandemic because others in their household were shielding? And what of students with sensory impairment, for whom there would have been additional learning loss through remote instruction? Research by the education think tank The Sutton Trust revealed that 40 percent of middle-class children had undertaken over five hours of schoolwork a day during school closures, compared to just 26 percent of those in working-class households.[23] Although some of this gap will have been driven by differences between the schools that these students attended, significant gaps were also likely to exist between middle- and working-class students within the same school, and indeed within the same classroom.

The difficulty for policymakers in considering grading fairness between individual students, however, was that it invited questions about examination grades that extended far beyond Covid-19. The attainment gap between students who are eligible for free lunches and their more advantaged peers had been shown to be growing rather than shrinking *prior* to Covid-19.[24] This situation had only worsened since.[25]

Policymakers may have considered trying to account for such systematic disadvantage by allowing teachers to raise grades beyond that for which they had evidence, based on extenuating circumstances. But how would these circumstances have been categorized, and what precedent would it have set for future years? Moreover, if sorting students into grades is merely a mechanism by which existing disadvantages in society are quantified and reproduced, then should it even be done at all? Students with graduate parents were found to be unfairly advantaged by teacher-assigned grades in 2020, illustrating how less standardized assessment systems may be more easily gamed by those with greater resources.[26] Nonetheless more standardized assessments, even if they are less easy to manipulate, are arguably still merely measuring the years of advantage that those with greater resources already have.[27]

## Looking Back and Looking Ahead

Deciding how to assign grades during Covid-19 in England required those with decision-making power to engage with significant practical and ethical dilemmas. One of the biggest of these was whether it was more important to prioritize fairness between cohorts, fairness between schools, or fairness between groups of pupils who experienced hardships to different extents during the pandemic. However, a second question about England's national examinations also rose to the surface of public debate during this time: Were they ever fair in the first place? Should exams be canceled again, how should the Department for Education in England respond? Do the issues with high-intensity, high-stakes examinations in England that were exposed by Covid-19 mean that changes need to be made whether another crisis occurs or not? And finally, if so, what might an ethical assessment and accountability system in England look like in the future?

# Conversation

**Hester Burn:** Welcome to our case study discussion on grading in a time of Covid. It's actually A Level results day in England today [August 18, 2022], which means we're about a full year after the time period discussed in the case study. But Covid still has a strong legacy, even this year, with students still concerned about the results, and policymakers having to grapple yet again with trade-offs about what will be included in examination papers, and how to set grade boundaries. This is very much going to be on our minds today. So thank you all so much for being here.

I was previously a maths teacher and I recall feeling very emotionally turbulent about assigning grades to my own students in 2020 and 2021. So I was interested to know: did reading the case study and returning to that period bring back any uncomfortable emotional memories for you?

**Josiah Isles:** Oh, yeah, lots. I moved schools in the interim between 2020 and 2021, and the approaches from school to school, top down from leadership, were so different. One of the biggest problems in the first year was trying to offer some parity to previous cohorts.

**Hester Burn:** Diana, do you want to talk a little bit about the dilemmas that universities were facing?

**Diana Beech:** Absolutely. When you asked the first question, I felt, first of all, relief that I wasn't in the front and center of things as a teacher. At the time, I was firmly part of the university sector, working for a large, research-intensive, high tariff [academically selective, elite] UK institution. And when the A Level results came out, there were more students who were predicted to have higher grades, because of the computer-generated results. But it wasn't a boon for universities, as the press were describing. Actually, there was genuine concern on the ground. How do we take all these students? How do we provide them a top-rate student experience? Have we got the accommodation? Have we got the staff? It wasn't just, "we've got more students, we've got more money," as I think some of the press were portraying it. Universities were really concerned about maintaining that high-quality student experience that they're known for, and to do justice to that cohort of students, which of course needed extra support, having come through the pandemic and adjusted to online learning as well. Can we make hybrid work? Can we cater for all students? And of course with international students, and travel restrictions that still exist to this day—how can we make sure we're providing an inclusive education experience, so they can join in and participate fully as well? Those were the questions I remember facing.

**Hester Burn:** Was there much of a concern about whether admissions procedures were going to be as accurate as they normally are?

**Diana Beech:** I think that was secondary. From the universities' perspective on the ground that year, they wanted to do what's right for those students who'd just overcome absolute turmoil. They just wanted to make sure that they had something secure for the future and that those who deserved it and wanted to go to university could. So I think the first year was just a mad scramble to do what's right.

**Tom Richmond:** It was always going to be very challenging for teachers. As a former A Level teacher, myself, I'm well aware of the pressures that teachers are under. But of course, the lockdown came in March 2020, when students were at the very end of their courses. They actually only missed probably about six to eight weeks of teaching at the end of a two-year course. So when the government said to teachers, can you tell us what you think those students would have got in the exam, which was basically the official instruction they were given, then that was a fairly reasonable request, given that teachers had access to two years' worth of assessment data. But of course, the following year, that changed very dramatically. The question that teachers got asked in 2021 was very different, which was, can you tell us what level these students are performing at? And the fact that these were two different questions escaped public attention and journalists' attention inevitably, because they were buried in guidance from the exam regulator to schools and colleges. At least in the first year, although there clearly was a political meltdown as much as a grading meltdown, teachers had a pretty strong basis to make decisions. But when it came to 2021, we'd had two academic years badly disrupted, and no exams, and students were told a long time in advance that they wouldn't have exams, and every school in the country just had to figure out its own answer. Universities were saying, hold on a second. How do we know which of these students is actually performing at a higher level compared to other students, when every school has come up with its own answer to "Should we use homework to judge students?," "Should we use mock exams?," "How many mock exams should we use?," "Should we include long term coursework assignments?" Everyone was coming up with different answers, and that just put teachers in a really difficult position, because they were, ultimately, the arbiters of their students' future. And I think one of the things we forget is that the anonymity of marking that we have with the public exam system is an incredibly important feature that we lost. We just said to teachers, you have to take on all the responsibility now. And I think that was incredibly unfair on teachers, and indeed, the school leaders and college leaders who then had to sign off on those grades as well.

**Josiah Isles:** Picking up on your points, Tom, about the process with regards to the fairness to school leaders and teachers, I would say that it brings into context the actual material that was used to assign the grades as well. When you go for an exam process, that material is so vigorous in terms of the content. I'm not convinced that in all subjects, across all our schools, across the country, that all teachers adhered to that level of detail. Because if you've got, for example, a really new and inexperienced faculty who has not been an examiner themselves, to then ask them to write enough material and to be quite vigorous with those grades is a difficult job. And that puts more emphasis on teacher judgment. And it's really quite evident that in some schools they've used materials supplied by exam boards and in some schools they have made their own, and it caused quite a lot of issues with regards to consistency across schools. It was quite a major issue with regards to whether students have been given materials in advance or given the list of materials to revise [review]. Even that small aspect still is different in different schools. So it was really quite a difficult position with not a lot of guidance about how to keep that additional scrutiny across schools really tight and consistent. Where's the parity between my school in Bolton compared to a school in Surrey, for example: we haven't discussed anything, there's no communication across maths departments, across English departments, between school leaders. So where's the parity coming from? Well, we're relying purely on that consistency or teacher approach. But that can't happen unless you've communicated in some way.

**Hester Burn:** What are the dilemmas that emerged about the UK education assessment system in general during this time?

**Dylan Wiliam:** Education researchers, particularly those focusing on assessment have moved away from the idea of validity as being a property of an assessment towards the idea that validity is a property of the conclusions that you draw. So there's no such thing as a valid test—a test is valid for some purposes and not others. And so validation needs to focus on: what are we entitled to conclude about a student from seeing how well they do on an assessment? I think if people had actually focused on that, we'd have had a more sensible debate. With A Levels in particular, there's an unspoken issue about whether they are meant to be measuring achievement or aptitude. If you want to apply to a British university, you have to apply to a particular department—that's not the case in the United States, where you typically select your major in your second or third year. In the UK, if you want to apply to do mathematics, you apply to the mathematics department, and they will want to see a high standard of mathematics achievement. But if you want to study law, they don't expect you to have studied law in school. So there's actually a massive variability in the kinds of requirements the universities have for specific achievement in subjects, even subjects that will be the focus of your studies. Often the focus is more on some measure of aptitude: is this person somebody who can learn?

The other thing that I think that is really quite important to get right, is that we've actually had a post-qualification system for many years in the UK and at many universities, because we tend to rely on predicted grades. When I was chair of the admissions committee at King's College London, we had a real problem that sometimes when we gave students offers, if they didn't eventually make the grades, we ended up rejecting them. And then we found we were short of students. So we went back to fill the places and we often ended up actually accepting students who were at a lower level than those who we'd rejected. So we actually started saying, "Look, if you've given them an offer, take them whether they make the grades or not," because the examination grade isn't as reliable as the kinds of processes that led to the offer in the first place. So I think there's several issues that need to be unpacked here, but the real problem comes down to this aptitude versus achievement issue.

I think that in Britain, we have a tendency at the universities to wait for talent to knock on the door, whereas in the United States, there's much more of a tradition of universities seeing it as part of their job to identify talent. If you score 1600 on the SAT you may actually get a contact from a top school before you've actually even got the results from the College Board. Here's the challenge for me. A Level is called the gold standard. But for me, the question should be: are A Level grades the only way of identifying talent? I think we should be highlighting that the A Levels are not perfect. The differences between subjects are really strange. We now know that chemistry, science and physics and mathematics A Levels are much harder than other subjects. What sense does it make to compare an economics A Level which is based on just two years of study and an English A Level where kids have been learning this subject for eighteen years? The other thing people don't want to talk about is the fact that some students don't get the same opportunities to learn as others. If you want to assess students then, fine, assess their opportunity to learn. But I don't want to certify doctors and airline pilots taking into account their opportunity to learn; I want them to be good at the things that we want them to be able to do.

All these tensions basically come down to defining the constructs more carefully: what it is we want students to be able to do. When people designing curriculum fail to specify the constructs, the people designing the assessments have too much power. So in terms of the ethics, with clear construct definition, assessment development should be a largely technical exercise, in that different people should be able to agree about whether a particular assessment is adequate or not. When the construct is not defined, reasonable people can disagree about the adequacy of the assessment. They think it's an argument about the assessment when it's actually an argument about the underlying construct. These debates are really about the fact that we don't actually even agree about what it is that A Levels should be assessing.

**Hester Burn:** We've got differences in the values, aims, and beliefs about what assessment of any kind is there to do. Does anyone want to talk more about the differences in values and aims for assessment in this country?

**Dylan Wiliam:** The case explains that we use assessments to certify the achievements and maybe the potential of individuals, but we also use them to hold schools to account. What's bizarre about this is that data from the Department of Education, and the Organization for Economic Cooperation Development, show that schools account for about 8 percent of the variation in student achievement. Ninety-two percent of the variation in student achievement is not caused by the quality of the school. So we use these results in ways that are completely illegitimate, in that the primary determinant of our kids' grades when they leave school is how much they knew when they started at that school. And that, I think, is the real problem. Average school grades are a really bad indication of how good that school is.

**Tom Richmond:** When it comes to the aim of assessment, the more aims you attach to a single assessment, the less it does any of them well. If you look at the assessments you have at age eleven, for primary school pupils, they are used for an eye-watering number of different purposes. And that places an enormous strain on them. This is sometimes used as a trigger for talking about university entrance exams in the UK and changing to a system, like they have in the United States, where they separate out the two roles: you'd have a test to get you into University, and a separate test to determine how students are performing in their school.

When you look at all the different actors who were in the system in 2020 and 2021, we had the government thinking that it was their job to hold schools and colleges accountable, and the exam regulator feeling the weight of their legal duty to uphold public confidence in the exam system, and also to make sure that standards are consistent over time. Then you had parents and students who were looking to get that highest possible grade, knowing that it might unlock doors at university or for employment. You have teachers and schools and colleges trying to make sure they were behaving with integrity and fairness in an extremely uncertain and unstable environment. And ultimately, with the greatest respect to everyone who was involved, you just can't achieve all of those things. I don't think politicians were honest enough with the trade-offs that were going to have to be made. They tried to go down one route in 2020, only to have to slam on the brakes in the face of enormous public opposition, because they weren't sure they understood the system very well themselves. That had a huge impact on 2021. That's why I think the two years ended up looking so different and posing such different ethical and moral challenges for teachers, and technical and technocratic challenges for the regulators.

**Dylan Wiliam:** It might be useful to compare the UK system to other systems like the ones in Sweden and Texas. In those systems, when you apply to university, you can actually take an aptitude test, the SAT in Texas or the SweSAT in Sweden. But you also apply on the basis of your grade point average, the grades your teachers give you. I think in Texas, if you're in the top 10 percent of your graduating high school class for GPA, you automatically gain admission to the state University of Texas system. In Sweden, you are automatically considered for a university place on whatever type of assessment gives you the best chance of getting in. The idea is to allow students to show us what they can do in a range of different ways. So maybe in the UK we should have multiple routes. And I think that would have been something that we could have done quite intelligently in 2020 and 2021, and let people let different users weight these components differently.

**Josiah Isles:** In the last couple years we've had some students who have had the opportunity to really show what they can do in the classroom, rather than in an exam, which previously they wouldn't have been able to. I'm a science teacher, and my students often find the chemistry, physics, and biology individual components of the A Levels really, really difficult. They are solid subjects. You often have students who are really good at science, but can't access the exam papers in a conventional manner. And I think over the last couple of years, these students have been able to realize that they're good at science in an unconventional way. The problem is that, in the UK system, the BTECS [Business and Technology Education Council vocational qualifications] that are offered for science are actually A Level in terms of content, just crammed into a format that is meant to be more accessible. And when it isn't, it's just as difficult. It would be helpful to get the opportunity to stop and think about how we can get some of these students through without writing them off and saying, "Because you can't access that A Level paper, science is not right for you." At the moment, either you can access the exam papers and do really well or you can't, and we let those students down. We allow them to do apprenticeships, which is wonderful, but there are quite a lot of opportunities that we could allow access to if there were alternative pathways.

**Diana Beech:** I wonder if we shot ourselves in the foot a little bit by the way we talk about A Levels as the golden ticket to higher education. Because, to pick up on something that Professor Wiliam said earlier, university admissions professionals in the UK do actually consider A Level results and BTEC results alongside a bigger basket of measures as well, to measure things that are not necessarily captured in testing achievement. And this does include the aptitude of our students, in the learning gains that they've taken to get their three A Stars, which could be dependent on their own personal circumstances: other commitments they're carrying, their school background, and other factors.

**Hester Burn:** Let's rewind, back to 2020, or 2021. Does anyone have any firm idea about which purpose of the A Levels should have been prioritized?

**Dylan Wiliam:** I would have actually administered traditional A Level exams and then put an asterisk next to the scores. So you keep the standard the same, and if the students fall short because of the disruption, you can take that into account. I would have made sure that universities understood this, and tried to give them some indication of the disruption. There's quite a lot of work about how much learning was lost as a result of the pandemic, including different estimates for different kids from different social groups. So you could actually tag it and say, if you're a middle-class kid, you probably lost two months of learning, if you're a kid from a much less affluent background, you probably lost four months. Then I think the admissions tutors could have taken that into account in deciding how to admit people. But once you change the standard, then it's really hard to figure out what these results mean. So I think even though it would be politically difficult, I wouldn't change the A Level standard, I would qualify and provide more support and contextualize it. You know, I wouldn't let people pass a driving test because they had a hard time learning to drive.

**Diana Beech:** That was going to be my initial thinking as well. However, I've got one niggling thought in my head and that is: what happens ten years down the line, when those students have graduated and are competing for jobs with people from two years previously? Are employers going to take that asterisk into consideration if they are looking at A Level grades as a differentiating factor?

**Hester Burn:** Can you talk a bit more about that? Where's the inequality or social justice issue that you might be seeing?

**Diana Beech:** Well, let's assume all these graduates come out with nice 2:1s and firsts. And let's take a five-year cohort. Some of the big employers do still look back to A Level grades as a differentiating factor for who they hire. And I just wonder, will it be in employers' consciousness that some of that cohort took their A Levels in the pandemic year? Do the students even want to be known as the pandemic generation? You would think there might be an issue of personal pride at play as well. People want to be in the position on their own merit. I don't think these students will want to feel that they're sort of dragged down by that asterisk, although, as Professor Wiliam said, it is probably the fairest thing to do in the short term.

**Hester Burn:** Do you agree that it should have been the priority to signal achievement, comparable to other years, even if it had to come with an asterisk?

**Josiah Isles:** Absolutely. I think that the students should have had an opportunity to actually just sit the exams. I don't see why that wasn't something that wasn't considered. It could have been rolled out quite easily and would have been fairer. Even if it was online, that would have allowed for a comparison to previous years and to their compatriots around the country. It would have been a wonderful thing to have done.

**Tom Richmond:** I'd very much echo that. I mean, the political considerations became overwhelmingly, and I would say disproportionately, important in the summer of 2020. But when it came to 2021, there was no reason why GCSE students couldn't at least have sat their English and maths GCSEs [taken at age 16]. Because when you're talking about the purpose of the assessments, there was an argument for saying, we need to get some core skills across these students and really test them because they're going to be going on to further study or employment or an apprenticeship. And that wouldn't have been impossible at all! Schools and colleges were open all around the country, and we could have offered students the opportunity to maybe sit two or three other subjects as an option rather than moving to teacher assessment. And for A Level students, maybe we could have let them sit one of their subjects out of their three or four, and had the teacher assess the grade for the other two. That would have given some grounding to the system, and maybe would have approached a system that people could trust and have confidence in. I think the biggest concern about what happened in 2021 is that nobody had confidence in the grades by the end of the process. And although as I was saying earlier, having an assessment with too many purposes attached to it is a massive problem, having an assessment that serves no purpose at all is probably even worse. If you'd go back and look at what was happening in the run up to the use of that so-called "mutant" algorithm in 2020, there were very few concerns being aired before exam results day because everyone knew it was a half decent solution to an unexpected and difficult situation. It was only when politics got involved that we moved away from that in a very dramatic snap and all of a sudden, we just couldn't really get back to any sensible conversations anymore. The results that have come out today are showing that we are in the process of returning back to normal, whatever normal now means. And by 2023, everything really should be back to pretty close as it was in 2019. Whether that means we've missed the opportunity for some quite important conversations is at the front of a lot of people's minds at the moment, because we have learned a lot about what the options are and what the benefits and drawbacks are of different models over the past couple of years.

**Hester Burn:** The one niggle that I've still got involves what influence schools have in this process. Dylan said at the beginning that they account for 8 percent variation in student outcomes, which is mostly determined already by where pupils are when they begin school. And yet there was quite big variation during Covid in what schools were able to deliver in terms of home learning. Is that something we should be taking into consideration?

**Dylan Wiliam:** The trouble for me is that, yes, we should, but allowing teachers to take those things into account produces a huge additional variability, because you have no idea just what to take into account. As a libertarian, my first question is, why is the government involved in examinations at all? Why is the government controlling this? Why isn't it a decision for individual schools and academies? I think that the debate I would want to have is at a system design level. What information do universities want? And the other thing I'd want to put into the equation is: Why is our qualification of kids at eighteen completely driven by universities? Is admission to university the most important reason to describe student achievement at the age of eighteen? I would like to see us deciding what it is we'd like to know about students at the age of eighteen, where the exam boards are just one of the partners involved and employers are others, but then, society as a whole needs to have some stake in how we're certifying student achievement when they leave school.

**Josiah Isles:** Is that fair? I think that there's quite a disparity coming to the fore with regards to learners who are from disadvantaged backgrounds. The lack of technology, the lack of a private work space, all of these factors have been exacerbated over the last two years. And just to add to that, these households might have experienced Covid deaths, or they might also be in situations where parents have lost work. That gap between parents who have graduate jobs, for example, and those that are coming from disadvantaged backgrounds is now increasingly more apparent. And I think that the "return to normal" doesn't take into account that for the learners who are going to be taking GCSEs, most of their time in secondary school has been disrupted. And their home life has been significantly disrupted as well. So they will be doing "normal" exams, and they will be having "normal" opportunities, but their emotional wellbeing and support networks are even more reduced than they would have been normal in a situation of disadvantage. What should we do for those students? And that's where the teachers come into play, but they can only do so much. Currently we are throwing money at this problem with tutoring programs in the hope that's going to improve results. But that isn't really going to improve anything if students try to do tutoring at home online, and they've got five brothers and sisters in the background, and mum's trying to find work for the family to get food. That doesn't take into account any of that, that doesn't actually fix the problem that some students are going hungry. We need to re-look quite heavily at that, because the results that come through for those learners when they sit their GCSEs, are going to be quite far from where we want them to be. And when they get through to A Levels the gap is going to be vast. We need to help with that home situation, which is quite a massive problem and needs to be looked at in more detail than just what we're doing in schools and with the exam policy.

**Diana Beech** *is Chief Executive Officer of London Higher, the representative body for almost fifty universities and higher education colleges across the London region. She was previously Policy Adviser to three former UK universities and science ministers and, before that, the first Director of Policy and Advocacy at the Higher Education Policy Institute.*

**Josiah Isles** *is the Assistant Headteacher at Ladybridge High School in Bolton, UK. A London born Science Teacher, he has a lifelong passion for helping disadvantaged learners to achieve their full potential.*

**Tom Richmond** *is the founder and director of the EDSK think tank, which conducts research on schools, colleges, apprenticeships, and universities in England. He is also a former teacher and former advisor to ministers at the Department for Education in London.*

**Dylan Wiliam** *is Emeritus Professor of Educational Assessment at the UCL Institute of Education. In a varied career, he has taught in urban public schools, directed a large-scale testing program, served a number of roles in university administration, including Dean of a School of Education, and pursued a research program focused on supporting teachers to develop their use of assessment in support of learning.*

# Discussion Questions

1 In 2020, policymakers used an algorithm to modify teacher-assigned grades, in an attempt to address concerns about consistency and fairness. What role, if any, do you think algorithms and/or other

technological solutions should play in the allocation of educational goods, like qualifications and university placements?
2   The pandemic highlighted the vastly different resources available to different schools and even to different students within the same schools. How much, if at all, should those disparities influence the ways that universities and employers use examination scores to distribute placements?
3   Ensuring that GSCE and A-level test scores are assessed consistently across grade-level cohorts is important partly because these scores directly inform hiring decisions beyond school. What role, if any, should standardized test scores play in hiring decisions?
4   Policymakers needed to find a way to balance being fair to the cohort impacted by the pandemic with being fair to both previous and future cohorts. How would you have balanced these different cohorts as you consider how to assign grades fairly in 2020 and 2021?
5   What inequities in the pre-pandemic testing system did the pandemic reveal? Would you describe the pre-pandemic testing system as more or less fair than the various pandemic-era approaches to testing? Why?
6   All school-age children were impacted by the pandemic. How, if at all, should policymakers think about accommodations or adjustments in future years for students whose education was also disrupted in the past?
7   How does this case help you think about the role that high-stakes standardized assessments play in your own national setting?

# Notes

1.  Students may also choose to study one or more Business and Technology Education Council (BTEC) qualifications, which are equivalent to GCSEs or A Levels and have a greater focus on practical, vocational skills.
2.  Students who are just a few marks short of a pass in their English GCSE are about 9 percentage points less likely to enroll in A Levels and 4 percentage points more likely to drop out of education entirely by age eighteen than they would be had they just scraped through. In Machin, Stephen, McNally, Sandra, and Ruiz-Valenzuela, Jenifer (2020). "Entry through the

Narrow Door: The Costs of Just Failing High Stakes Exams," *Journal of Public Economics* 190. https://doi.org/10.1016/j.jpubeco.2020.104224

3. For more information. see Taylor, Nick (2022). "The Real Story behind University Entry Requirements," *The Uni Guide*, Accessed June 14, 2022. https://www.theuniguide.co.uk/advice/ucas-application/the-real-story-behind-entry-requirements

4. Coughlan, Sean (2020). "A-levels and GCSEs: Boris Johnson Blames 'Mutant Algorithm' for Exam Fiasco," *British Broadcasting Corporation*. https://www.bbc.co.uk/news/education-53923279

5. Fazackerley, Anna and Savage, Michael (2021) "Parents in UK Prepare for Legal Action over A-level Results," *The Guardian*. https://www.theguardian.com/education/2021/may/30/parents-in-uk-prepare-for-legal-action-over-a-level-results?CMP=Share_AndroidApp_Other

6. This process is called the Comparable Outcomes Framework. It allows some adjustment for differences in the difficulty of examination papers and for the prior attainment of specific cohorts. For more information, see Balaban, Corina, Lloyd, James, and Surridge, Phoebe (2021). "Comparable Outcomes: Setting the standard?," *AQI*, Accessed June 14, 2022. https://www.aqi.org.uk/briefings/comparable-outcomes-setting-the-standard/

7. Students in England are in the same cohort if they begin school in the same academic year, usually when they are age four. Moving between cohorts is very rare, so these students are usually taught together until they leave compulsory full-time education.

8. Richardson, Hannah and Sellgren, Katherine (2020). "Pupils Get GCSE Grades as BTEC Results Are Pulled," *British Broadcasting Corporation*. https://www.bbc.com/news/education-53833723. In addition, Murphy and Wyness (2020) provide some evidence to support this assumption. Analyzing data from years not affected by Covid-19, they find that 75 percent of students are predicted A Level grades—which determine offers of university places in England—which are higher than those they actually receive. Nonetheless it is important to bear in mind that the contexts of these A Level predictions are not the same as teacher assessments in 2020 and 2021. See Murphy, Richard and Wyness, Gill (2020). "Minority Report: The Impact of Predicted Grades on University Admissions of Disadvantaged Groups," *Education Economics* 28:4: 333–50. https://doi.org/10.1080/09645292.2020.1761945

9. See Weale, Sally, Hall, Rachel, and Adams, Richard (2022). "First Post-Covid School Leavers Face Fight for Fewer University Places," *The Guardian*. https://www.theguardian.com/education/2022/jun/11/first-post-covid-school-leavers-face-fight-for-fewer-university-places

10. Lough, Catherine and Gibbons, Amy (2021). "GCSE and A Level Results 2021: What Did Teachers Learn?," *Times Education Supplement Magazine*. London: The Times. https://www.tes.com/magazine/news/secondary/gcse-and-level-results-2021-what-did-teachers-learn
11. The algorithm was based on the Comparable Outcomes Framework as well as the historical results of the school. In practice, teacher assessments were automatically scaled up or down so that they replicated the average proportion of grades that the school's previous three cohorts had achieved.
12. Universities UK (2020). "Universities UK Response to NUS Letter Calling for 'No Detriment' Exam Policy," *Universities UK*. https://www.universitiesuk.ac.uk/topics/covid/universities-uk-response-nus-letter
13. Otte, Jedidajah (2021). "'I'd 100% Prefer to Sit Exams': Pupils on Teacher-Assessed Grades," *The Guardian*. https://www.theguardian.com/education/2021/feb/25/pupils-on-teacher-assessed-grades-a-levels-gcse-england
14. In reality, 40 percent of teacher-assessed grades were initially downgraded by the algorithm in 2020. See Office of Qualifications and Examinations Regulation (2020). "Awarding GCSE, AS, A level, Advanced Extension Awards and Extended Project Qualifications in Summer 2020: Interim Report." Great Britain: Office of Qualifications and Examinations Regulation. https://assets.publishing.service.gov.uk/government/uploads/system/uploads/attachment_data/file/909368/6656-1_Awarding_GCSE__AS__A_level__advanced_extension_awards_and_extended_project_qualifications_in_summer_2020_-_interim_report.pdf. See also Coughlan, Sean (2020). "A-levels: Anger over 'Unfair' Results This Year," *British Broadcasting Corporation*. https://www.bbc.co.uk/news/education-53759832
15. Packham, Alfie (2020). "NUS President Larissa Kennedy: 'I Worry Universities Won't Put Student and Staff Safety First,'" *The Guardian*. https://www.theguardian.com/education/2020/aug/31/nus-president-larissa-kennedy-interview
16. Bremner, Juliet (2020). "'They're Robust, They're Good': Boris Johnson Defends England A-Level Results as Thousands of Students Degraded," *Independent Television*. https://www.itv.com/news/2020-08-13/a-level-results-day-number-of-students-accepted-to-university-rises-amid-exam-results-controversy
17. Coughlan, Sean (2021). "A-levels and GCSEs: Boris Johnson Blames 'Mutant Algorithm' for Exam Fiasco," *British Broadcasting Corporation*. https://www.bbc.co.uk/news/education-53923279
18. Del Bono, Emilia, Fumagalli, Laura, Holford, Angus, and Rabe, Birgitta (2021). "Coping with School Closures: Changes in Home-Schooling

during Covid-19," *Institute for Social and Economic Research*, University of Essex. https://www.iser.essex.ac.uk/files/news/2021/little-inequality-homeschool/coping-with-school-closures.pdf

19. Children's Commissioner (2020). "School Attendance since September," London: Children's Commissioner for England. https://cco-web.azureedge.net/wp-content/uploads/2020/12/cco-briefing-on-school-attendance-since-september.pdf

20. Oxford Cambridge and RSA (2021). "Consultation on How GCSE, AS and A Level Grades Should Be Awarded in Summer 2021: The OCR Response," *OCR*. https://www.ocr.org.uk/Images/609621-summary-of-the-ocr-response-to-dfe-ofqual-consultation-how-gcse-as-and-a-level-grades-should-be-awarded-in-summer-2021.pdf

21. McCall, Alastair, Griffiths, Sian, and Rodriguez, Nick (2022). "Private Schools 'Gamed' Covid Rules to Give Their Pupils More Top A-Levels," *The Times*. https://www.thetimes.co.uk/article/6bf66e7c-85fd-11ec-9c9e-c5f8451b2970?shareToken=7a9ad0e8241d545e98106d6ee8317344

22. Lumby, Tommy (2022). "GCSE and A-Level Grade Appeals Soared in 2021, Ofqual Data Shows," *Wales Online*. https://www.walesonline.co.uk/news/uk-news/gcse-level-grade-appeals-soared-23128647

23. In the UK, "middle-class" can be broadly understood to refer to those who work in managerial or professional occupations and "working-class" to those who work in routine and manual occupations. The statistic is taken from Cullinane, Carl and Rebecca Montacute (2020). "Covid-19 and Social Mobility Impact Brief: School Closures," *The Sutton Trust*. https://www.suttontrust.com/wp-content/uploads/2021/01/School-Shutdown-Covid-19.pdf

24. Hutchinson, Jo, Mary Reader, and Avinash Akhal (2020). *Education in England: Annual Report 2020*. London: Education Policy Institute. https://epi.org.uk/publications-and-research/education-in-england-annual-report-2020/

25. The attainment gap between more and less privileged students grew further during the first year of the pandemic such that it reversed almost ten years' progress. See Renaissance Learning and Education Policy Institute (2021). "Understanding Progress in the 2020/21 Academic Year: Complete findings from the Autumn term." London: Department of Education. https://assets.publishing.service.gov.uk/government/uploads/system/uploads/attachment_data/file/1062287/Understanding_progress_in_the_2020-21_academic_year_Complete_findings_from_spring_term_Oct2021.pdf

26. One example of this is that Anders, Jake, Macmillan, Lindsey, Sturgis, Patrick, and Wyness, Gill (2021). "The 'Graduate Parent' Advantage in Teacher Assessed Grades," *UCL*. https://blogs.ucl.ac.uk/cepeo/2021/06/08/thegraduate-parentadvantageinteacherassessedgrades/
27. Freedman, Sam and Hares, Susannah (2021) [Twitter] 31 May. Available at: https://twitter.com/samfr/status/1399485039440760841?lang=ar (Accessed June 1, 2021).

# 5

# Remaking the Grade: A District's Quest for Equitable Homework Policy

## Janine Bempechat and Sara O'Brien

*This nonfiction case explores a controversy that erupted when a school district in the United States revised its homework policy. In the United States, grades for homework assignments often count as a portion of students' overall grades in their classes, though the nature of these homework assignments and how heavily they are weighted in overall assessment are left up to individual districts, schools, or even teachers. In addition to indicating how well a student has mastered academic content, homework grades often depend on how timely the student's homework completion is. In many places, students lose points when they hand in homework assignments late. Teachers sometimes let students earn extra points to count toward their overall grade by completing homework assignments for "extra credit." These extra assignments, completed in addition to regular homework, are generally academic in nature, though not always clearly connected to course concepts. In recent years, some districts across the United States have begun to question these common homework practices, spurred in part by a popular book by Joe Feldman titled* Grading for Equity: What It Is, Why It Matters, and How It Can Transform Schools and Classrooms. *In his book, which influenced the policy described in this*

---

We conducted ten interviews for this case study, with district leaders, parents, and educators. Some of the people we interviewed wished to remain anonymous. In these cases, we have identified them only by their role in the district.

case, Feldman argues that grading homework for content is counterproductive to student learning; encouraging students to focus on the correct answer makes them more likely to cheat and less likely to think deeply about their own academic growth. Moreover, Feldman argues, grading homework down for tardiness unfairly punishes students whose personal circumstances make it challenging for them to complete work in a timely manner. Feldman's ideas have been influential in many places, though not everyone agrees with him.

--

Located across the Potomac from Washington, D.C., the Arlington Public Schools in Virginia faced a challenge. As a high-performing district so close to D.C., APS was sought after by families looking for quality public schools. And for many students, the schools delivered a quality education.[1] But some students found themselves left behind. To help close this gap, in 2020–21 APS convened a working group with seven members to center equity in their five-year review of policies specific to homework and grading. In November of 2021, the working group released its draft policy to the schools. Among the key recommendations for grades 6–12: no grading of homework, no late penalties for homework, no extra credit assignments, and unlimited redos and retakes.[2]

A firestorm quickly followed. Within days, several teachers at Wakefield High School anonymously issued a statement condemning the proposal. They argued that, if adopted, these modifications to homework policy would cause a "decline of high expectations and rigor" and that the all-important "accountability piece of the learning process" would exist "in theory only."[3] The proposal made local and then national news when Jay Mathews, education columnist for *The Washington Post*, characterized the proposal as a "catastrophe" and the anonymous Wakefield educators as "smart teachers fighting a dumb plan." Rather than fostering equity, Mathews argued, abolishing grades on homework would "hurt the neediest kids."[4]

## A Heterogeneous District Seeking Equity

While Arlington was known for its highly educated, middle-class population,[5] it was not a homogenous community. Low-income families and families of color tended to be disproportionately clustered in South Arlington, south of Route 50 bisecting the city. By some measures, their students were doing well. For example, Wakefield High, which served many students of color and low-income students,[6] was ranked in the top 2 percent of schools nationally, as measured by AP and IB participation.[7] Indeed, across the district, 94.4 percent of economically disadvantaged students graduated on time in 2021.[8] Jay Mathews of the *Post* used his column more than once to praise the district for "chang[ing] the lives of impoverished students."[9] However, these overall data obscured a significant academic achievement gap—or what Gloria Ladson-Billings termed "education debt."[10] In Arlington, many students were not in fact achieving at the levels these statistics would suggest. "We are not educating Black and Brown kids," argued Symone Walker, Vice President of the Arlington Special Education Advisory Committee (ASEAC), Executive Committee Member of the Arlington NAACP, and Co-Chair of the NAACP Education Committee. Walker had data to support her assertions. For example, on state tests in 2018–19, only 72 percent of Black students and 66 percent of Hispanic students in grades 3–8 were proficient in reading, compared to 94 percent of White students; only 54 percent of students with disabilities were proficient.[11] While Arlington boasted strong results for students overall, those results were not equally shared by traditionally marginalized and disadvantaged groups.

Some work had already been done in the district to address these disparities. In 2017, for example, Principal Lori Wiggins had noticed a disproportionate number of students of color at the lowest end of the grading scale at Gunston Middle School, which served a diverse population in South Arlington.[12] At that time, Dr. Wiggins initiated a staff-wide study of the school's grading practices. As a result, Gunston joined a number of schools in the district that had adopted standards-based grading. In 2020, APS' Chief Academic Officer (CAO) Bridget Loft invited Dr. Wiggins to join the new working group that would examine the district's homework and grading policy. The working group also included two other school principals, Dr. Erin Russo and Tony Hall; two other district administrators, Sarah Putnam and Tyrone Byrd; and English teacher Kelly Dillon. According to a presentation the group made to the school board in October 2021, equitable grading practices in Arlington should be "accurate," "bias-resistant," and "motivational."[13] The new grading policy would "provide guardrails for our teachers so that we're clear that all students have similar consistent experiences when it comes to grading," according to the superintendent.[14] The new homework policy specifically would help ensure that grades "reflect student achievement and not student behavior,"[15] since teacher perceptions of student behavior can be impacted by implicit bias.[16]

One month later, in November 2021, the working group released its draft policy to the schools. The proposal identified four key recommendations to make homework and grading practices more equitable, three of which struck some as quite radical: (1) *no grading of homework*, as students "are less likely to take risks when they fear they will be graded down for making a mistake and more likely to cheat or copy when homework is graded"; (2) *no late penalties for homework*, as these "lead to inaccurate grades, as they reflect student behavior, not achievement," and "lead to biased grades, penalizing students with learning differences and fewer resources"; and (3) *unlimited retakes and redos*, which would "reduce pressure on students to constantly be at their best, motivate students to continue learning by offering redemption, and increase rigor by insisting that all students achieve mastery rather than accept failure."[17] In making these recommendations, APS joined other districts from Massachusetts to California that were considering eliminating homework grades, including Marlborough,[18] Los Angeles, Sacramento,[19] and San Diego.[20]

## Whose Vision of Equity?

While the proposal's advocates and critics all agreed that APS' achievement gap for Black, Brown, and low-income students needed fixing, they disagreed about whether the new homework policy was the right solution. District leaders deemed the existing homework policy "so broad that it encourages inequitable grading practices" through "a lack of consistency."[21] Thus students in different classrooms could earn the same grades for vastly different performances, even within the same subject. "How is that equitable for students?"[22] wondered Dr. Wiggins. By setting consistent standards for ungraded homework, the district sought to create a new, equitable policy that would benefit all students. But critics argued that this consistency actually worked against equity goals, leaving no room for individual cases. A middle school teacher argued that removing consequences for late work would "take away structure from the kids who need structure."[23] One Wakefield teacher worried that under the new policy teachers "would very quickly lose a lot of students who need an incentive to practice."[24] Indeed, some feared the new policy would exacerbate the challenges teachers already faced in reintroducing students to structures and routines after the disruptions caused by Covid-19. Moreover, the consistency of the new policy felt more like a constraint to some. One teacher deemed the revised policy "a creativity crusher."[25]

Beyond establishing consistency, district leaders also believed the new policy would particularly benefit low-income and other historically marginalized students. When teachers grade students' homework for timeliness, Bridget Loft explained, "We're also grading the capacity of their environment at home."[26] While some students had parents at home to monitor their assignments, other students lacked even a quiet space to complete their work. Moreover, some students had jobs or took care of siblings after school, which reduced their time for homework. In the current policy, district leaders saw "bias towards school-independent kids," alongside the policy's failure "to recognize that our kids have very different home experiences."[27] By eliminating late penalties, they hoped that students whose home lives made homework completion more challenging would no longer be penalized for those circumstances.

However, others questioned whether the new policy would actually benefit the students it was designed to serve. While abolishing late penalties might boost the grades of students who struggled to complete their work, it would not give them time, space, or resources to get their assignments done. Plus, some teachers who had already abolished homework grades and late penalties when their schools shifted to standards-based grading reported "a drop in the quantity of formative work that's been handed in."[28] Would the new policy make it any easier for students without a quiet workspace at home to complete assignments on time? Would equitable policy instead do better to require that assignments be doable "without support at home," as one district administrator wondered?[29] Others wondered: while the policy was designed to benefit low-income students, how much input from low-income families went into its creation? "If we are searching for equity in our educational system," said John Stewart, a Wakefield teacher who didn't sign the open letter, "then I want to hear the voices of parents whose students do not have access to tutors and free time at home or quiet spaces to do schoolwork. But it's not the voices of those parents that we get to hear."[30] While the district aimed to promote equity, the reasoning behind the new policy seemed rooted in a deficit view of low-income families as compared to middle-class families. Did the new policy perpetuate prevailing assumptions about the forms of family support that were valuable to school? Or did it simply attempt to level the playing field given the reality that some APS students lacked the resources that their more privileged peers enjoyed?

Other parents questioned whether a revised homework policy was the best vehicle for tackling inequity. For Symone Walker of the NAACP, equity concerns in APS had nothing to do with homework, but rather were rooted in more serious systemic issues. Inequities in the district, she argued, have to do with "the quality of instruction" and supports that students might not be receiving, particularly students of color and students with disabilities. "Through a prolonged practice of social promotion and failing up," Ms. Walker argued in the local paper, "APS has a sordid history of graduating generations of Black students who are functionally illiterate."[31] For Ms. Walker, Arlington's achievement gap "is not a homework issue—it's a preparation issue."[32] Would the new homework policy be an important step toward addressing systemic inequities? Or was it simply a distraction from larger problems?

Different groups in the district also clashed on the issue of accountability. Some parents and teachers questioned whether abolishing grades and late penalties for homework would leave students unprepared for the demands of higher education and the workplace, where there are consequences for unfinished work. "If you don't allow kids to live the reality they're going to face as they get older," one parent explained, "you're just going to delay the inevitable."[33] There were also concerns that some parents would simply fill that accountability gap, requiring their children to complete assignments on time despite the new policy, while students without those structures at home would find themselves at a disadvantage. "Such results are anything but equitable," the Wakefield teachers argued in their letter. "Conversely, they offer our most needy students reduced probability of preparing for and realizing post-secondary opportunities." Advocates of the new policy, however, pointed out that preparing students for the demands of higher education and the workplace didn't necessitate replicating those demands. "Our job is not to bootstrap our kids to be ready for college," Ms. Loft argued. "Our job is to teach adolescents and to recognize the wide spectrum of readiness and executive functioning skills that are in front of us, and to accommodate them accordingly."

In addition to questioning the new policy's efficacy for meeting equity goals, critics felt frustrated by the lack of input from key constituencies in its creation. In particular, teachers felt the policy was part of a long line of decisions in which they had little say. "We're at a particularly challenging moment with teacher morale," one teacher noted. "And consistently Arlington has not been great about listening to teachers or asking for input when making these big changes."[34] Teachers who were already experiencing challenges with standards-based grading in their schools reported feeling "demoralized" that the district had not worked out the logistics of tracking student work completion without homework grades. Their students felt "overwhelmed" trying to keep track of their assignments, and the "backlog of work" was a struggle for teachers and students alike.[35] Parents, meanwhile, had their own concerns. One school board member reported that even after three years of standards-based grading at his child's school, he still struggled to understand their academic progress: "If I don't see a grade, I don't understand what 'approaching mastery' means."[36] Would the new policy stymie parents wishing to track their children's performance?

The new policy's advocates and critics were also divided on the very purpose of homework, with the distinction between academic and socioemotional skills at the center of the debate. The district's procedures policy stated that grades "should reflect student achievement and not student behavior." Bridget Loft argued that "punitive obstacles," such as giving students zeroes for missing a deadline, "run counter to the motivation that's required to work towards proficiency." Indeed, some research has found motivation for doing homework diminishes and cheating increases when students perceive the teacher as controlling rather than supportive of their autonomy and responsibility.[37] Tellingly, students report completing homework assignments they find meaningless solely because homework completion counts in their final grades. These students may seem engaged in their schoolwork, but their negative affect around homework suggests they are not deeply absorbed in learning.[38]

In their open letter, Wakefield's teachers countered that in addition to developing knowledge and understanding, homework helps students develop "organizational, time and stress management skills and grow as responsible, civically engaged, and considerate young adults." Eliminating grading and late penalties would likely undermine the development of critical "work habits (timely attendance, work completion, positive participation in group activities) that make for successful careers."[39] These teachers' concerns are supported by some research. Homework that is graded or otherwise carefully monitored by teachers enhances conscientiousness and achievement, especially in less attentive students.[40] And students report that they appreciate graded homework because it provides them with clear and frank feedback.[41] Similarly, students are more likely to adopt homework management strategies when they know teachers will grade their homework assignments.[42]

## What Happens Now?

Given the intense pushback from teachers, the district adopted a new approach that would give educators latitude around homework and grading practices. As of April 2022, the office was working on a second draft of the proposal, which would allow teachers to continue grading homework assignments because, as Sarah Putnam, Director of Curriculum and Instruction, put it, "people aren't in a place yet to think about shifting their practice." A goal for 2022–23 was to encourage principals and instructional lead teachers to consider new approaches to grading practices as a whole: "Try something different, and see what it does for kids."[43]

The debate about homework reverberating through Arlington can also be heard in communities across the country. In December 2021, for example, nearly 900 people in La Grange, Illinois, signed a petition to reinstate graded homework after a local high school changed its policy to make homework reflect "practice," not "achievement."[44] It seems clear that the controversy around homework and its uses will continue to be contested by educators, parents, and academics. Given the competing concerns, how should the Arlington County School Board, and leaders in other communities, write equitable homework policy? Whose input should determine what these policies say? And how will schools know that their policies are serving marginalized and disadvantaged students well?

# Conversation

**Janine Bempechat:** Natasha, will you get us started? What you do think are the key dilemmas in this case and for whom are they dilemmas?

**Natasha Warikoo:** I think that perhaps the biggest and most obvious dilemmas are around this juxtaposition: on one hand, you have a desire to have kids practice what they've learned at school beyond the limited time in the day—practicing the skills but also teaching kids punctuality. On the other hand, kids have unequal resources at home and unequal time because some may be working or taking care of siblings. They have unequal parental supervision because parents may be working, and unequal assistance because parents have different fluency in English. Kids have different experiences with the academic content and different access to a quiet place to work at home. This is a dilemma, obviously, for classroom teachers and also the administration that is trying to set guidelines for what the teachers are doing.

I think there is also a dilemma because we want all kids to achieve their personal best, no matter what, given their resources and their background. But some kids start further ahead than others, and so that inequity could lead to unequal outcomes. And I think there is a question mark around the purpose of homework in the case. Are we trying to help kids get to mastery? Are we trying to build good study skills or good work habits? Are we trying to differentiate kids by grading them? The purpose of homework is unresolved for this district.

**Colin Rose:** When I think about the working group that was tasked to come up with a policy, it seems like there was only a month in between them announcing their charge and then them coming out with a policy. They are to create something that is going to touch every student, every family, every administrator, and everybody in the ecology of the school system. And it doesn't seem like they've had enough time or have a process in which they use data and engage stakeholders in a way that informs their decision and prepares them for the pushback they face in the case.

It feels like they were also asked to create this policy with those constraints without that process around equity. And in a space where there doesn't seem to be a North Star for the purpose of homework, what is the purpose of grading? And how does it connect with the outcomes we want for students in this district?

Policy should be undergirded by practices and values, and it doesn't seem like there is a consensus in this jurisdiction about the purpose of homework, and the purpose of grading. And on top of that, as noted by Symone Walker from the NAACP, it's unclear whether even focusing on homework solves the equity issue that they are dealing with. It's missing the forest for the trees.

In this case, most of the kids are graduating on time, but the district is noticing that even though kids are progressing, competencies are not necessarily following, as measured by some of the examinations. So, in my experience, homework might not even be in the top ten issues that may be affecting that actual problem.

So, I think any time you have conservative columnists and the NAACP both throwing rocks at you, you didn't go through a thorough process and it's time to step back to your corner and regroup. Hopefully, there's not so much scar tissue that you can't move forward.

**Karen Mapp:** I'm going to use a movie scene to describe the biggest dilemma for me. In *Raiders of the Lost Ark*, there's a scene where the opposing group is digging for the ark with all this equipment. And Harrison Ford realizes that they are digging in the wrong spot because they hadn't looked closely enough at the evidence that they had. And I quite frankly feel that the dilemma in this case is that the district is looking in the wrong spot.

I find it interesting that a lot of times when school systems identify equity issues, they look at what the students are doing and they don't look at what they're doing themselves.

I'm quite perplexed as to why this conversation isn't actually about what we want kids to know or be able to do, and looking at our teaching and learning to then discuss how homework aligns with our goals and our vision. Homework is supposed to be a way to extend your pedagogical journey with kids. You don't start with a conversation about homework.

For me, the dilemma has to do with what the district is looking at. Because this is supposed to be about equity, I just think that their vision is misplaced. They're looking at a symptom.

**Amanda Jimerson:** I noticed that the case set up the changes to homework policy as the dilemma, but they don't discuss how homework is graded across the district, whether that's consistent across teachers. But I think that first we should be thinking about why we're doing homework in the first place. Is it helping students? Because if the issue is independent practice, I think the argument always goes to why aren't they doing that practice in our instructional time. As Natasha said, we have this finite amount of time in the classroom. But if at the end of the day only some students are able to get support it is always going to be inequitable.

For us math teachers, Photomath popped into existence about five years ago. This is a free app: you can take a picture of any problem or worksheet, and not only does it give the answer, it also shows all the steps. So even if you're requiring students to show work, if that's your only way of doing independent practice at home, it'd be ridiculous to think that your students are completing this. So, they are getting nothing out of that homework, unless it's for compliance reasons.

So, years ago I moved to a choice board where students had to select their own homework assignment, like writing their own word problem. And this is the first year that I've moved to independent practice in class, because it's our job to make sure students are getting that independent practice during our time with them, instead of putting additional pressures on their home life. So for me the dilemma is more about the purpose of giving students homework, rather than the grades.

**Natasha Warikoo:** I feel like there is a lot we don't know empirically in this case. Are the current homework practices exacerbating inequality? There was no evidence in the case that they are. And do those changes that the district proposes decrease these gaps in equity? If that's the goal, does that happen? I don't know that we know that yet.

So, I think we can also think about this in terms of what are the empirical gaps that are leading to these dichotomies that maybe actually aren't dichotomies. It's just different ideas about what will happen and what does happen, rather than being about values and priorities.

**Sara O'Brien:** Natasha, you said you don't see it as a dilemma, but I think you are in fact raising dilemmas here. How do you frame a problem, and what data are you using to identify where the problem lies? As Karen put it, how do you know you're digging in the right spot? And I think that's what Symone is pointing to in the case as well when she says that the equity issues aren't about homework at all. And you all pointed out this question: what is the purpose of homework in this district? And how is it contributing to inequality? I'm curious to hear whether you all see dilemmas for other groups, not just the district leaders.

**Natasha Warikoo:** The case mentions the teachers, but of course, there is also the family, the kids, and the parents. I think it's just so important to help parents understand the purpose of this change and get their views. What do families see as the obstacles to homework completion? What did they think would be a solution to those obstacles? That's really what I wanted to hear, and then to hear from the kids as well of course.

**Janine Bempechat:** Those are the missing voices. As to the purpose, for me, the teachers who wrote that anonymous letter were quite adamant about this dual purpose of homework for building not only understanding but also self-regulatory skills like planning and organization. I wonder, Amanda, does that resonate with you?

**Amanda Jimerson:** I worry that some students are penalized more than others for not being able to meet deadlines, if homework is worth 50 percent of the grade in some classrooms, for example, but only worth 5 percent in others. But at my school, we have quarterly grades, so at some point there has to be a deadline because I have a deadline to submit a grade. We are a brand-new high school here, and a restorative practice school, with no late penalties, any number of retakes as long as it's by the end of the quarter. But without that outside pressure, we could probably allow for more time, more opportunities. With what Arlington is doing in the case, grading a year's worth of assignments in June sounds awful for teacher workload.

**Natasha Warikoo:** Amanda, for me there's a dilemma around deadlines. I feel like deadlines are helpful for some people, and I know that some things work for some kids and not for others. If it's the night before the end of a quarter, they're going to get that work done. If they have until the end of the year, now it's an almost impossible task to catch up. That can be very anxiety-provoking for some. For others, who may be ended up having work or a family crisis, the flexibility works and they're able to get it done.

I also think that the dilemma is often that there's no one grading system or system of homework that is going to be the best for every single child. That's the reality of teaching 20 or 30 kids at once. So, we just have to figure out which method is going to work for teachers' workloads and most kids and that pays attention to equity in terms of knowing that there are different learning styles, different workstyles, and different motivations.

**Colin Rose:** It's tough to talk about policy without knowing what the purpose of homework is. When I was a teacher, I expected students to hand in their homework the next day because I try to make it very relevant both to the students and to our class work. I had students connecting their learning to things at home. We did a lot of group work in student-centered learning, so homework completion was part of the ethos of the classroom. We're all contributing meaning, so if you're not bringing what needs to be brought into the class, you're kind of letting other folks down in the classroom because everybody is a teacher.

So when students couldn't do their homework, how could I support their getting it done so that I could hit the targets that I have in my classroom? It's not about this almost binary choice around grading or not grading. It's more around the process of students gaining competency. It's important to find a policy that undergirds our philosophy that we're working with, with input from the community.

**Karen Mapp:** There's no indication in the case that anybody talked to parents in the first place about any of this. I write cases and I also teach cases, so when I read this case, I tried to figure out how I would use it in a classroom. And of course, I teach family and community engagement, but I also have taught leadership classes. And to be quite honest, my angle on this would be: how do districts try to deal with issues of equity?

In this case, I think the district focused on homework without really doing their due diligence. Sometimes, well-intentioned people end up reacting when they are accused of not being equitable. We look for some quick way to solve the problem. That's how I would teach the case: how did this district decide that they were going to make homework the way that they were going to solve the accusation of not being equitable? And then what should they do next?

They went wrong when they didn't involve any of the people. They could have done focus groups with kids and parents. There are no co-design attempts here at all, no piloting, no engagement with families.

**Colin Rose:** There was no process. I see no evidence of them speaking to parents or community or teachers. Because of the blowback, it seems like they haven't run any of these ideas past anybody.

**Karen Mapp:** Nope.

**Colin Rose:** Even the folks who will be directly implementing it. That is not a way to make a decision. I've seen this many times, and I'm sure you have, Karen, in a district where folks sit in a room who might be very smart, highly educated, and liberal-minded, but they do not attempt to engage the folks that are most affected and the folks that will be in charge of actually implementing the policy. So it falls flat on its face. And usually the ingredients are: you didn't look at data, you didn't have a well-formulated goal, and you didn't engage any stakeholders before you proposed a policy, let alone use strategies to mitigate the pushback and rally folks to be on your side. Unless you do that, you don't have a chance for an initiative that's going to touch every student and every family in a district. It could be the greatest idea in the world, but you didn't engage anybody and it's over. It's over before it started.

It's also fairly technical, right? Are we grading or not? We don't have to agree on the philosophy of homework; we could just not grade it.

**Karen Mapp:** It's seductive to pick the homework issue because it looks like it's a problem. But when there's no process to do a root cause analysis and you don't involve any of the stakeholders, then you end up with this mess with the parents upset, the teachers upset, probably the students upset. The case to me is about the lack of process.

**Natasha Warikoo:** It seems like we've sort of identified two different issues. One: is this policy solving the problem that the district leaders were trying to solve? But the second piece, which is both separated and interrelated, is the process. Even if you have, as Colin said, the best policy in the world, if you don't go through this process, you might do the opposite of what you intended. In my research in another suburban district, I spoke with parents who were upset about a new homework policy that actually eliminated homework altogether. A lot of parents that I spoke with said they were mad, but when I gently asked whether they talked with anyone in the school district about the policy, they hadn't tried to. They just started saying, "Well there's no homework in elementary school now, I'm going to send my kids to supplementary academic classes, Russian School, math or Kumon or what have you." If that's what happens, then you're going to exacerbate the gap. So I think it's important to solicit that parent voice, go out into the community and ask them about what they see, especially to reach parents who are not used to feeling they can have a stake.

**Sara O'Brien:** What values are at stake in the case? What were the values that you saw the folks in Arlington attempting to make real with this policy?

**Amanda Jimerson:** I think the district saw this change as a positive thing. There is a lot of evidence to suggest that students who have multiple siblings or jobs at home, which is 90 percent of the students I have, don't have the support for homework. They can't even stay for afterschool tutoring because they need to go pick up four siblings from three different bus stops. So it does affect equity. But then some people said that the new policy takes away from students' work ethic and we're not preparing them for the real world because in the real world they need to turn in finished products on a deadline. But am I preparing students for the workforce? Should their grade in Algebra II be reflective of how ready they are to work a 9-to-5? Or that they're learning algebra?

**Colin Rose:** I saw the policy a little bit as paternalistic because I think value is very culturally-laden. From my experience, my father is from the West Indies, and if you told him that we would not have any homework, he would have a problem with that. He's from the British system. So, as the district talks about shifting towards the more progressive way of doing things, the assumption can't be that just because someone is Black or Latino Hispanic or low-income, they share a progressive liberal view.

I think that's why when I think about equity, it's not just an outcome, it's also a process, because the community has to be part of thinking about the strategies for themselves. And if you're thinking about one sample of a subgroup of the community especially, we should be oversampling. We should be in folks' households asking them about their aspirations and needs and goals and vision. If equity is a value, you should have that core group of folks behind you as you go and try to do something that's pretty global. So, I see a little bit of paternalism in the attempt to be equitable in this case.

**Karen Mapp:** Another value I saw people considering was fairness: what is fairness? For me, it comes back to the question of what homework is for. Is there a way to make it rigorous and relevant, as Colin alluded to when he was talking about his own classroom? But in this case, instead of looking at the relevance to make it fair, they seem to be looking at the timing and *when* it's done, instead of *what's* done.

I like how in the case when some people saw this policy, they wondered, "But wait a minute, isn't this playing into stereotypes about this whole deficit-based thinking around families and what kids can do?" I found myself thinking about Jeff Duncan-Andrade's piece on Critical Hope. Sometimes people think, "Oh well, the kids can't do it, so we're going to make it less hard." And that's racism. So exactly what was the district thinking about the value of the homework? I'm just not sure.

**Amanda Jimerson:** I want to reiterate that these students shouldn't be denied the opportunity to do the practice, but it's putting more work on the teachers to make sure they're getting that independent practice during our time with them, instead of putting the additional pressures on their home life.

I liked what Colin said about asking people what they need. That's something that I know I need to do more of but struggle with.

**Colin Rose:** That's kind of how you move away from stereotypes. If there is a real need in the community, there's a need in the community. Maybe the community is saying, "Hey, our kids have three jobs, you can't give them hours' worth of homework." That's authentic. But it's a problem when you make assumptions about people's needs.

**Amanda Jimerson:** Right.

**Colin Rose:** It isn't course-responsive, it's not engaging and that's not equity.

**Amanda Jimerson:** Especially if your reaction to your assumption is preventing the students from interacting with the content at the same level as other students.

**Natasha Warikoo:** I think that we need to think outside the box as well in terms of solutions. If there is that child who needs to be picking up siblings, are there after-school programs for those siblings? And why does that family not have access to those after-school programs? If you can get the siblings an after-school program, they can get the support that they need for homework and after school, and then the older child can also stay after school and get extra support. Families need supports that go well beyond homework or even education, because we know that what's coming into the classroom is creating inequality.

**Karen Mapp:** The first paragraph of the case says, "For many students, the schools delivered a quality education, but some students found themselves left behind. In order to close this gap, APS convened a working group to center equity in their five-year review of policy specific to homework and grading." So, if we look at a logic model, basically what they're doing is looking at the outputs. They've decided to look at the outputs instead of the inputs.

I find myself wondering if maybe we are trying to avoid the hard work of turning the mirror on ourselves. Is this a pattern of looking at the outputs, going to the students instead of looking inside at why there's a gap? Basically what they're saying is there's a gap because of the homework. I don't think so. That's not the first place we should be looking. I find it interesting in and of itself that they decided that this was the thing that they were going to look at and not what's happening in the classroom. Have we asked parents what's happening? Have we asked the students about it?

**Sara O'Brien:** Let's move into thinking about what could be done in this case.

**Karen Mapp:** I have a clarifying question, though, for that question. There's obviously not one right answer here. I don't know if I want to give you an answer because you don't want just one answer—you want people to be creative.

**Sara O'Brien:** That's true—there's definitely not one right answer. But we're curious to hear from folks with different kinds of expertise: what do you think should be done in this case and which values do you think should be prioritized? We're curious to hear your different answers and then people reading this can discuss further possibilities.

**Natasha Warikoo:** Now that the district has put a pause on the new policy, it's important to just collect some data. Go and do some focus groups with parents living in different neighborhoods, with parents from different social classes and racial backgrounds. Do some focus groups of kids, to get a sense of how they are spending their out-of-school time. Get more input beyond the seven people in the original group. For teachers, as well as getting their input, there needs to be a discussion around the goals of homework. It might be that there are different goals for the math teachers and the English teachers, for example.

Then, what do we know about the research on afterschool programs and homework or achieving these equity goals? We find out the research and get the community input and put that all on the table before they make any more decisions or take any actions.

**Amanda Jimerson:** I would agree with Natasha, but I would put more of an emphasis on the data. They need data to see if the homework holds the correlation that they're implying by this radical change. Is there a correlation between their homework completion and their student outcomes? If not, then the homework policy may be a band-aid that they're trying to place over their equity issues. They need to research the issue that is causing this opportunity gap.

**Colin Rose:** Similarly, I think they need to step back and ask themselves: what are they trying to accomplish and what is the problem? They could try to re-explore homework, but I feel that in reality they've expended a lot of political capital and taken a pretty public shellacking around this policy. Is it even worth trying to jump into that arena again if the homework policy isn't dealing with the issue that is at hand in Arlington?

So, I would say they should just step back, talk about the actual problem that they have within that district, and then have an honest conversation around the big leverage points they have to change that. And that has to be done in consultation with teachers, and with families and community, before they jump back into another kind of initiative that is going to be so third rail and widespread.

**Natasha Warikoo:** That's a really good point, Colin: not starting with homework, but starting with the equity problem that they are trying to address.

**Karen Mapp:** I think one of the things the district has to do is apologize. They're going to have to gain trust again with all of these groups that are now not happy with them. So they're going to have to find some way to say, we're sorry because we do see that there are some errors in the way that we approached this. Then I think they're going to have to go back to square one and put together a process for trying to interrogate the reasons for this gap. Ask for help from outside groups that could help them learn how to interrogate the problem. And make sure that the group doing that is a diverse group that includes students, parents, community members, and teachers.

There's plenty of wonderful information out there about how to do co-design; there's a process for trying to solve these problems. And they need a longer timetable than they had developing the policy in this case.

**Sara O'Brien:** Many values are raised in this case: accountability, consistency, equity, fairness. But what strikes me after this conversation is the key value of community. How does a district serve a community and welcome them into the conversation?

**Natasha Warikoo:** Democracy. Civic participation.

**Karen Mapp:** Districts signal whom they value by whom they put on that team. That's a value, whose voices are meaningful to us.

**Colin Rose:** And I would say there are a lot of values but very little consensus. These people teach next to each other in the same buildings, in the same district, but there seems to be no solid way that we view what teaching and learning are in this district and how homework interacts with that.

**Sara O'Brien:** What do you hope people will take away and continue thinking about after this conversation and after this case?

**Karen Mapp:** There's a business school case about the Mount Everest disaster that happened a few years ago where quite a few people died because there were these two very competitive teams. And they wanted to make sure that they took all these people up to the top, and at all costs, and they wouldn't listen to the Sherpas who were the people from the community who know the mountain. And a lot of people perished because of it.

So, I hope people remember that you have to listen to the Sherpas—you have to listen to the community. You have to value the voices of the people who are closest to the problem. It's the value of process, the value of community voice, and the value also of not just reacting to a problem but thinking about giving yourself time to figure out what the problem is.

**Colin Rose:** You can't speak to equity unless you have an intentional process that is engaging folks, especially folks that are most affected by whatever you're trying to make a decision around. It's important to be very intentional around your planning, embedding equity within each step of that planning, and making sure that you're able to justify the decisions that you make by the research, the data that you mine, and the engagement that you embarked on. That gives you a chance to be brave and do more "controversial things." Without that, you have no armor, and it is not going to go your way most likely.

**Natasha Warikoo:** I would add the importance of looking at a few different kinds of data. What are teachers using homework for, and what are their goals for homework? What do we know about the bigger problem that this district is trying to solve? What do we know about the research on homework? What happens when we assign homework the way we do? Is it doing what we think it's doing? What is our theory of change? What do we want to happen? What data are we going to collect to know if it's not working?

Data is so much easier to collect than it was two decades ago, and we can learn a lot from it. It's important to look at the evidence and to make clear what the theory of change is as well.

**Amanda Jimerson:** I agree, but I focused on the who. Who should be making these decisions? It definitely shouldn't be seven people with two months behind closed doors. It should be a larger conversation over much more time, with a lot more facts and figures and data. So, they should be thinking more about the who. Who should be involved in these equity conversations?

***Dr. Colin Rose*** *(PhD) is the Founder and CEO of Perennial Education Consulting where he supports leaders to build coherence and operationalize improvement with a strong focus on excellence and equity. Prior to his consulting work, Dr. Rose was an Assistant Superintendent at the Boston Public Schools, USA wherein he was able to build a legacy of groundbreaking policies, effective systemic initiatives and professional development, meaningful programming, and innovative school models.*

***Amanda Churchill Jimerson*** *is a veteran mathematics teacher and department chair in central California, USA, working in exclusively Title I schools. She is a passionate advocate for homeless and foster youth and has firsthand experience with the foster care system as a child, parent, and teacher.*

***Karen L. Mapp*** *(EdD) is a Senior Lecturer on Education at the Harvard Graduate School of Education (HGSE), USA. Over the past twenty-five years, Dr. Mapp's research and practice focus has been on the cultivation of partnerships among families, community members, and educators that support student achievement and school improvement. She is the author and co-author of several articles and books, including* Beyond the Bake Sale: The Essential Guide to Family-School Partnerships *(2010), and* Everyone Wins!: The Evidence for Family-School Partnerships and Implications for Practice *(2022).*

*Natasha Warikoo* is Stern Professor in the Social Sciences, Department of Sociology, at Tufts University, USA. She is the author, most recently, of Is Affirmative Action Fair? The Myth of Equity in College Admissions *(Polity Press, 2022) and* Race at the Top: Asian Americans and Whites in Pursuit of the American Dream in Suburban Schools *(University of Chicago Press, 2022).*

# Stakeholder Guide

| Setting |
|---|
| Arlington Public Schools (APS) in Arlington, VA, serving approximately 28,000 students ages 4–18. |

| Primary Figures | |
|---|---|
| **Bridget Loft**: APS' Chief Academic Officer<br>**Symone Walker**: parent, district advisor, and NAACP member<br>**Lori Wiggins**: principal at Gunston Middle School | **John Stewart**: teacher at Wakefield High School<br>**Sarah Putnam**: APS' Director of Curriculum and Instruction |

# Discussion Questions

1. One group of stakeholders whose voice is largely absent from the case is students themselves. What dilemmas do you see students facing in the Arlington Public Schools?
2. What role should family voices and preferences play in the decision-making process in this case? How should schools and districts respond when their views conflict with families' views?
3. Advocates for adopting the new homework policy argue that grades "should reflect student achievement, not student behavior." What do you think teachers and schools should take into account when assigning grades?
4. The case highlights many values at play in the debate over the new homework policy: equity, of course, but also consistency, accountability, rigor, antiracism, and achievement. Which values strike you as most important as you evaluate the new homework policy?

5 One district administrator suggests that requiring all homework be doable "without support at home" is a better policy. How might schools and districts create more equitable homework policy beyond eliminating grades and late penalties?
6 District leaders believe that the new homework policy is an important step toward "equity" in the Arlington Public Schools. What conception(s) of equity do district leaders seem to hold? What conceptions do others in the district hold—both those who support the policy and those who oppose it?
7 How does this case help you think about the role that homework plays in your context?

## Notes

1. Districtwide, in 2018–19, 84 percent of students in grades 3–8 scored proficient on statewide reading exams, compared to 76 percent across the state. In math, 87 percent of students scored proficient, compared to 82 percent of students statewide. See: Virginia Department of Education (2020). "Arlington County Public Schools—Virginia School Quality Profiles," *Virginia School Quality Profiles*, Accessed November 10, 2023. https://schoolquality.virginia.gov/divisions/arlington-county-public-schools#desktopTabs-2. (After the disruption of the pandemic, APS did see some falling scores for standardized tests. To give a more accurate reflection of achievement in the district, this case uses scores from before 2020.) In 2020, the average SAT score for seniors was 1198, compared to 1116 statewide and 1051 nationwide. And in 2021, 94.4 percent of seniors graduated on time.
2. The working group relied heavily on Joe Feldman's 2019 book *Grading for Equity*, which argues that students' grades should be tied to achievement, not behavior. In our interviews with educators and district leaders, many mentioned the strong influence that Feldman's work had in the district.
3. For the full text of the Wakefield teachers' letter, see: Minock, Nick (2022). "Va. Teachers Push Back on Equity Proposal to Abolish Some Grades, Late Homework Penalties," *WJLA*, January 2, 2022. https://wjla.com/news/crisis-in-the-classrooms/va-teachers-push-back-on-equity-proposal-to-abolish-some-grades-late-homework-penalties.
4. Mathews, Jay (2022). "Abolishing Grades on Homework Will Hurt the Neediest Kids," *Washington Post*, January 30, 2022. https://www.washingtonpost.com/education/2021/12/26/homework-grading-curve-arlington-assignments/.

5. In 2022, the median household income in the district was around $120,000, and 75 percent of residents held at least a bachelor's degree. See: https://www.apsva.us/wp-content/uploads/2022/01/APSQuickFacts-update0122.pdf
6. At Wakefield, around 41 percent of students were eligible for free or reduced lunch (see: https://www.apsva.us/wp-content/uploads/2019/11/SNPMonthlyEligibilityReport.pdf) and 76 percent of students were non-White. See "How Does Wakefield High School Rank among America's Best High Schools?," https://www.usnews.com/education/best-high-schools/virginia/districts/arlington-county-public-schools/wakefield-high-20363.
7. Also, in 2018, 56 percent of Wakfield's graduating seniors passed at least one AP final exam, nearly three times the national average. See: Mathews, "Abolishing Grades on Homework Will Hurt the Neediest Kids."
8. https://schoolquality.virginia.gov/divisions/arlington-county-public-schools#desktopTabs-4
9. Mathews, "Abolishing Grades on Homework Will Hurt the Neediest Kids."
10. In her influential 2006 address to the AERA, Dr. Ladson-Billings pushed back against the widespread focus on an "achievement gap" for students of color and English learners, arguing that educators, scholars, and policymakers should instead consider the education debt owed to these students, which has been accumulating for generations. Ladson-Billings, Gloria (2006). "From the Achievement Gap to the Education Debt: Understanding Achievement in U.S. Schools," *Educational Researcher* 35:7: 3–12.
11. https://schoolquality.virginia.gov/divisions/arlington-county-public-schools#desktopTabs-2. It's also useful to note that districtwide, the on-time graduation rate for Hispanic students was only 85.5 percent in 2021, compared to 98.4 percent for White students. See: https://schoolquality.virginia.gov/divisions/arlington-county-public-schools#desktopTabs-4.
12. 37.4 percent Hispanic, 30.5 percent White, 18.6 percent Black, 7.6 percent Asian, and 5.7 percent representing multiple races. Almost one-third of its students are economically disadvantaged. See: Virginia School Quality Profiles, n.d. "Gunston Middle—Virginia School Quality Profiles." https://schoolquality.virginia.gov/schools/gunston-middle#fndtn-desktopTabs-enrollment.
13. The group's definition of equitable grading drew heavily on Joe Feldman's *Grading for Equity* (2019), published by Corwin. For the presentation to the board, see: https://go.boarddocs.com/vsba/arlington/Board.nsf/files/C7XLVB557627/$file/101421%20School%20Board%20Work%20Session%20-%20Grading%20%26%20Homework.pdf.
14. Dr. Francisco Durán, school board meeting on October 19, 2021. You can find a recording of the livestream from this meeting here: https://www.apsva.us/school-board-meetings/school-board-work-sessions-meetings/

15. APS PIP I-7.2.3.34 PIP-2, 11/29/21. This language directly echoes Feldman's language in his book.
16. Staats, C. (2014). *Implicit Racial Bias and School Discipline Disparities: Exploring the Connection*. Columbus, OH: The Ohio State University, Kirwan Institute for the Study of Race and Ethnicity.
17. These four quotations are from a presentation to the school board on October 19, 2021. https://go.boarddocs.com/vsba/arlington/Board.nsf/files/C7XLVB557627/$file/101421%20School%20Board%20Work%20Session%20-%20Grading%20%26%20Homework.pdf
18. To read about controversy surrounding homework policy in Marlborough, MA, see: Razzaq, Zane (2021). "Marlborough School Committee Votes to Not Have Homework Be Graded," *MetroWest Daily News*, October 15, 2021. https://www.metrowestdailynews.com/story/news/education/2021/10/15/homework-not-graded-under-new-marlborough-school-policy/8435608002/
19. For homework policy in Los Angeles and Sacramento, see: Jones, Carolyn (2021). "Why Some California School Districts Are Changing How Students Earn Grades," *EdSource*, December 14, 2021. https://edsource.org/2021/why-some-california-school-districts-are-changing-how-students-earn-grades/664226
20. Esquivel, Paloma (2021). "As Ds and Fs Soar, Schools Ditch Inequitable Grade Systems—Los Angeles Times," *Los Angeles Times*, November 23, 2021. https://www.latimes.com/california/story/2021-11-08/as-ds-and-fs-soar-schools-ditch-inequitable-grade-systems
21. Personal interview with Bridget Loft.
22. Personal interview.
23. Personal interview.
24. Personal interview with John Stewart.
25. Personal interview.
26. Personal interview.
27. Personal interview with Bridget Loft.
28. Personal interview.
29. Personal interview with Sarah Putnam.
30. Personal interview.
31. See Ms. Walker's full column here: Walker, Symone, and Symone Walker (2021). "ED Talk: The Miseducation of Black Students in Arlington | ARLNow.Com," *ARLnow.com* | Arlington, Va. Local News, April 16, 2021. https://www.arlnow.com/2021/04/16/ed-talk-the-miseducation-of-black-students-in-arlington/.
32. Personal interview with Symone Walker.
33. Personal interview.
34. Personal interview.

35. Personal interview.
36. David Priddy, school board meeting on October 19, 2021. You can find a recording of the livestream from this meeting here: https://www.apsva.us/school-board-meetings/school-board-work-sessions-meetings/
37. Trautwein, U. and Ludtke, O. (2009). "Predicting Homework Motivation and Homework Effort in Six School Subjects: The Role of Person and Family Characteristics, Classroom Factors, and School Track," *Learning and Instruction* 19: 243–58.
38. Galloway, M., et al. (2013). "Nonacademic Effects of Homework in Privileged, High-Performing High Schools," *The Journal of Experimental Education* 81:4: 490–510.
39. For the full text of the Wakefield teachers' letter, see: Nick Minock, "Va. Teachers Push Back on Equity Proposal to Abolish Some Grades, Late Homework Penalties," *WJLA*, January 2, 2022. https://wjla.com/news/crisis-in-the-classrooms/va-teachers-push-back-on-equity-proposal-to-abolish-some-grades-late-homework-penalties.
40. Trautwein, U. and Ludtke, O. (2007). "Students' Self-Reported Effort and Time on Homework in Six School Subjects: Between Student Differences and within Student Variation," *Journal of Educational Psychology* 99:2: 432–44.
41. Peterson, E. R. and Irving, S. E. (2008). "Secondary School Students' Conceptions of Assessment and Feedback," *Learning and Instruction* 18:3: 238–50.
42. Xu, J. and Wu, H. (2013). "Self-Regulation of Homework Behavior: Homework Management at the Secondary School Level," *Journal of Educational Research* 106:1: 1–13. See also Núñez, J. C., et al. (2015). "Teachers' Feedback on Homework, Homework-Related Behaviors, and Academic Achievement," *The Journal of Educational Research* 108:3: 204–16.
43. Personal interview with Sarah Putnam.
44. Giuliani, David (2021). "LTHS Grading Policy: Hundreds Object to Changes," *La Grange, IL Patch*, December 9, 2021. https://patch.com/illinois/lagrange/lths-grading-policy-hundreds-object-changes.

# 6

# Caught in the Web: Educational Risks and Rewards of Online Learning

## *Douglas Yacek*

*This case study takes place at a fictional school in Bavaria, the southernmost province of Germany. Selma Morgenstern, the main character in the case, is a principal or* Direktorin *at a type of school called the* Gymnasium, *which is the university-track secondary school serving grades 5 through 12. The non-university, vocational track schools in Germany, the* Realschule *and the* Hauptschule, *offer a reduced educational schedule compared to the* Gymnasium. *The* Realschule *offers grades 5 through 11, while the* Hauptschule *offers grades 5 through 10. At the end of 12th grade in the* Gymnasium, *students take the* Abitur, *a national standardized examination in several subject areas that qualifies them for enrollment at universities. In an effort to modernize their educational offerings, schools at all levels in Germany are quickly implementing educational technologies and virtual learning opportunities, for which Germans use the term* Digitalisierung. *The school in this case is responding to a funding program released by the Bavarian* Kultusministerium—i.e., Bayerisches Staatsministerium für Unterricht und Kultus—*which is roughly equivalent to state departments of education in the United States. Although the program is fictional, it is in line with the existing approaches to school funding in the Bavarian "Master Plan Digital II," which already includes several funding programs to improve technological infrastructure, introduce IT administration in schools, and purchase devices for students, among other things.*[1]

--

When Selma Morgenstern, principal of the humanities-oriented Meister-Eckhart-Gymnasium (MEG),[2] received the email about the highly competitive new funding program for hybrid learning initiatives from the *Kultusministerium*,[3] she wasn't surprised. The push for more blended models of teaching and learning—which would shift more of students' learning time both in and out of school onto online platforms—had been coming for a long time.[4] But until now, it had always seemed to be put off by some more burning issue or problem, at least at MEG. Covid-19 changed that, exposing on a grand scale just how unprepared schools like hers were for creating productive and satisfying online learning environments. Now the *Kultusministerium* was offering schools financial support, up to 750,000 Euro[5] per school, for compelling hybrid learning programs developed by principals around Bavaria. Successful schools would make up a group of "Digital Lighthouse Schools" to serve as public examples of effective digitalization[6] in the school environment. Participating schools would offer what the state was calling a "hybrid curriculum," meaning that at least 50 percent of the learning time in school would occur in online spaces and platforms, with additional allotted time for classes in coding and programming. Although applying would be taxing and time-consuming, Selma was excited that she would have some freedom to create a plan tailored to her own school. MEG's move in the last few years toward emphasizing the digital humanities really seemed to resonate with parents and others in the MEG community, and she had already begun hatching some ideas for expanding their approach in case something like this came along. Putting the proposal together would be a perfect task for the summer break coming up in just a few weeks, when her husband would take the kids to his parents.

Although Selma was looking forward to getting started, she was a little daunted as well. Funding programs like this always came with strings attached. If MEG were successful, she would have to submit bi-yearly reports to the *Kultusministerium* on the progress of implementation and its impact on student satisfaction and performance. Also, the money could be used only for "structural improvements" in the school: new classroom technologies, approved online learning platforms, some technical support staff, and only an initial technological training course for teachers. She worried about her teachers' willingness to adopt the new technologies, especially if they didn't have adequate training. Several had already expressed frustration with MEG's finicky new smartboards.

Moreover, just last week, she had to sit in a steering committee meeting on the issue of cyberbullying. Several students had created fake and highly offensive Facebook pages that posed as a 10th-grade girl's profile; the girl missed several days of school to receive psychiatric counseling in the aftermath.[7] In the same meeting, teachers called for more restrictive online protections on the school's computers, since several 12th-grade boys had been caught looking at pornographic material in the computer lab. Selma had also experienced first-hand how difficult it was to reach many of the school's weakest-performing students when instruction moved online during the lockdowns in April 2020 and between December 2020 and June 2021. The model of instruction they adopted relied on students having adults at home to help them structure their online days—but not all families could provide such intensive support. Several did not even have an internet connection in their homes. Even the students who regularly showed up to online class rarely turned on their videos or interacted with the class as a whole. Thus, many teachers expressed concern that these students had missed the equivalent of a year of learning. Although Selma was still hopeful that a systematic blended learning program could work, her experience showed her that digitalization brought with it thorny issues of equity and distribution.

With a mixed sense of caution and excitement, Selma decided to talk to a few colleagues about how much online learning was right for students. She made her way, first, to Edith Kranz, the school psychologist who had dealt with the cyberbullying problem. Selma hoped that Dr. Kranz might have some academic insight on the issue, as she would regularly cite psychological research to support her positions in school policy meetings. Dr. Kranz was happy to voice her opinion about the matter.

"Well, there are pros and cons of hybrid learning models from a psychological perspective, Frau Morgenstern," Dr. Kranz said. "Hybrid learning can help students who are more passive and shy in traditional settings gain a sense of self-efficacy in their education, and it can allow them to learn in the spaces, timeframes and manners that suit them. Also, online learning allows for gamifying course material, which many students really respond to."[8]

Selma nodded, but sensed the cons coming. "What about the downsides, then?"

Dr. Kranz sighed, "Unfortunately, when students are required to be online for their learning, they spend even more time on social media than they already do. Social media can be a major distraction from students' learning activities."[9]

"Can't we do something about that?" Selma queried. "What about social media locks, mouse motion detectors, or even eye-trackers? I thought there were technologies to monitor when students begin to veer off task."

"Unfortunately students are quite adept at finding their way around these things," Dr. Kranz replied. "Especially at home, students have no help from professionals to keep them on task and away from misinformation and harmful content. It seems to me that we need to reach students somehow with real human support even in these spaces, but it can be so difficult."

Overhearing Kranz's worries, Hilde Schmidt, a social studies teacher and enthusiastic climate activist, burst into the office with her usual gusto. "That's what I've been trying to tell you, Frau Morgenstern!" Hilde exclaimed. "We need to get students off their devices and spending real, quality time in *nature*. Kids belong in the garden, in the fields, in the forest—not cooped up in front of a monitor that's making their eyes square!"

Selma couldn't help but chuckle at that. "Come on, Frau Schmidt. Screens don't make eyes square."

"I don't *really* think screens make eyes square," Hilde acknowledged. "But my point is the same. We are divorced from the slower, natural processes of life because we're fixated on our phones, tablets, laptops, TVs and whatever else. Why do you think we have a climate change problem? Because we don't know how to care for the environment anymore. It's not as flashy and fun as that ridiculous smartphone game Candy Crush. If we as a school encourage even *more* screen time, don't you think we are missing a chance to help students to develop a relationship with the natural world?"

"It's a really important point," Selma admitted, "but do the two necessarily exclude each other?"

"That's a tough question," Dr. Kranz remarked. "I'm not sure they do, but I do agree with Hilde's worries about screen time, if for a slightly different reason. Cyberbullying has been on our minds, of course, but I'm also worried about how normal it has become for adolescent girls to share explicit pictures and videos of themselves to boyfriends and sometimes complete strangers online. I do wonder whether students get themselves into this kind of thing because they're just looking for something exciting. Boredom often begets stimulation-seeking behavior, even if it does not bring the person pleasure per se."[10]

Selma sighed again as she turned over Dr. Kranz and Hilde's points in her head. She admittedly felt relieved when they both headed off to break duty. With ten more minutes of the break period, Selma sought out the teachers' lounge. Across the room, she saw Tarik Demir and Jonas Müller in conversation. Jonas and Tarik were good friends—both had the subject combination Physics and German and both were almost universally loved by students.[11] They were also some of Selma's closest colleagues at MEG, and she was excited to get their take on submitting an application for the funding program. As she approached, they paused their conversation.

"Yes, Selma? What's on your mind?" asked Jonas, smiling.

"Is it so obvious that something's on my mind? I'll have to work on my poker face. Well, I'd like to put together an application for this new funding program for hybrid learning that the *Kultusministerium* just released. They are offering close to a million Euro to update our technological infrastructure, but I do have some reservations. I mean, our students did not do well with online learning during the Corona lockdowns. They were practically begging to come back to school, even the 12th graders!"

"Oh I wouldn't worry about that," replied Jonas. "That was a special situation. I've been using the flipped classroom model for a long time, and my students love it. It frees us up for hands-on project work in class. Plus, students' performance in the learning-check assignments I use can be recorded and measured with my analytics software, and it sends me automatic notifications whenever a student is falling behind. It's pretty sweet."

Selma relaxed a bit, grateful for the positivity. "Well, what would you focus on in the application? What does our school really need?"

Jonas was eager to continue: "You should definitely put in a budget line for high-quality laptops. So many of our kids were trying to do their online learning during the lockdown on their smartphones. It was a disaster. And tablets just don't work as well as a full-powered computer. It's crazy that we can't offer all our students the tech they need to learn in the 21st century."

"So would you be for moving most of the curriculum online, then?" asked Selma.

"In my opinion," Jonas urged, "the more online learning we have, the more individualized, dynamic and flexible instruction we can offer our students, not to mention the innovative games, activities, and performance data. There are always downsides to things like this, but the tools available to us there are invaluable."

Jonas broke off, his eyes flicking to the door. "Oh," he said, "Maria just poked her head in the door. She probably has a question about our Projectiles Project. Do you mind if I invite her in really quick?"

"Sure," Selma and Tarik both responded.

"Hi, Herr Müller!—uh, guten Tag, Frau Dr. Morgenstern, hallo, Herr Demir. Sorry to bother you. I just have a very quick question for Herr Müller.

There's this great animation of projectile motion that I found on Reddit, but I can't find the source behind it. It was just posted by some random user. Can I use it for our Projectiles Project anyway?"

Jonas nodded, "Well, that depends, Maria. Have you checked whether the science is even accurate? What initial conditions are modeled? I'm happy as long as it accurately portrays projectile motion given appropriate initial conditions. Check up on this, and then just put as your source the URL of the page."

"Thanks!" Maria exclaimed.

As she whirled to go, Selma burst out, "Wait! I have a question for you about digitalization at our school, Maria. If I gave you unlimited money, what would you do with it to update our learning here at MEG?"

"You're asking me? Hmm. I've really liked Herr Müller's flipped-classroom approach. Maybe we should encourage this more often? It's cool seeing how much we can learn online. Also, with more flipped classrooms, maybe we'd have more time for social projects and initiatives, like that organic food drive the SMV[12] did last Christmas or the fair-trade events we've held in the past. We call ourselves a fair-trade school,[13] but we could definitely do more to advance that cause."

"Good point. But come on, Maria," Tarik teased. "Are you trying to tell me that my technology-free in-person classes are *that* boring?"

Maria laughed, "No! Hmm, I guess that's a good point, too. I wouldn't want to miss out on those hilarious re-enactments of Faust that Herr Demir does with us. Hard to do those online. Plus, don't sell yourself short! You do use the chalkboard."

"Thanks, Maria," Selma laughed, dismissing her. After Maria was out of earshot, Tarik continued the discussion.

"Maria's great. But I want to get back to our original topic. One thing I think you overlooked, Jonas, is all the issues students like Maria were having with their classwork during the COVID lockdowns. I had so many students tell me that the material seemed more abstract or just more difficult to grasp in the virtual environment. Maria herself complained that online learning was a real chore, and she's one of my most motivated students."

Jonas interrupted, "Well, yes that's true, but … "

"Hear me out," urged Tarik. "The students I talked to reported sitting for hours on end in front of their computers, completing assignments that were only ever graded by a web app, and they really missed the face-to-face interaction with teachers and other students. Some students even mentioned feeling listless and having trouble getting out of bed.[14] When learning becomes such a dehumanized affair, we lose so much of the motivational power of the student-teacher relationship. When I teach my German classes, I want my students to feel a part of something that matters—a living, breathing community of people who think Schiller is just as cool as Justin Bieber. Online, this stuff just seems like one more thing to learn for a test."

"Aren't you overreacting?" Jonas asked.

"Look, digital technologies are tremendously powerful in some ways, but very weak in others. Unfortunately, we tend to overemphasize what they can do and forget what *we* can do as human beings, person-to-person, without screens involved. Think about how transformative a passionately-told personal story can be, or a well-orchestrated discussion, or a spur-of-the-moment decision to follow the interests and insights that students share spontaneously. I think students get enough of the 'this is what technology can do' message from the world outside, and they seldom hear how their flashy interfaces and user-friendly algorithms can limit and distort their experience. That's why I try to give my students something different—something non-algorithmic, screen-less and uniquely human—in my classroom."

Selma glanced at the clock. "The break is ending, but thank you for thinking this through with me. I do have to admit, though, that I think I'm more confused than when our conversation began!"

Laughing, they went their separate ways. Selma returned to her desk determined to at least get something down on paper today. But she found that her efforts were foiled by a flurry of questions swirling in her head. Should she apply to this program at all? Would increasing learning time on digital platforms expose her students to more moral and social hazards than they already faced? What would be gained and lost in the transfer of learning and instruction to online spaces? Could the school balance the risks and rewards of online learning?

# Conversation

**Doug Yacek:** What are some of the key dilemmas you saw in this case?

**Drew Chambers:** I think that the main dilemma is about Selma Morgenstern [the school principal] deciding whether to apply for the grant—in other words, whether hybrid learning will disadvantage or harm students or support their learning and development, while at the same time keeping them safe. But on another level, each of the adults in the case study has a personal dilemma in terms of their advocacy. They're representing the interests of students, but also their own interests as professionals or as educators. In the case of Dr. Kranz being a school psychologist, she also has a personal dilemma about what her professional duties dictate in terms of advocating to Morgenstern.

**Nicholas Burbules:** I think one of the flaws in the program design, as described in the case study, is that the head of school is the one who submits the proposal. But the head of school isn't a technology expert. There's this strange dynamic where she has the accountability, but she doesn't have the expertise. Other people have the expertise, but not the accountability. They don't have to make the decision about whether to submit the proposal. And they have the luxury of saying, well, I'm concerned about X or Y, or Z—all legitimate concerns—but someone has to still make the decision about whether to actually accept some of those dilemmas or compromises and go forward with the proposal anyway. One of the consequences for the case study, then, is that unless the users are going to help to draft the proposal, they don't really have to take responsibility for what ends up being in the proposal and ultimately applied in the school. For Selma, there are both positives and negatives, and someone has to make a decision about how to keep those in some state of balance or creative tension with each other.

**Doug Yacek:** The talk of accountability and responsibility touches on an issue of justice, or equity. I wonder, as you're thinking through the dilemmas embedded in this case, to what extent they impinge on these issues of justice and equity or others you might have seen?

**Eva Simon:** I can understand the psychologist, for example, who said, "Okay, students could be distracted when using hybrid learning technologies." Cyber bullying is one problem that always comes up when we talk about online learning. It's not a dilemma, but a problem that we have to talk about because there's a positive and a negative side there. Spending too much time inside in front of the monitor is another problem. Not spending enough time outside. These were some of the main [problems and dilemmas] that I found.

**Doug Yacek:** So, for you, the key dilemma was really about the kind of impact the new program may have on students' relationship to technology. With Kranz and Hilde Schmidt, Kranz was more balanced, while Schmidt was really going hard at its potential negative impact on students' relationships. Did you find Hilda's argument convincing that the more online learning we're doing has a potentially negative impact on our relationship to nature?

**Eva Simon:** I mean, spending too much time in front of the monitor is not necessarily good for students. But they spend a lot of time in school as well. It would just shift the time spent listening to the teacher to sitting in front of the monitor. In the afternoon after school, there should still be enough time to go out in nature.

**Johannes Giesinger:** I want to add that you can also use the online tools in nature. You can go out in biology class and go to a brook, look at the surroundings, and use online tools to do experiments. My main question is whether online teaching is good for students, whether it has educational advantages, or other kinds of advantages, or what kind of dangers are involved.

Another issue that was not touched on so far is that Selma is put in a bad position unnecessarily because this Bavarian funding program is just crap. I mean, why not support schools in a positive way and not put them in the situation where they have to decide whether they want to apply for funding? It takes time, and it's complicated, and they have to do all kinds of stuff, and also report afterwards what they have done! It also is clear from the program that only a limited number of schools can benefit from this. Why not just do it for all schools in a reasonable way? I also think this 50 percent demand is just pointless because you cannot do it in percentages. She's a poor woman, Selma, and in this position I wouldn't be able to tell her whether she should apply for the grant. Although generally, I would say she should try to digitize her school.

**Drew Chambers:** The program does not put Selma in a position to rely on her expertise. And she may have areas of expertise that are certainly relevant for applying for grants, right? Maybe she understands her faculty; maybe she understands human resources are needed. But the grant is restricted to structural improvements. And it seems to me that this pigeonholing of the grant into just structural improvements, even if it's for the intention of digitalizing a school, seems to be narrow-sighted because there are certainly many ways to modernize a school or introduce digital media or digital technologies. For example, with a move to more hybrid learning, students need more social-emotional support. There might be a case for more counselors to help students process these sorts of issues and to help teach them social-emotional skills. But the grant prohibits that money being used for that purpose, and I think that's an instance where the grant isn't trying to leverage the real expertise of schools and principals.

**Nicholas Burbules:** That's a great point, Drew. And I think it's even worse than that. One of the myths of this area of reform is that technological problems have technological solutions. Many of the problems that are outlined—self-image issues, pornography issues—suggest that if you want to really reform teaching and learning with technology, you have to put resources into professional development, into psychological counseling, social-emotional learning, and other factors. The reason some of these problems arise is because we're putting computers and technology into the hands of kids who don't have the maturity or experience or critical wherewithal to use them prudently. That problem is not a technological problem. This whole idea of structural investments artificially slants the discussion into what you can fix with the technology itself, and that's not the nature of a lot of these problems that are being recounted in this case study.

**Doug Yacek:** But what about the counterargument that, in allowing only structural improvements, the state is basically enabling schools to develop their own pedagogical and curricular framework for how to use those technologies? Also, the particular technologies themselves are not stipulated in the grant, so there is quite a bit of freedom for customizing the program to the school's needs. What if the state replied to your worries by saying, "Look, this program is how we can allow schools to develop a tailor-made pedagogical approach that is modern and digital." Would you buy that argument? Or does that have any merit for you all in addressing some of the issues of accountability? You could imagine, for example, a school using some of the technological infrastructure to provide counseling at home. There's an app they can use to contact a school psychologist that's on call between 2 p.m. to 4 p.m., for example. What would you all say to that?

**Nicholas Burbules:** I think that's great. But that takes resources, too. That would be my concern there. I like the fact that they're not mandating a specific use or approach. But look, this school has expertise. A lot of schools aren't going to have people on staff who have this background. So where are they going to develop their pedagogy from? Or are they going to import it from somewhere outside without really understanding it?

**Doug Yacek:** Eva, as a K-12 teacher, if you wanted to update your pedagogy, would you prefer that you got a "full package" deal that provides you with specific technology and applications? Or would you rather have a budget for buying the technology that you think would work best in your class?

**Eva Simon:** I would probably take the latter approach. Of course, it's easier to get something that is already done. But it might not be a fit for my students. So it's probably better to construct it myself, even if it's much harder and it takes more time. It also depends on the age of the students because they have to be able to take responsibility and to work independently. I think the younger students from the age of ten to, I don't know, maybe fourteen—most of them are not mature enough to be able to handle these technologies themselves. For the older ones, I think it can be a huge advantage for them to decide when they do their work, to prepare their stuff at home, instead of doing it together in class and just listening to the teacher.

**Drew Chambers:** Just to follow up on your question, Doug. I see the program as it's set up in the case sort of splits the difference. It allows the money to be used for technologies as the principal sees fit, but the string attached to that plan is that 50 percent of the actual education be virtual. There's quite a big difference, from my perspective, when a teacher can say, "Have I seen the benefit of having laptops that are accessible to my students? Yes, absolutely. Have I seen the benefit of smartboards? Absolutely," as compared to having to commit to teaching half the class online. I mean, that's quite a big rider with this grant.

**Doug Yacek** This is such an interesting cost-benefit sort of thing. On the one hand, you have pedagogical freedom that we want to protect. And, on the other hand, you have the very real burden of pedagogical work associated with adopting the program in real classrooms.

I'd like to move slightly later into the case study and focus on the discussion between Tarik and Jonas because they bring up slightly different issues than the ones we've been talking about so far. If you remember the debate between the two, we have Jonas who seems like he's an early adopter. He's been using the flipped classroom model for a while with good success. They're both well-liked by their students, but Tarik is somewhat more suspicious of the tech. So instead of asking who you agree with, first, what I'd like to know is, what do you think their disagreement is based on? Do you think they have the same values, but they understand them in different ways? Or do you think they have very different values?

**Nicholas Burbules:** What strikes me is that the ethical issues that are raised here are very different types of ethical issues. There are what are called, broadly, equity issues. Different students have different kinds of access to technology at home or are differently motivated, so one set of concerns has to do with equity and whether what looks like the same class is experienced as the same class by all students. Another cluster of concerns has to do with the negative side effects of technology use–self-image issues, pornography issues, self-esteem issues, cyberbullying issues. Those are also ethical concerns, but they are ethical concerns of a very different sort. And then there's the kinds of concerns that Hilde raises, which are that you're not learning enough about this other area of the curriculum. That's really important. And so I think they're all motivated by what's in the best interest of the students, but I think they mobilize different kinds of ethical frameworks and different ways of defining what is in the interests of students.

**Drew Chambers:** What's important to remember is that both teachers are universally loved by parents. We see a student, Maria, come in, and she's clearly loving Jonas's flipped classroom. This isn't an instance where one teacher cares about students or student learning and the other doesn't. In some ways, they do have shared values, right? As Nick said, they care about equity and access to education. Jonas is mentioning the fact that the flipped classroom provides students with skills that they're going to need to thrive in the twenty-first century. He emphasized the individualized nature of online instruction that he thinks it affords something over and above in-person instruction. And then Tarik is emphasizing that there are certain motivational goods, certain existential goods, maybe even certain civic goods that are only realized in face-to-face community engagement. It's important to remember that advocates of virtual learning and advocates of non-virtual learning are acting with the best interests of students in mind.

**Johannes Giesinger:** What strikes me here is that the discussion seems to be about remote teaching, and I don't see that remote teaching is identical to digital learning more generally. If it's about being at home in front of a computer, I would totally agree with Tarik that this form of learning is dehumanized. There's a motivational problem: students always have their smartphone open, their Instagram account open. There are equity problems: different situations at home, different technology situations. I'm opposed to remote teaching, but not to digitalization at school, which takes a lot of thinking about how you organize it, the spaces, temporal structures, social structures, and how you individualize it, how much self-directed learning you put into it. You need a pedagogical program to structure this digital learning.

**Nicholas Burbules:** Just to create a little disagreement, I have a different view than Johannes does. I think that one of the virtues of a flipped classroom or a hybrid classroom is that you can do some effective learning activities at home at a distance. But it's not either/or. Flipped, hybrid, all those models suggest you do certain things in the classroom, you do certain things at home. It's how those activities relate to each other that is important. I'm a big fan of diversification of approaches, and I think hybrid classrooms allow us to combine different kinds of activities in ways that are customized to students' age and development but that allow us to do different things in different ways.

**Eva Simon:** I think Tarik and Jonas just see each other as different kinds of teachers. I think Jonas is the one who sees himself as a mentor for students after they have learned something at home, and Tarik sees himself as the presenter of the topic. He seems to be very passionate about helping students feel excited. That's the biggest difference between them. Jonas seems to be very popular among the students. And because he seems to be the advisor, he also wants to teach the students in a different way. He wants them to debate on the topic. He wants to make them discuss, to talk deeper about the topics and the knowledge they have gained at home.

**Drew Chambers:** One more complicating factor here is age. When we think about university education, the flipped classroom is the ideal model. Students go home, they do their reading, maybe they do some writing, and then they come to a seminar where they're ready to workshop ideas. That works because students are motivated to do the work at home, but also because they have the self-efficacy to do it. A complicating factor here is that, in its ideal form, the flipped classroom is really effective, but you have to instill the capacity in students and keep them accountable. That can be really difficult.

**Nicholas Burbules:** Flipped doesn't … there aren't just two contexts, the school and home. Mobile devices allow learning in a lot of different locations, as Johannes said. You take it out into nature, or you do oral histories in your neighborhood. Part of the whole point of these distributed networks is that you can do learning in many different contexts and environments, and then bring that information back to the classroom where you analyze it, synthesize it, and do the things together that are best done together, face to face.

**Doug Yacek:** I want to play devil's advocate. I'm thinking about something that I heard from Johannes earlier, about going into nature with your smartphone, and using it to look up the names of trees or plants or other biological information. And while I think I understand what you're talking about on a theoretical level, I find that if smartphones are involved with me when I'm in the forest—well up to just a week ago, I didn't have a smartphone!—but when my wife was, it was generally eating away at the experience to a certain extent. There was something lost when the technology, even just its sheer presence, was there. There was a level of distraction. Heidegger calls this "enframing," some people call it "brain drain." That's based on a study that actually found that if your smartphone is in the same room—you don't even have to be able to see it—you experience a decreased capacity for attention. These powerful technologies have a certain effect on us, and they might have an effect on our ability to teach a lesson that would be better or more compelling had we not used technology. Does that hold any weight? If you have a directive from your school principal to do 50 percent online or online supported learning, is there anything lost there? Or is there a gain when we bring in the technology?

**Nicholas Burbules:** I bring a certain kind of moral framework to discussions like this. In my worldview, when you get things you want, it often comes with things that you don't want. I just think that's a general thing about life and about the moral dilemmas that we deal with in life. I think this is one of those examples. I think all of those potential downsides are real. But the affordances, and the benefits are also real. The underlying question is the inevitability of tradeoffs: How do we get the things that we want, while accepting the fact that there also are going to be consequences that we don't want? That's a different kind of question than "is online education a good thing or a bad thing?" As somebody who's done a lot of it, it's a really good thing for some students, but it's not a very good thing for other students. That's a more complicated moral framework than, "Are we going to do it or are we not going to do it?"

I also think as a teacher, you really have to *try* to teach in a technology-free way. The more devices are around, the more you have to take care that devices disappear sometimes. For instance, one of our teachers held an outdoor class, under a tree in front of the school, and it's really different to go out there and have a philosophical discussion than to do it in the classroom with the smartboard and everyone's computer open. The more the technology develops, the more you have to take care to get rid of it for certain purposes.

**Eva Simon:** Technology is taking over our world. I think that the task of the school, of the teacher, is to make students aware of the struggle they can have with these technological devices. But it can also be highly motivating for them to actually *work* with the smartphone rather than just using it for normal free-time activities.

**Drew Chambers:** An integral part of my class, both as a philosophy instructor but also when I was a secondary English instructor, is people talking with one another. I think that that's totally possible to achieve in a virtual context. But it does require some careful thinking about the parameters that you're going to set on what occurs in your class. What I'm trying to do if I'm teaching a class online is make sure that students have their cameras on, making sure that students are talking with one another, and making sure that students are talking back to me. Breakout rooms have been an incredible resource for doing that and making sure that students are held accountable to the work.

On an abstract level, the thing I care most about being in person is that we're embodied individuals. That means we come to know each other in reference to our bodies. And when we're online, everything about us is being mediated by technology. In this discussion, all your voices sound different than they do in person, what you look like looks different. I just am seeing a two-dimensional screen in front of me. I don't know how you occupy a space. We can't have an organic conversation where I can pick up on the cues that you're about to say something.

What I'm doing if I'm teaching a virtual class is thinking about all the ways that I can allow my students to come to know each other just as they might in an in-person class. If I'm 50/50, that means I'm going to have to work especially hard to make sure that the 50 percent online is as meaningful as the 50 percent in person so that students are really coming to know each other as individuals, fellow peers, as colleagues, as fellow citizens, as moral individuals. And I think that is difficult online. But I do think it's possible.

**Nicholas Burbules:** I do want to underscore the fact, and Johannes has made this point a couple of times too, the 50/50 figure is extremely arbitrary. I mean, I'm an advocate for the blended or hybrid model. I'm not sure if 50/50 is the right mix. And even more specifically, I'm not sure it's the right mix for every student. To me, one of the advantages of technology is the ability to pursue multiple different modalities and different pedagogical approaches that fit different students' situations, as opposed to a one-size-fits-all model.

**Doug Yacek:** What would you like people to really take away from thinking about these issues after engaging with this case study?

**Drew Chambers:** When we're trying to decide how to proceed in any context—whether it's a question that just has to do with a particular lesson or something very, very large like whether to digitalize a school—we have ballast points that are going to, whether we are conscious of it or not, tip the scales in favor of one course of action or another. I think for me that the takeaway that I have—and I would want anyone reading this to have–is to think about what their ballast points are. It might be the case that when you go back to the first principles for what made you want to be a teacher, the first principles for what you think education is all about, you realize that, in this particular case, your ballast point is in the wrong spot. If you prioritize something else, you'll see different outcomes. I think that's the biggest takeaway for me, and the most important aspect of any sort of case exploration.

**Eva Simon:** I would say technology shouldn't be seen as a competitor to the conventional way of teaching but as enrichment. The time students spend in front of the monitor should be limited and their online habits should be controlled by the teacher. But it can be a huge advantage for everybody if you are open-minded.

**Johannes Giesinger:** For me, it's just very clear that schools should be digitized. I think the problem that Selma has is about whether it should be done by the state. One term, which is sometimes opposed to digitalization, is "digitality." It means a culture that evolves when we are digitized. What does it mean that our culture is a digital culture? This changes students' attitude towards information and knowledge: there's just so much information all around, and it's so easy to access. Even if we don't have a digital school, students will Google at home on their smartphones or whatever, and this changes their attitude to knowledge. How does this change the role of the teachers? Some would say teaching is not necessary anymore because the information is all around. We should also engage in these questions against a background that school is digitizing anyway.

**Nicholas Burbules:** I really liked the way Johannes just put that. Here's what I would add. I think it's important not to romanticize the traditional classroom. The traditional classroom also has equity issues and injustice issues. It also has unintended negative consequence issues. So the enemy isn't technology, but neither is it the conventional classroom. To me, the enemy is our desire in education to seek a one size fits all approach. We see that in a traditional classroom. We see it in certain approaches to technology. To me, the great advantage of technology is the ability to diversify and to allow some range of customization and choice on the side of students to different mixes of technology, face to face, etc. in light of their learning styles, their interests and so on. I want to broaden the question: how do we develop a hybrid model that is a diversified model? And I think that, to me, one of the greatest advantages of these technologies is that we can adopt some degree of customization, flexibility and choice in how students communicate and access information. In that, I think we have a chance to remedy some of the equity issues that are raised by trying to treat all students the same way.

**Nicholas C. Burbules** *is the Edward William and Jane Marr Gutgsell Professor in the Department of Educational Policy, Organization and Leadership at the University of Illinois, Urbana-Champaign. His primary research areas are philosophy of education, the ethics of communication, teaching through dialogue, and technology and education. He is the Education Director for the National Center for Principled Leadership & Research Ethics and a Fellow of the International Academy of Education.*

**Johannes Giesinger** *is a research affiliate at the University of Zürich's Center for Ethics. He also teaches philosophy and German at the Kantonsschule Sargans (Switzerland). His research interests lie in philosophy of education and the ethics of childhood.*

**Drew Chambers** *is a PhD candidate in Philosophy and Education at Teachers College, Columbia University. Formerly, he was a high school English teacher and now teaches in the Teacher Education Program at Barnard College.*

**Eva Simon** *is a Physical Education, English and Ethics instructor at the Johannes-Scharrer-Gymnasium in Nuremberg, Germany, where she has been teaching students ages 11–18 since 2015.*

# Character Guide

| Setting |  |
|---|---|
| Meister-Eckhart-Gymnasium (MEG), a university-track secondary school in Germany serving ages 10–18. | |
| **Primary Characters** | |
| **Selma Morgenstern:** *Direktorin* (principal) | **Hilde Schmidt:** social studies teacher |
| **Edith Kranz:** school psychologist | **Jonas Müller:** physics and German teacher |
| **Tarik Demir:** physics and German teacher | **Maria:** one of Jonas' students |

# Discussion Questions

1. Many characters in the case highlight the struggles that both students and teachers experienced when the Covid-19 pandemic pushed the school into remote learning. How should Selma take these pandemic-era challenges into account as she thinks about applying for the new grant?
2. Selma must navigate a range of conflicting views—about online learning, about the nature of social connection, about the place of nature in the curriculum—among the teachers at her school. As a leader, how can she honor teachers' different beliefs and values while nonetheless establishing a shared vision and set of practices around technology use at the school?
3. Meister-Eckhart-Gymnasium (MEG) has a "humanities-oriented" mission. What implications does this mission have, if any, for Selma's decision about whether to shift 50 percent of learning time into online platforms as required by the grant she's considering?
4. How is online learning distinct from in-person learning? What are the similarities between the two?
5. Jonas points out that not all students have reliable access to the technologies that they need for online learning. How should this inequity impact Selma's decision whether or not to apply for the grant?
6. Different characters present technology as either a method of connecting people or a barrier to in-person connections. How have you experienced technology as building versus hindering connections with others in schools? Are there particular practices or policies that you have found particularly helpful or harmful?
7. How does this case help you think about educational technology and digital learning in your own school, community, or national setting?

# Notes

1. For examples of existing funding programs, see: https://www.km.bayern.de/lehrer/foerderprogramm.html
2. German *Gymnasia*—the university-track secondary school which includes grades 5 through 12—typically has an orientation toward the humanities (*humanistisches Gymnasium*) or toward modern languages

(*neusprachliches Gymnasium*), but other types exist as well: e.g., science- and-technology-oriented, music-oriented, athletics-oriented or "European" Gymnasia.
3. The *Kultusministerium*—i.e., *Bayerisches Staatsministerium für Unterricht und Kultus*—determines curricula, grading standards, administrative procedures, professional development goals, and so forth.
4. As an example, the *Bundesministerium für Bildung und Forschung* (BMBF) issued its *Strategie "Bildungsoffensive für die digitale Wissensgesellschaft"* in 2016, which calls for a "digital transformation of the educational system" (p. 5). This program supports moving more learning time in and out of schools into digital settings. See: https://www.bmbf.de/files/Bildungsoffensive_fuer_die_digitale_Wissensgesellschaft.pdf
5. Slightly more than $850,000.
6. Digitalization—in German, *Digitalisierung*—is the term that is used for applying technology in educational spaces.
7. According to the "Jugend, Information, Medien"-Study 2019, one in five school children report having had false information about them distributed through digital channels. A case similar to the one described is reported in an article from the November 26, 2020, edition of the *Süddeutsche Zeitung*: https://www.sueddeutsche.de/politik/cybermobbing-wenn-das-internet-zur-qual-wird-1.5128418
8. These are some of the standard advantages that are associated with online learning in its various forms. See, for example, Northeastern University's list of "The Benefits of Online Learning," which plugs its online degree programs: https://www.northeastern.edu/graduate/blog/benefits-of-online-learning/. For research on the link between gamification and online learning, see: Antonaci, A., Klemke, R., and Specht, M. M. (2019). "The Effects of Gamification in Online Learning Environments: A Systematic Literature Review," *Informatics* 6:3: 1–22.
9. According to the "Jugend, Information, Medien"-Plus Study 2020, German students reported using friends via chat as the top source of help with online assignments during the 2020 online learning phases resulting from the Corona lockdowns. See: https://www.mpfs.de/fileadmin/files/Studien/JIM/JIMplus_2020/JIMplus_2020_Corona.pdf. For research supporting the distracting influence of social media in online learning, see: Hollis, R. B. and Was, C. A. (2016). "Mind Wandering, Control Failures, and Social Media Distractions in Online Learning," *Learning and Instruction* 42: 104–12; Wood, E., Zivcakova, L., Gentile, P., Archer, K., De Pasquale, D., and Nosko, A. (2012). "Examining the Impact of Off-Task Multi-Tasking with Technology on Real-Time Classroom Learning," *Computers in Education* 58: 365–74.

10. See Bench, S. W. and Lench, H. C. (2019). "Boredom as a Seeking State: Boredom Prompts the Pursuit of Novel (Even Negative) Experiences," *Emotion* 19:2: 242–54.
11. Bavarian teachers are required to have at least two subject specializations in which they offer courses.
12. SMV stands for *Schülermitverwaltung* and is the equivalent of student government.
13. Schools in Germany can take part in various special programs such as the fair-trade program in Nuremberg in order to develop a unique pedagogical profile. Other programs include civic educational programs like "Schule mit Courage," which is devoted to combating racism in schools.
14. Diagnoses of depression and anxiety disorders among school-age children increased in Germany during the Covid-19 lockdowns by around 10 percent compared to pre-lockdown rates. See: Kostev, Karel, Weber, Kerstin, Riedel-Heller, Steffi, von Vultée, Christian, and Bohlken, Jens (2021). "Increase in Depression and Anxiety Disorder Diagnoses During the COVID-19 Pandemic in Children and Adolescents Followed in Pediatric Practices in Germany," *European Child & Adolescent Psychiatry*: 1–7.

# 7

# Remote Control: Blurred Boundaries in the Zoom Classroom

## *Alysha Banerji and Winston Thompson*

*This case is set in the United States of America at a public (i.e., state-funded) primary school. The 4th-grade students in this case are likely nine or ten years old. Due to the Covid-19 pandemic, public schools across the United States closed to in-person learning in March 2020. When schools reopened in fall 2020, many relied on either remote instruction or hybrid learning, in which students learned from home on some days and at school on others. While most schools across the country were fully reopened for in-person learning by fall 2021, some districts continued to offer remote learning options. Other districts looked for ways to continue the hybrid model of learning. For example, some districts decided that students would learn remotely when extreme weather forced schools to close, or when widespread illness made in-person learning challenging or unsafe.[1] Other districts, like the fictional one in this case, looked to remote learning for part of the school week as a way to address teacher shortages, which were exacerbated by the pandemic.[2] Also exacerbated by the pandemic was the "dual pandemic" of systemic racism in the United States.[3] In the United States and around the world, the "Black Lives Matter" movement gained momentum during the pandemic, generating a widespread call for racial justice in the face of systemic racism. In the United States and elsewhere, "All Lives Matter" has evolved as a charged response to Black Lives Matter, both the phrase and the social movement.*

"You're muted, Sarah," said Emir, the grade representative for the 4th grade at Riverside Elementary.

" ... right at 1pm today ... Oh no! Sorry! Can you hear me now?" responded Sarah.

"No problem," Emir chuckled. "You were saying?" Even after all their time meeting in Zoom rooms during the Covid-19 pandemic-related transition to virtual instruction, there was always some incident involving the mute button.

"Oh, I was just asking how long we were going to meet. I have to get my kids from camp at 1pm," said Sarah.

This was the second preparation meeting for Riverside's 4th grade team. Over the summer, their district had decided to adopt what they were calling "Virtual Fridays"—a one-day-a-week practice of online instruction. On Virtual Fridays, teachers were expected to teach synchronously during the mornings, with the afternoons reserved for student and family conferencing, professional development, and/or planning. There were a handful of reasons for this decision, though staffing shortages and teacher burnout were two of the biggest ones. Coming out of emergency remote instruction during the pandemic, schools across the district—and across the country—had lost a number of veteran teachers and were having trouble filling all of their vacancies.[4] While other places had adopted a four-day week to attract teachers and manage burnout, the district worried that such a move would exacerbate pandemic-related learning loss.[5] School and district leaders believed their plan constituted a smart middle ground.[6]

Staffing issues, however, were only one set of reasons that Riverside was embracing Virtual Fridays. Ultimately, remote instruction, in one form or another, was here to stay. First and foremost, some students and their families found that remote instruction actually worked for them. In fact, this success had prompted the district to create an online-only school available to all families.[7] Additionally, their new inclement weather policy explicitly named synchronous remote instruction as a key strategy for ensuring students met state-mandated instructional time targets. And, of course, no one could guarantee that a new variant wouldn't emerge, prompting a new round of school closures.

While teachers had been given opportunities to provide feedback and express concerns about the new policy, now that the decision was final and before the school year officially began, school teams needed to create policies and practices that would structure Virtual Fridays. Building on previous conversations about classroom rules on Zoom, the purpose of today's meeting was to recommend a camera policy to the school principal.

"Ok," said Emir, "we only have an hour, so I want to get straight to it. Principal Jones has asked each grade's instructional team for feedback on some of the proposed policies around Zoom norms. I know that we've previously had some disagreement about whether we should have a camera policy, but I'm hoping we can come to a consensus by the end of this meeting."

"Hold on," said Ana, a veteran teacher at Riverside. "I thought we'd already agreed that on Virtual Fridays we were going to require students to keep cameras on?"

"Technically, that's true ... but we know that in the past this has been challenging for everyone to implement," replied Emir.

"Yes!" said Grace, one of Riverside's newest teachers. "I was ready to pull my hair out with some of my students. Despite my reminders, Nadia was constantly turning her camera off. She was one of the students who received a laptop and had internet enabled at home through the district last year, so I knew it wasn't a technical issue."

"Exactly!" Ana replied. "We were inconsistent in our camera policies last year. We really need to avoid making that mistake again this year."

Sarah's face scrunched. "I hear that concern, but I worry that being really consistent with this issue is easier said than done."

Like Ana, Sarah had been at the school for a long time, and the other teachers often looked to her for guidance. This wouldn't be the first time she and Ana had disagreed, but they were good friends and respected each other's often divergent positions.

Sarah continued, "Last year, I found out that one of my students, Rodney, was keeping his camera off on his mother's orders. I did talk to his mom, but she was adamant, and I honestly wasn't sure what else to do."

"Did Rodney's mother offer any explanation?" asked Emir.

"She just kept saying she didn't want a camera transmitting the inside of her home for hours a day. Honestly, I didn't fault her. Frankly, it felt weird and invasive that we required students—and their families—to comply with a school policy that is essentially exercising authority over their homes."

"But remote instruction means that we have to treat them as if they are at school, otherwise we're just giving them a three-day weekend!" said Ana. "I don't love that going virtual gives the students an intimate view of my kitchen, but that's just the way it is. Our chief concern has to be the quality of their instruction. If we can't even see students, how can we tell if they are present or paying attention?"

"I hear you, Ana. I really do," responded Emir. "Grace, do you want to talk about the incident with Chris last year? I feel like that's really relevant to this question."

"Oof, yeah," responded Grace. "We had a tricky situation with Chris during the pandemic. At one point, he was doing classes in the living room, and I noticed an "All Lives Matter" flag on the wall. Now, I would never place or even allow something like that on our classroom walls, but I hesitated to do anything. People can have whatever they want on the walls in their homes, right? It seems weird to try to control that—even if it ran against the class norms I was working to set up. Luckily, he went back to calling in from his bedroom, and the situation resolved itself. Honestly, I can't imagine what I would have done if other students or their parents noticed that."

"You keep teaching!" Ana shot back. "Look, I don't think an "All Lives Matter" flag in someone's house has to be a problem. Some people would be fine with placing it on a school wall to communicate that everyone is welcome and valued. Even if you, or me, or another teacher disagrees with that phrasing, people have a right to express themselves in their homes. I'm not sure why we're fretting about one poster that didn't even cause any problems!"

"Come on, Ana!" Sarah exclaimed. "What if a kid's parent had a poster with sexually explicit or violent content on the wall? If we're actually going to take your idea seriously—that we treat kids like they're at school during remote instruction—we need to think about issues like this."

Listening to Sarah and Ana, it was hard not to be drawn back to the memories of the early days of emergency remote instruction. Emir loved his job, but teaching virtually during the first two years of the pandemic was like pulling teeth. He felt like he couldn't connect with students anymore, and desperately missed all the little moments—the conversations between classes, run-ins in the hallways, eating lunch together .... Teaching had been his passion, but teaching remotely felt purely transactional.

"Consistency and instructional quality are the priorities," Ana replied slowly and deliberately. "We can't treat turning your camera off differently from breaking any other school rule. We need to make sure we're all holding the line on this so kids aren't getting different messages."

After a pause, she added, "And we can't let small political differences get in our way."

Among the matrix of faces on the screen, there were roughly equal amounts of head nodding and frowning following Ana's statement. Ana's reputation for strictness was well known among students and teachers. While students often grumbled about her toughness, they knew it came from an unwavering commitment to their best interests. The walls of her office were filled with cards and tokens of appreciation from her students, many of whom returned to visit her even years after moving on to middle and high school.

"I do agree with Ana that we need to be consistent," Emir jumped in. "I'm also thinking about what might happen if we had to go back to virtual learning for longer periods of time. My daughter Julie just found out that her fall semester of college is going to be mostly online—a huge hurricane this summer destroyed much of that area, and they're not sure exactly when they can bring students back to campus. We had a few worrying storms last year here, too, and I can imagine us being in a similar position at some point in the future. Unfortunately, extreme weather events are now just something we need to keep in the back of our heads when we do our contingency planning." Sarah looked concerned.

"O.K., but *can* we be consistent here? I mean, isn't the fact that we all struggled with this issue indicative that maybe it wasn't the right approach? As much as we try to treat all kids the same ways in school, we've always known that our kids are coming from different circumstances and have different choices. And honestly, remote learning highlighted those inconsistencies like never before—the students could see it too!

"I remember when Dmitri gave us a tour of his parents' basement. They had just refurbished it a few months before, and it was the perfect place for him to do his classes virtually. He had a ton of space down there. They even have a foosball table—you can imagine the looks on the other kids' faces when they saw that!"

The teachers chuckled.

"And then I compare that to Troy, sitting at the kitchen table with both of his siblings. Whenever he unmuted, we could hear his brother or sister in the background doing their own classes. The kids' grandmother lives with them, too. It's such a full house! I worry about how Troy can focus when we're virtual. I don't know how Troy feels about showing the rest of the class how cramped his house is, but I have to believe that navigating his home and his classmate's perceptions must be a distraction!"

Emir half-smiled to himself, thinking of his own efforts to curate the perfect Zoom background. If this was something that he was aware of, it was hard to believe the students wouldn't be self-conscious about what their classmates were seeing, too. Although teachers had tried last year to encourage students to use the background blur feature, they quickly found that strategy didn't work for students using older computers. Too often, those students would find their own faces or torsos blurred along with everything else. In his own experiments with background blur, Emir had no technical troubles but quickly found seeing his own image staring back at him against a mostly blank border too distracting to be worth it.

"For me," Sarah continued, "the differences between students' home situations make it hard to know how to respond when the usual rules—or these new ones—are broken. How can I hold all students to the same expectation, when I know that the remote camera policy carries such different weight for them?"

The group seemed thoughtful. After a brief pause, Sarah finished. "It's always been true that factors at home influence what happens in our classrooms, but now, at least on Fridays, what's happening at home *is* what's happening in our classrooms."

"I think that last point is particularly critical," admitted Grace. "When we employ remote instruction, the student's home becomes an extension of the classroom. That's a fundamental issue. I'm really worried about the prospect of teaching to a bunch of black boxes, but we need to think about how to manage this. I mean, I still don't know what I'll say to Chris's family if that poster pops up again."

"I think we should be able to say to the family that that sign isn't an appropriate Zoom background. Is that taking a political stance? Sure! But the more I think about it, the more I realize we just need to now!" Sarah stated.

"I don't know," said Emir. "That worries me a little."

"Let's be real here," Ana said, barely concealing her exasperation. "We have to focus on helping the kids make academic progress. They've lost a ton of instructional time in the last few years, and I don't know how to help them meet grade-level benchmarks on time if we start holding students to different standards, or picking unnecessary political fights. Flexibility has its advantages, but relaxing our expectations isn't good for anybody, least of all our kiddos who have fallen furthest behind."

"Ok, so ... say we decide that our official policy is to keep cameras on, but kids' parents are telling them not to ... what can we do?" asked Grace.

"We have rules for a reason. I'm sorry that some parents are telling their kids not to follow school rules, but the right response is simple: 'Breaking the rules results in consequences: end of story,'" replied Ana.

"Consequences for whom?" asked Sarah. "If the child is following their parent's instructions, is it really fair to punish them for that? We don't punish them for coming to school late, because we know that's out of their control. How is this different?"

Ana leaned closer to the camera. "What are you suggesting, Sarah? That we make the rules optional? Doesn't that set a dangerous precedent? If we let students—or their parents—choose whether or not they want to follow our remote learning policies, how can we require all students to wear the same uniform, or do the same assignments, or even accept the same curriculum?"

It was almost 1 p.m., and Emir knew the teachers would have to sign off in a minute. He'd anticipated some disagreement but had hoped that they'd be able to reach consensus by the end of the meeting. Instead, it seemed like discussing the school's "camera on" policy had suddenly spiraled into a constellation of new issues. Was the Zoom classroom an extension of the school building? Should the school hold students accountable to school rules while in their homes? How should teachers navigate situations where school policies and standards were in tension with students' families' expectations?

"So what should we recommend?" Emir asked.

## Conversation

**Alysha Banerji:** What are the dilemmas in this case?

**Laura Oxley:** They need to make a decision about whether they ask the students to have their cameras on or not, and there's conflict within the staff over how and why they should make that decision, with two strong differing opinions.

**Ben Paxton:** Building on what Laura said, one underlying dilemma is whether or not the home can become a legitimate extension of the school and the classroom space. Underneath that, what kinds of rules and expectations are legitimate within the classroom? And do they extend into the home?

**Will Kuehnle:** There are also interesting questions about how to manage the fact that students can now see into one another's home and, in some cases, see that there are significant inequalities in wealth between families in the same school community.

**Ben Paxton:** I'll just add that I've noticed, in this and many other normative case studies, an ongoing discussion about the basic aims and purposes of education.

**Alysha Banerji:** Can I ask you to expand on that?

**Ben Paxton:** It stuck out at me that teachers at various points mentioned not just school policy but higher level policy and the aims of education. We need to meet certain benchmarks. We need to keep students on task. We need to have them focused on academic goals. And there are a lot of other interesting issues being raised about what ought to be the focus of the educational experience. The teachers view their camera dilemmas as distractions from these educational goals. Perhaps, however, they should see solving these dilemmas as a community as part of the educational experience. Thinking about how we treat one another. Thinking about the messaging that we're sending to one another. Thinking about whether we're treating each other with kindness and respect. The teachers frame these issues as distractions, but they may actually be something we should reconsider as central themes.

**Winston Thompson:** Laura, you mentioned that there were two strong differing opinions. Could you articulate these two opinions and how they relate to the dilemmas here?

**Laura Oxley:** One teacher, Sarah, who was trying to be inclusive, explained that there's a student who might be embarrassed to give peers a view into his house and wouldn't be able to keep his camera on. Another teacher, Ana, was saying, "You know, I don't really like the students in my kitchen either, but that's just what has to be done to teach effectively." It came across in the case like there was a significant conflict between these two teachers. If I were a school leader in that situation, I would think that any decision we made would need to be managed quite sensitively because at least one staff member wouldn't be happy with the outcome.

**Ben Paxton:** That also brings up the issue of socioeconomic inequality. One child is sitting at a kitchen table surrounded by their siblings in a smaller home, and one child has a home with a refurbished basement and a new foosball table. Is it the intention of schools to hide that from students? Are we protecting students from the effects of inequality in schools? Why are our schools sterile places? It may serve very good purposes, like protecting students. But virtual instruction brings these issues into the school when the school had heretofore been able to carve out a little space for itself where it didn't have to deal with these issues.

**Ivelisse Ramos Brannon:** I would add that we can consider the social dynamics between the teachers as a dilemma. There is something in the case study about how Sarah and Ana are colleagues who have disagreed in the past but who generally get along. How do teachers navigate their own social relationships in schools in moments of conflict, and what are the implications for the community, especially when conflicts arise?

**Alysha Banerji:** That's a helpful segue. Who are these dilemmas for? Is everybody facing the same set of dilemmas? Are different people facing different dilemmas?

**Will Kuehnle:** I introduced this case study to a number of undergraduates. They felt that these fourth graders faced their own ethical dilemmas. The issue they were stuck on was the possibility that a student might have a teacher instruct them to put the camera on while a parent instructs them to keep the camera off. Now, it's the student dealing with the dilemma.

**Laura Oxley:** There's also the parents' perspective. They may feel that they don't want to have the camera on but they also don't want their child to get in trouble. They don't want to be seen as not supporting the school. But there may be valid reasons why they wouldn't want to have a camera on in their house. That might be tricky for them to navigate. How can they raise that with the teachers?

**Ivelisse Ramos Brannon:** I want to go back to the ethical dilemmas facing students. Some of them are taking classes at the same time as their siblings. When there are multiple students taking classes in one house, to what degree can each child engage? How do they navigate participating in the class while not distracting their siblings or the other children in the house?

**Ben Paxton:** In addition to the teachers, the students, and their families, we also have unnamed actors–the other faculty and staff at the school, the school administrators, the school board, the community at large. And, of course, none of these cases occur in a cultural and historical vacuum. We can ask even deeper questions about societal expectations about what should happen here and the influences that these expectations have.

**Alysha Banerji:** What are some of the values or principles creating these dilemmas?

**Laura Oxley:** The value of privacy. If there's a policy in place that requires the students to keep the camera on, that's essentially invading the privacy of the home because the teachers are then seeing the home environment and seeing whoever else may be there. And families might not want that.

**Ivelisse Ramos Brannon:** My interpretation is that Ana values preserving the integrity of the classroom experience in an online space, whereas some of the other stakeholders value the agency of families to make decisions about keeping cameras on or off.

**Will Kuehnle:** I think Ana definitely values integrity. That's a good word for what I've been trying to think of. But I also think Ana has a conviction that norms ought to be universal, that there should be consistency. It seems that she's concerned about allowing for exceptions to the camera policy and the possibility of an infinite spiral of exceptions.

**Alex Pittman:** It seems that Ana wants a kind of a one-size-fits-all way of handling this–not just the camera, but the learning in general. She talks about meeting grade level benchmarks, standards, and expectations. To me, one-size-fits-all thinking is always a dangerous pillar to stand on because there is no standard child. They're all different and have different needs. I respect her wanting to, as you said, protect the integrity of the classroom. In doing so, however, she should think about the individual needs of each student.

**Ben Paxton:** I also saw this distinction emerging between a real concern for the rules in the classroom and consistent policies versus a broader conversation about good education that meets the needs of students and families.

I also think it's important, as others have mentioned, that there's this very practical dimension having to do with the four teachers simply working together as a team. Working together as a team has its own set of ethical implications. You have to think hard about how to go about working together well as a team. Consistency, for example, is often a very important part of teamwork. You don't want one person doing something that other people are not doing, right?

**Ivelisse Ramos Brannon:** There's also the social political context. The All Lives Matter flag is in the background. These teachers are teaching in a moment of elevated racial tension. Figuring out how to respond is an important dilemma.

**Alysha Banerji:** I'd love to hear more from you on that. What do you see as the dilemma for teachers teaching in this context?

**Ivelisse Ramos Brannon:** There's so much to talk about here. On one hand, Grace brings up this problem about her student, Chris, whose All Lives Matter flag is flying in the background. This problem emerges in the context of a broader argument about whether they should require cameras, against the backdrop of elevated racial tensions complicating this already challenging experiment with virtual Fridays. It's important to parse out the flag issue from the other issues surrounding cameras. You have the issues of privacy, the issues of agency, but you also have free speech issues. I think that's an important conversation that requires a whole other meeting. What do we do when students have posters or flags or are wearing clothing that is offensive or harmful to other students?

**Will Kuehnle:** We're discussing a new version of the question about speech in schools. For the most part, when we are concerned with student speech in schools, it's the student who has decided to say something or to wear something. But in this case, we can imagine a student who's zooming from home, and there's any number of political messages in their living room. And maybe they can't zoom from their bedroom because the internet's not good enough. That student might think, "I don't agree with this message, but my mom put it in the living room, and that's the only place I can zoom from." In this case, there's an issue of speech that concerns and relates to the student but that isn't endorsed by the student. Another actor has brought speech into the educational space. We need to expand our focus beyond just student speech.

**Laura Oxley:** Yes, the children might not be choosing what posters or pictures go up on the walls, especially if they're little. How far does the school's responsibility extend in this case? Can the school ask parents to take something off their wall in their own home?

**Ivelisse Ramos Brannon:** I can't help but think that this is also surfacing another dilemma related to political division. In the case study, Ana says, "Come on, consistency and instructional quality are the priorities." She doesn't even want to engage in a conversation about how the flag might be harming children, particularly children of color, in this moment. Why? There can be many reasons, but it's a problem that folks in the meeting, namely Ana, don't even want to confront this possibility.

**Laura Oxley:** I wondered whether Ana understood the implications around the flag because she said some people would be fine with placing it on a school wall to communicate that everyone is welcome and valued. Maybe that lack of understanding is why she wasn't wanting to engage with the political questions about having an All Lives Matter flag in the background of a Zoom call.

**Ben Paxton:** Teachable moments screamed out to me throughout. Why do we have to move past these big issues in order to get on to ... what was the quote? "State-mandated instructional time targets." So we're going to skip past the inequality issues, the child safety issues, the education for democratic citizenry issues–everything–so that we can meet the state mandated instructional time targets. That's a fascinating debate, and it's a very real one that people are having.

**Will Kuehnle:** I think we are now bringing up another point I had been thinking about–what is it that the teachers do and don't find worth talking about? What individual actors in this dilemma find worthy of discussion and what they don't and then how they collectively move on from a topic is one of the problems of the case.

**Ivelisse Ramos Brannon:** My own experience tells me that these teachers are likely competing with institutional constraints around timelines. They have a job to do, and they have to create policies around Virtual Fridays, but they're unearthing all of these issues. And what do they do with them? Like you said, which issues are they going to skip over? And how much time do they have to do this? The clock is ticking.

**Alex Pittman:** I was thinking about issues of leadership. It seems like Emir has been tagged as the leader of the group, but he is a teacher as well. As a former public school educator, I know that a lot of times we are given decisions to make, but we don't actually have the authority or autonomy to make those decisions or we have very tight constraints to work within. It goes to thinking about representation, about who's at the table, or in this case in the Zoom space. The actual teachers in the classroom don't have the authority to make certain decisions.

**Alysha Banerji:** I think that last comment helps us transition into thinking about some of the policy or practical considerations that are shaping these dilemmas. What are other practical considerations that contribute to these dilemmas?

**Will Kuehnle:** I believe the Virtual Fridays themselves are partly the consequence of a labor issue. And then the other looming background issue that comes up—on the first page I think—is the threat of climate as a catalyst for future virtual learning. There's the real possibility that a hurricane, for instance, may send us back to our computers for a month, so we need to be very clear about our policies for online learning.

**Laura Oxley:** The point about workload is an important one. One of the key issues raised by teachers during the pandemic is the increase in workload and the diversification in workload that they're having to manage in order to adapt their lessons for effective online teaching. On the first page of the case, we can see that Virtual Fridays were in part a response to teacher burnout. Perhaps rather than removing some of the pressure from teachers, these virtual lessons actually put additional pressure on teachers and contribute to burnout. It would be helpful if the district leaders or school leaders were able to remove that pressure from teachers, but it doesn't seem like that's something that they would be willing to do in this case.

**Ben Paxton:** Another dilemma that popped up for me concerns the tension between the real and the ideal. If we view this from a very practical perspective, we have four teachers with fifteen or twenty minutes to decide what to do. There are things that we've thrown out that are, I think, valuable and worth considering, but is it really practical for these teachers to consider massive social issues? Even if they wanted to, and they're committed to it, where do they have the time and the space and the resources and the support from their administrators? I think from a practitioner's point of view, there's a dilemma between what I might like to do, even in terms of thinking through this dilemma, and what I can actually do and what I have time to do. I have to triage and identify the most important thing that needs to be done within the next week and what we can revisit during our annual review.

**Alysha Banerji:** So what should Emir recommend?

**Ivelisse Ramos Brannon:** I think that he should recommend that they continue this conversation with additional stakeholders, including families and students. I don't think that they can make a definitive decision in this meeting given all of the issues that emerged. I think it would do a grave injustice to the students. This is one full day a week of instruction, and there's much at stake in the decisions that they're making.

**Alysha Banerji:** Ivelisse, I'm going to push on that a bit. Even with the limited stakeholders they have in the room, there's already so much disagreement taking them further away from the decision point. How would they navigate having additional stakeholders? Wouldn't that potentially take them even further away from coming up with one decision? I'm also wondering why you think they need more meetings. What will more meetings help them do? Is there specific information you think that they're missing?

**Ivelisse Ramos Brannon:** I think that you're right. There's always … what's that phrase? Many chefs spoil the broth. And I agree that it will take longer for them to make these decisions. But is it really fair? Is it ethical of them to make this decision that will impact students without any family input? I think the answer is no. It's not fair or ethical. It will take longer, and it will complicate the decision-making process, but that extra time and complication is in service of children and families. What's missing is the family perspective. These teachers are making assumptions based on one or two instances. Who knows why Rodney's mother wanted the camera off? Maybe let's ask the parents and the family members. I'm also curious about the positionality of these teachers. What is the composition of this group? I have so many questions about who these teachers even are and what they look like with respect to what their students look like. I don't know how carefully this group was constructed. I have more questions for you than answers, Alysha.

**Winston Thompson:** Ivelisse, you raise some good questions here about process. I think we could also think about the outcome. It's possible that even with a different process, we might still arrive at the same outcome–being at loggerheads with one another. Given that, the question that Alysha posed earlier is quite a good one. What additional information could these folks have that they don't already have?

We know that some parents seem okay with the cameras on, and some parents want the cameras off, but we don't know exactly why some parents want the camera off. Should that matter? Earlier, Laura mentioned privacy as a value. Maybe it doesn't matter why the parents want the camera off. The fact that they want it off is sufficient. I'm encouraging us to think about whether the process that you're describing may still result in a conflict of values? And what is it that we're after that might allow us, might allow these characters, to arrive at a decision that we think could be endorsed?

**Will Kuehnle:** On the one hand, I see value in including more stakeholders—parents, for example, or even students. I think a parent explaining some very genuine reason why they don't want their child's camera on in their home might change Ana's mind, for example. That said, it seems like we have a decision that's been kicked down to the level of the teachers who are already held accountable for everything—from learning loss to the failure of a student. What I would really like to see is a meeting where there are administrators who have to sign off on the decision. When values clash, there should be an administrator who takes the heat, rather than Emir or Sarah or Ana. I think you're right, Winston, that much of the information is already available. What's lacking is the proper person whose job is to help manage the inevitable tension. And I think that, among other things, that's one of the roles of the administrator in schools today.

**Ivelisse Ramos Brannon:** I feel like these teachers are making this really important decision based on anecdotal evidence. Where's the discussion about what's best for kids? What does the research say about whether we should require children to have their cameras on or off? These are actual conversations that folks were having during remote learning during Covid-19. Let's look at what the experts say about this and go beyond what happened in my classroom. To be clear, I do think these stories are important. Context counts, right? The individual experiences of students count. It just feels like there are a lot of feelings in this meeting.

**Ben Paxton:** We have a multiplicity of stakeholders and a multiplicity of dilemmas that we've identified. Maybe we also need a multiplicity of solutions? For example, we might need to develop a short-term solution because we're dead in the water until we have a camera policy. When schools were doing virtual instruction five days a week, we couldn't simply suggest that we stop everything until we resolve these questions, right? So we need a short-term policy, and then we need a longer-term policy. We might list all of the dilemmas that we discussed, sort them into categories, and develop solutions. Maybe some of those solutions, for example, could be townhall meetings that involve students and parents and other constituencies from the community. Maybe there are more formal professional development sessions with administrators, teachers, social workers, and others at school who are thinking about these issues and bringing in the information that they have.

Teachers and other school employees like social workers are aware of the social conditions in their communities. Hearing from these folks, gathering all of the relevant information, and having conversations may be a really important piece of our strategy that has to extend over a longer period of time.

**Alex Pittman:** Perhaps they should develop some kind of survey asking the fourth grade families: Does your child have a place that you would deem appropriate to conduct virtual learning? Do you feel comfortable with having your camera on and why? And then when you have that second meeting, you would have more than just anecdotal evidence about someone who saw a flag or someone's siblings in the background. You wouldn't have a full picture, but you would have a more complete picture of what families are thinking, which could inform the decision that you ultimately have to make.

We also have to think about whether teachers are going to enforce a rule that they feel hurts their students. I've had to make a decision like this when I was a high school teacher responsible for carrying out my school's tardy policy. Are you going to slam the door and lock it the moment the bell rings? And let your students get swept up and receive an in-school suspension, or potentially an out-of-school suspension? I decided not to enforce this rule. I'm still going to handle tardies and hold my students accountable, but I'm going to do it in a way that I feel like is going to be most beneficial for the students and the families that I serve. And so I think, when you're making this decision, you have to think about what you're going to do when teachers—perhaps Sarah, or someone else—don't enforce this rule. That has to be part of the consideration. I would not feel comfortable enforcing a rule knowing the negative impact it would have on my students' learning or on their family dynamic. That's a difficult choice.

**Ivelisse Ramos Brannon:** I support Alex's idea that no decision can be made until there's some kind of community questionnaire. If they rush through this decision, they're going to have to triage when new challenges emerge, right? So why not just be a little more thoughtful now?

**Winston Thompson:** What if they request feedback, and the results show that people are split? Some of the parents say one thing, some say another. The reasons that are offered are compelling and gut wrenching. So we find ourselves having kicked the can down the road, but we've still got the can. I'm curious. What are your immediate responses about what to do at that decision point?

**Laura Oxley:** I would err towards saying, "We encourage you to have your cameras on, but it's okay if you choose not to. There won't be a consequence for that." Alongside that, I would advocate for building educational workshops about the benefits of keeping the cameras on to try and persuade people.

**Alex Pittman:** I agree with Laura that the drawbacks of forcing cameras to stay on outweigh the potential benefits. I also think that additional information about why students or families don't want their cameras on will allow us to think about alternative paths forward. If the focus really is on student learning, you want to know that you're not just talking to an empty, black box. There are a variety of ways you can have students respond, however. There are polls. There's the chat box. Again, if you're really concerned about whether they're picking up what you're laying down, there are other kinds of feedback you can look for beyond a nodding head in the square.

**Will Kuehnle:** As a teacher, my inclination is that rules are good. That said, I think my gut answer is that I can see going either way. I don't know this school. None of us do. I'm going to go back to the responsibility of the school administration. I believe there should be an administrator whose job is to say, "I know this school very well. I know these families, and it's my job in these moments of collective tension to become the voice of the general will, which is something beyond just the kind of collective expression of every individual. I take on the risk of pushback and the real possibility of becoming a community scapegoat."

That's how I envision the role of the administrator. They can become a kind of personal solution to the ethical dilemma by becoming the potential ritual victim. That's my response. I can see a good administrator going either way on this question, depending on this community that we've only seen a snippet of. The job of the teachers is to teach, not to take on hard decisions like this.

**Ben Paxton:** Early on in my career, I focused primarily on political philosophy, so I appreciate the reference to the general will. Part of the reason I chose philosophy of education as my path is because I've always committed to educative solutions to problems rather than coercive ones. I think Alex raised the issue of control at the beginning of our discussion. There's tension between the teachers about whether or not control is appropriate, and how much control needs to be exercised. That immediately throws up red flags for me. If we do need to exercise control, I think the rationale for that control needs to be educative. There is a strain within education, in my experience, that seems to want to push control for the sake of control, without any real educative value. Often, actually, this undermines the value of education. My question is, what can we do in this situation that's educative? What's going to allow people to learn and grow from this experience?

In some of the previous casework that I've done, participants sometimes encounter a dilemma and become uncomfortable. You want a resolution, and you want to get back to a place of comfort. Perhaps that's not realistic, or that shouldn't actually be the goal. We need to do more to make people feel okay with the fact that the lack of comfort is going to last for a while. And we have to ask some serious questions about who owns this dilemma. Alexander made a great point that, at one level, each individual is going to have to make decisions for themselves about what they're going to do. Those decisions are difficult. You can't simply wait around for the community or the school or the administrator to solve the problem for you, but I think that's sometimes what people are hoping for. I'm just thinking out loud as an ethics educator. You can't abdicate from those individual decisions, and you shouldn't abdicate from them. The individual teacher is going to have to make decisions at some point about whether or not the choices of their school administrator, their fellow teachers in their department, the school board, or their local community mesh with their own values and moral commitments. And if not, what are they going to do?

**William Kuehnle** *is a graduate student at the Ohio State University. His work explores the political and theological interpretations of personal relationships between students and teachers.*

**Benjamin G.S. Paxton** *(PhD) is an educational ethicist. He currently teaches philosophy, ethics, and history of education at the University of Virginia.*

**Alexander G-J Pittman** *has nearly a decade of secondary teaching experience as a social studies and history teacher. Currently, Alexander is pursuing a doctoral degree in education, specifically focusing on Multicultural and Equity Studies in Education at The Ohio State University. His research focus centers on the intersections of race and social justice in the context of preparing preservice educators.*

**Laura Oxley** *is a Research Associate and Senior Teaching Associate at the University of Cambridge, UK. Her research interests are in behavior management and teacher well-being.*

**Ivelisse Ramos Brannon** *taught High School English Language Arts in New York City for fourteen years where she also served as a teacher leader, mentor, and coach. She is currently a doctoral student at the Harvard Graduate School of Education.*

# Character Guide

| Setting |
|---|
| Riverside Elementary School, a public school in the United States serving children ages 5–11. |

| Primary Characters | |
|---|---|
| **Sarah:** 4th-grade teacher | **Nadia:** 4th-grade student |
| **Emir:** 4th-grade teacher and grade team representative | **Chris:** 4th-grade student |
| | **Rodney:** 4th-grade student |
| **Ana:** 4th-grade teacher | **Dmitri:** 4th-grade student |
| **Grace:** 4th-grade teacher | **Troy:** 4th-grade student |

## Discussion Questions

1. Inequality in income, wealth, educational attainment, home context, and many other domains impacts the quality of education children receive. How should teachers and schools think about these inequalities when planning instruction—whether remote or in-person?
2. To what extent is the Zoom classroom an extension of the school building? To what extent is it an extension of students' homes? How should educators respond to the dual nature of the space?
3. What is gained or lost when students come together physically in a shared classroom space versus when they join together virtually from home or other spaces? How is equity advanced and/or impeded by these different spaces?
4. What are the minimal requirements for a safe and viable space for a student to engage in remote instruction? How should schools respond if not all students have access to such a space?
5. How do different characters in the case conceptualize equity? Which conception(s) of equity align most closely with your own views?
6. Ana emphasizes the importance of consistency, not only for the camera policy but for other expectations like school uniforms. How do you understand the relationship between consistency and equity?
7. The teachers in the case disagree about how much control parents should have over whether their children's cameras are on—and, by extension, about the extent of parents' rights to direct their children's upbringing. How should schools respond when families make decisions or requests that oppose school policies?

## Notes

1. Sullivan, Emily Tate. "Under the Right Conditions, Can Remote Learning Be an Asset?" January 24, 2023. EdSurge. https://www.edsurge.com/news/2023-01-24-under-the-right-conditions-can-remote-learning-be-an-asset
2. Fortin, Jacey and Eliza Fawcett. "How Bad Is the Teacher Shortage? Depends Where You Live." August 29, 2022. New York Times. https://www.nytimes.com/2022/08/29/us/schools-teacher-shortages.html

3. Jones, Janine M. (2021). "The Dual Pandemics of COVID-19 and Systemic Racism: Navigating our Path Forward." School Psychology 36 (5). doi: 10.1037/spq0000472. PMID: 34591591. https://pubmed.ncbi.nlm.nih.gov/34591591/
4. Fortin and Fawcett, 2022.
5. Evidence on the impact of the four-day week in schools is still sparse. See: Barshay, Jill. "Proof Points: Seven New Studies on the Impact of a Four-Day School Week. August 29, 2022. The Hetchinger Report. https://hechingerreport.org/proof-points-seven-new-studies-on-the-impact-of-a-four-day-school-week/
6. The number of schools adopting a four-day week has approached 25 percent in some states. See: Benincasa, DC. "Four Day School Week? In Rural Missouri, More Districts See It As a Way to Recruit Teachers." June 11, 2022. Missouri Business Alert, KCUR. https://www.kcur.org/education/2022-06-11/four-day-school-week-in-rural-missouri-more-districts-see-it-as-a-way-to-recruit-teachers
7. Boston, for example, has opted to open a virtual school in part due to the success some students had during remote instruction. See: Woolhouse, Meg. "13 Mass. School Districts Propose Offering An All-Virtual School Option Next Year."May 14, 2021. Boston Public Radio. https://www.wgbh.org/news/education/2021/05/14/13-mass-school-districts-propose-offering-an-all-virtual-school-option-next-year; More broadly, remote schools have become an increasingly common practice in many big school districts. See: Belsha, Kalyn and Matt Barnum. "Sticking Around: Most Big Districts Will Offer Virtual Learning This Fall, A Sign of Pandemic's Effect." June 6, 2022. Chalkbeat. https://www.chalkbeat.org/2022/6/6/23153483/big-school-districts-virtual-learning-fall-2022

# 8

# School Choice in Hong Kong: Peking Ducks or Rich Expats?

*Liz Jackson*

*This case study takes place at a cooked food market, a popular place to eat in Hong Kong. In this case, a group of friends with diverse local, international, and educational backgrounds discuss the three types of schools available to Hong Kong families: local schools, private international schools, and direct subsidy scheme schools (DSS). Local schools include those fully organized and supported by the Hong Kong government, as well as "aided" or "grant" schools, which were originally founded by religious or charitable organizations, but also follow government curricula. Most local schools teach in Chinese, but some have options for English medium of instruction. Some are elite and competitive, while others have poorer reputations and are relatively easy to join. International schools may teach in a variety of languages, including English, Japanese, and Korean. Non-local children can only apply to international schools; they are not eligible for local or DSS schools. DSS schools generally follow the local curricula, with classes taught in Chinese, but they are more independent than local schools in terms of curricula, staffing, and admissions. All schools in Hong Kong charge tuition and have competitive admissions, but vary in terms of cost, educational requirements, language of study, and values.*

--

It had been several months since Cindy and her husband Benny had met up with their friends for dinner, and she was looking forward to it. As usual, they were going to the cooked food market in their neighborhood. While everything there was delicious, they also liked that it was traditional—so traditional that the waitstaff only spoke Cantonese. Actually, that's probably why it had become their favorite place. While everyone in the group was a Hong Kong resident, only Cindy and her colleague William could speak fluent Cantonese. Their colleague Puja, an Indian Hong Konger, could speak a bit, while her husband Mark, an Australian, only spoke English. Benny, and William's wife, Iris, were Chinese, but since they both grew up in North America, their Cantonese was not fluent. So it was a special treat for the group to enjoy the food together, while Cindy and William took care of ordering in Cantonese.

Plus, Cindy had news to share: She and Benny were expecting their first child. As their friends already had children, she was sure they would have good advice for her as she began planning for the baby.

When they arrived at the food market, Cindy and Benny did not see their friends anywhere, so they got a table. As they began rinsing their utensils and cups in hot water, Puja and Mark rushed over.

"Sorry we're late," Puja said breathlessly, as she plopped down across from Cindy. "We were trying to get the kids to bed, but it was a joke. They never want to go to sleep these days."

"They never sleep," Mark added. "I don't know where they get their energy."

Just then, William and Iris arrived. "Hello everyone, long-time no see, Cindy!" William rolled his eyes. Cindy and William had just been in a boring meeting together that afternoon. "I hope you haven't been waiting long," Iris added as they sat down.

"Not at all," Cindy replied. "We haven't even gotten the menu. Although we probably don't need it!"

"Yellow chicken, beef noodles, bok choi, … seafood?" William rattled off their usual orders.

"Let's get fried tofu and eggplant," Puja added.

"Yes," Mark nodded. "And salt and pepper squid."

"I think it's too much, but let's see," William said as he waved the server over. After William listed the items in Cantonese, the server confirmed the order.

"Let's also get three rice," William added, "and one … two … three large beers." The server ran off, and immediately returned with the beer. As Iris collected everyone's cups, William poured some beer into each and passed them around.

"None for me today," Cindy said, suddenly feeling embarrassed.

"Oh yes," Benny smiled. "Have you told them?"

"Not yet," Cindy began …

"You're pregnant!" Puja shouted. Cindy nodded as the table erupted in oohs and ahs and the clinking of small cups of beer.

"Welcome to the club," Puja said.

"Yes, now comes all the fun," Mark nodded. "Helpers and tutors, finding an apartment with two bedrooms that can fit beds in them … "

" … and best of all, preparation for school interviews and exams," Puja added.

Mark rubbed his eyes and shook his head.

"Yes, we have a lot to do," Benny smiled, taking his wife's hand beneath the table. "First things first." Cindy felt relieved by this gesture.

Soon food began appearing: Bok choy, eggplant, and tofu. Everyone dived in to try each.

"Just curious," Puja said as she filled her bowl with eggplant. "Do you know what type of school you want your child to go to—local, international, DSS?"

Cindy nodded. "We'll go to a local school.[1] We just need to decide whether we want to move to another neighbourhood for better school choices in the coming years."

Benny nodded rapidly. "I really want him or her to learn Chinese. My parents figured sending me to California for my education was best. But it's embarrassing that my Cantonese is not that good. You know, I can't really read or write. I want my child to fit in here."

Puja gazed at Benny and Cindy with sympathy. "We wanted the same for Dev. But for us it hasn't been easy. Even though I grew up here and went to local schools, I didn't get to learn Cantonese. Today they still segregate ethnic minorities into English medium-of-instruction local schools, or English-medium classrooms. It's really a problem. Not speaking Cantonese limited what I could study at university—I wanted to work in the health field, but the medical system and social work system are all in Chinese."[2]

"Yeah, that's been the hardest thing," Mark agreed. "Our children will have to compete for jobs here with people who speak Chinese and English. But teaching Dev Cantonese, when we don't speak it ourselves, is impossible. We tried a private tutor, but since Dev doesn't use it socially, it's really hard for him to learn it well."

Puja interjected. "We want Dev to be 100% a Hong Kong person, but now I'm afraid he'll be caught in-between worlds."

"Even for us, schooling has been a challenge," Iris added, nodding. "Kenneth was in a local school, but we recently decided to switch to an international school."[3]

"What happened?" Cindy asked.

William chimed in. "I was not happy with what they were doing there. It's the stuffed Peking duck approach."[4]

"I know what you mean," Benny jumped in. "The students here are so focused on memorizing information, that they don't really think about how to apply it. It's the opposite of what I'm trying to do with my students in my university classes—passive versus active learning."

Iris nodded. "Teachers are really focused on teaching students how to learn to succeed in exams—how to give exactly the answer the teacher is expecting. Every tiny difference from the 'right' answer has to be corrected. If you spell one word wrong, you need to rewrite the whole sentence again three times and turn it in to pass dictation."

"I don't know how children here do it," Mark shrugged. "I was just average at school. I would not have survived here. In Australia it is much more laid back. Everyone is okay in the end."[5]

"There was just no time, even for us as his parents," Iris continued. "One dictation for English and one for Chinese, every week. At least an hour, usually many more, of homework every night. On Fridays, Kenneth would have thirteen homework assignments. There's no time for sports or games or outside reading ... In second grade, he was so stressed out about the tests. We were all miserable." She sighed.

"The system-wide assessments are crazy," William explained. "These tests are not supposed to be evaluating the students. But the students and teachers worry so much about them that everything else gets ignored."

"But test scores are important to get into university, right?" asked Cindy. "If they don't teach students to work hard and do well on tests, in the long run it will be impossible for them to get into university. It's not a bad thing."[6]

Iris nodded. "We really debated it. In general, people here value hard work, and this is also reflected in the schools. I wish I had studied harder when I was growing up in Canada. In Canada, we didn't have a sense of dedication, to work hard in difficult subjects. But now we also like the Western approach, where children have more freedom to just be children."

William went on. "The problem is that if we say, 'no worries, you don't have to be perfect,' that actually makes things worse for Kenneth. The school demands parent involvement and support to do all the homework perfectly every time. So the teachers disapprove of us, and Kenneth. And Kenneth felt anxious and ashamed. We didn't like that."

The conversation briefly paused as the server returned with more food and beer. Cindy poked at her food and reflected on what had been said. She remembered feeling stressed out when she was at school and pressure to do her best so she could go to university. But she had never dreamed of her children going to international schools. She shook her head. "I'm not sure we can afford an international school. Aren't they really expensive?"

"Sooooo expensive!" Iris whined. "ESF costs nearly $150,000 per year. It's not even the most expensive. It's definitely not possible for most people."[7]

William nodded. "We knew another couple at the local school, Westerners who wanted their children to integrate and learn Cantonese. They said that they can internationalise their children by taking them skiing in Hokkaido in the winter and to America every summer, with the money they are saving by going to the local school."[8]

Iris looked doubtful. "Right, but are you really going to choose a school just so you can go on holidays? It's your child's future you're talking about … ".

"Another option is DSS,"[9] Puja said.

"What's that?" asked Benny.

"Direct Subsidy Scheme," Puja explained. "They're for local students, and they take Hong Kong examinations, but they can also have international subjects and tests. They can be a little cheaper. Like an international school for local students who already speak Chinese."[10]

"It's a nice idea," Mark added. "They also emphasize more traditional values about studying hard and have high standards. But they can also be really hard to get into."

"But I heard some bad things about some religious DSS schools," Iris interrupted. "One of my friends has terrible stories of being caned at a Catholic school."[11]

Puja raised her eyebrows. "I don't think that happens now, but maybe it happened in the past. In our case, we wanted Dev to feel like he belonged, and to have international exposure. Plus, we have to prepare him in case he wants to study or live outside Hong Kong when he's older."

"That makes sense," Benny replied. "I think that some of my students at university would have a difficult time studying abroad."

"That's one side of it," William interrupted, "but on the other hand, for Kenneth, now he's becoming too international. He hardly speaks Chinese at home anymore!"

"And some of Kenneth's school mates come from really wealthy families," Iris added. "Now Kenneth has this sense of class division. These expat kids,[12] they are completely focused on holidays, phones, and all the latest toys."

Puja nodded and grimaced. "There's also a sense that students in international schools 'can't take it' in local schools—that they are coddled, because the international schools have a more western approach to academics."

"There's no easy answer," Mark said. "But let's not upset Cindy now. They'll be fine. First, they have the baby, then they get started on kindergarten interviews."

Puja laughed.

"And we haven't even mentioned names," William added. "Of course, I already know it will be William if it's a boy!"

The group broke out in laughter.

As the evening progressed, Cindy could not get the issue of schooling out of her head. After dinner, she and Benny walked through the neighborhood, and she brought the conversation up again. "What did you think about what they all said about the local schools?"

"I never thought about it that much before," Benny admitted. "I can see their point—the local system is not perfect. But I also don't want my child to be in the situation I am in now, not even fluent in Chinese."

"No, me neither," Cindy agreed. "If William struggles with Kenneth's Chinese, we would be in the same position."

Benny nodded. "There's nothing wrong with western values, but there's nothing wrong with Hong Kong values, either. Sometimes international culture is treated as superior to the local system. I wish there was a way to have the best of both worlds: low stress, but also high commitment to excellence. But when I compare my experiences in school in California with Hong Kong, I don't think you can have both."

"My only worry," Cindy continued, "is that what if our baby does want to go abroad when they grow up? Would we be depriving him or her of opportunities, like you said?"

"It's hard to say," Benny frowned. "But still, I would feel bad depriving them of opportunities to succeed in Hong Kong."

Cindy gazed at the sidewalk in front of her. "Now that I think of your experience compared to mine, I never realised that our parents made such a big difference to our future with these decisions. Your parents were sure California would be best, but here you are today. How do we decide on behalf of a baby that is not even born, about what is best?"

Cindy and Benny and their friends' struggles are not unique but are shared across many families, in Hong Kong and around the world. Beyond financial considerations, child well-being, cultural values, and academic achievement are all important aspects of education. An even more fundamental issue is whether it is appropriate for different parents to make different choices about their children's education, or whether there is one best answer regarding school options that is relevant to all members of society. What rights do parents have, if any, over their children's futures? If this is not only a personal choice for parents, what other considerations do you think should take priority?

# Conversation

**Liz Jackson:** Before we get into the discussion, I would like to ask each of the participants to give a little bit of an introduction of where they are from and why this case is relevant to them.

**Jan Gube:** I think there's an interesting question here: where do you call home? My home is Hong Kong, and my background is Filipino. My parents are both Filipino, and I went through the local education system through the Chinese medium schools. So I find the case very interesting.

**Chi-Ming Lam:** I was born in Hong Kong. I find this case very relevant and interesting not just because I am interested in talking about ethics and values in education, but also because I'm a parent.

**Emma Buchtel:** I also have very intense personal connections to this case. I have a very complex, multicultural family. I'm American, all my education was in the public schools in the US. My husband is from mainland China. My children were born here. They are nine and eleven now, and I sent them to the local primary school which is a Mandarin Chinese medium of instruction primary school. And now, as they get towards secondary school, I'm taking them out of the local system and going to an international school. This has been a giant dilemma and I'm not happy, really, about almost any decision that we make.

**Eric Layman:** I can relate to what Emma just shared. I'm originally from the US, but I've lived almost my entire adult life in East Asia. I was an English teacher in Hong Kong, Taiwan, and then mainland China. My wife is originally from Taiwan. She grew up in South Africa. For my dissertation, I interviewed a number of couples about their schooling choices, and I found, similar to Emma, that many wanted to do primary school in an East Asian setting and switch into something that was more "Western" for secondary school. And so that's kind of what my wife and I have ended up doing with our three children, with mixed results.

**Liz Jackson** Thank you! Alright, what's the dilemma in this case?

**Chi-Ming Lam:** If we represent local schools in terms of Hong Kong values, and international schools in terms of Western values, there is apparently a dilemma between Hong Kong values and Western values, and between local schools and international schools. Obviously they have differences, but maybe their differences are over-generalized or exaggerated in this case. I'll use one example. When we talk about local schools, we say the value of attending local schools is to learn Chinese or Cantonese more effectively. But at the same time it's not impossible to learn Chinese or Cantonese in an international school. Many international schools offer Chinese as a foreign language, just like French and Spanish. And students could learn English in local school, and Chinese in an international school with English as the medium of instruction. Of course, in a local school, the language-rich environment is incomparable, but this is just for me a matter of difference in degree rather than a matter of difference in kind.

**Jan Gube:** The question for me is, what kind of motivations? I always think about my past experience, when I was struggling to learn Chinese when I was a kid. The motivation for me back then did not come from the curriculum itself. I was motivated to learn Chinese because when I was able to pick up some Chinese, then the kinds of conversations that I was able to have with my classmates increased, right? For example, if I could talk to them about what we were watching, cartoons in the Chinese channels, that also meant I could play with them more, I could interact with them more. There was a very social aspect to that process.

**Emma Buchtel:** I will say that language is not the only thing that we're worried about kids learning, but it is something sort of unique about Hong Kong, where it is quite technically difficult to learn Cantonese. And then if you don't look Chinese, you get very little encouragement to speak it, because people will speak English to you. My experience living in mainland China was completely different from my experience living here. In mainland China, I learned Mandarin Chinese because I could not talk with people unless I learned it. But here people speak to me in English or I get by in Mandarin Chinese and English. I imagine if you're going to the international schools, it's going to be hard in Hong Kong culture to experience external pressure to improve your Chinese.

**Eric Layman:** My wife and I are both Mandarin and English speakers. So that was a big factor—we really wanted our kids to learn Mandarin and we thought that there wouldn't be any way unless they were in a Mandarin immersion environment. We just moved back to Hong Kong a year ago, after two years in Taiwan and a couple years in the States. The experience that our kids had in Taiwan was wonderful. All three of our kids were thriving, they were picking up Mandarin easily, feeling very confident. So when we moved here, we thought, well, of course, we're just going to throw them in the deep end in a local Cantonese school. We've had a chance to live in a number of different places, we love Hong Kong, we want to be here long term, we want our kids to be able to learn Cantonese. But, I've got to be honest with you, it's been quite difficult. I really like the local school where my kids are. People have been very supportive, going out of their way to offer extra tutoring or any extra support that we need. But just in terms of practicality, they don't really seem to know what to do with a non-Cantonese speaker. Even one who has parents who are very motivated, very involved, saying, "oh, what can we do to help?" I have met a lot of people who are very interested in getting their children into Cantonese culture, saying, "We love being here. We want our children to be integrated." And there almost seems to be, at times, a surprise about that from some of the local Cantonese population. Like, "What? No, everyone here is on their way out! They want to go to Australia, or go to England, and you want to enter our culture?" So pedagogically they aren't always prepared to help people make that integration. And I'm not saying that they aren't welcoming, but pedagogically, taking people step by step, scaffolding ways to learn Cantonese, I haven't seen that in the curriculum. My wife and I are both teachers, and we come home, and cumulatively, all three of our children have maybe, not exaggerating, five hours of homework. And thinking about how to walk with them through engaging with a Chinese text, a lot of times, it just becomes, "Okay, this one's C, just circle C. This one's A, just circle A." I don't have time to explain, or to do any kind of Socratic "what do you think is the right answer?" because we're just so exhausted. And I imagine that there's a lot of parents in Hong Kong that are in a similar situation, where it's just, it would be so much energy to try to keep up with the homework.

**Chi-Ming Lam:** I think we've come to a very important point, the concept of motivation. I think motivation is more important than language. But motivation is affected by many factors, including parental choice. Whether the language can be learned effectively in a local school or international school sometimes depends on the motivation of the kid, and also the parents. It's not just the job of the school teachers. Just like when you compare the English language of students in a local school with an international school, you will not find that all the best students can be found in international schools. We have some very good local schools that train students to be good English speakers and writers, even better than students in the international schools, which we see in the public exam results. If the students have a very high motivation to achieve a high standard, they will try their best, they have a kind of dedication to excellence. Some schools have the authority or the encouragement that can help students to move in that direction. But some schools are more free. Maybe the Western style of teaching in the international school may not have such strong requirements of students to have this kind of dedication.

**Emma Buchtel:** Many of us also have this concern about cultural identity: are our children going to feel they are from Hong Kong? Are they going to feel they are Chinese? And this is also a complex aspect of motivation for learning. Eric, it was interesting to hear you say that your children went to a Hong Kong school but they are not learning Cantonese. I wonder if it's also partially that people don't expect them to speak Cantonese. With children, they always think of them as non-Chinese speakers. They're classified "NCS." My kids are not happy about this classification, but that's how many of the teachers see them. I sent my kids to the local school. The environment—not the language environment, but the cultural environment, how people interact with each other, how they speak to each other, how they treat each other, what topics they're talking about—they are actually learning to be Hong Kongers, but it's ironic: their feeling about themselves is the opposite. After first grade, I asked my son if he felt Chinese and he said, "No, I'm English." And I said, "English? If there's anything that you're not, it's *English*, like, you could be American, you could be Chinese, you could be Hong Kong … " but that was his choice. In his mind, he was either a Chinese speaker or an English speaker, therefore, he is English. And so they actually got this reactionary identity. Very sadly, they identified as being other, as not local.

**Jan Gube:** When I was a kid, I was told very explicitly, you are a Filipino. My parents taught me to speak Tagalog, and I still speak it, that's my first language. My second language is English, then Cantonese, then a little bit of Mandarin. So yes, identity is a really big question to me, Emma. I know that I'm a Filipino, Hong Kong-Filipino, Filipino-Hong Kong, whatever you like. In terms of day-to-day interaction with people here in Hong Kong, my experience as a kid was that people wouldn't necessarily speak to me in English right away, they would sometimes give me a weird look, and speak to me in Cantonese at first. So, I would respond to them in Cantonese, you know, as much as possible. Fast forward, some of my colleagues still speak to me in English, but I say to them, let's just switch to Cantonese.

**Liz Jackson:** So far, we've discussed language, motivations, and identity a lot. Are there any other values or principles that come up in the case? What are the other reasons why you would want to pick one school type or another school type?

**Emma Buchtel:** Do you mind if I share my screen and talk about homework?

**Liz Jackson:** Sure!

**Emma Buchtel:** Okay. I'm just showing the English dictation book from my son when he was younger [when he still attended the local school]. This is about culture and the culture of learning, specifically. You can first see that I'm supposed to sign every single dictation. Parental involvement is really high. Now I have my son in the international school, there is no homework, almost no parental involvement at all. Chi-Ming talked about the drive for excellence in this environment. In the local school, there's still so much focus on just getting things done. Every single sentence, if you make a tiny mistake, you have to write it two times, often three times. This is a huge amount of time. A large proportion of the time that the parents are spending with their children is doing this kind of homework. Very detail-oriented, learning that you need to do what the teacher told you to do.

This is also part of the dilemma for me because on the one hand, this is a really intense form of education There's a lot of focus on studying, on spending the time, on working really hard, and also failing, actually, and being okay with failing, and just continuing to try. There's a lot of focus on perseverance and accuracy. But it doesn't make for a happy home life, I think, for most people, at least not for me. And I will just say that at the time when my kids were doing this, my friend's kids who were going to an international school were doing a unit on leadership, writing arguments about how women can become better leaders and getting praised for their reasoning. I think that this type of homework in the local schools is focused on doing things right according to what the authority has said. And the international schools, it's focused on being a leader. I think it's actually related to the socio-economic status background of students at international schools. If you send your kids to international schools, I think there's just a large proportion of very rich kids with very elite parents who have lots of choices. And that's not the case in the local schools. That's why I wanted to choose the local schools, because I feel like it's more "normal people." But there's really dramatic differences in the types of attitudes they're teaching the kids through things like homework.

**Eric Layman:** I absolutely concur with that. I recall in the case study the characters talked about how much money they would save by sending their kids to local school, and all of the things that this would free up. But I think people need to think honestly about what it is going to involve for you and your family life, to send your kid to a local school, with all the support that needs to happen with homework. Some of the homework expectations are quite unhealthy in terms of how exact they need to be and the volume of work that needs to happen. Like you said, it doesn't create for a happy home life, especially if you have a child who's struggling. One of our children, we haven't been able to identify any specific learning disabilities, but he just likes to take his sweet time to do anything developmentally. No matter what, he goes at his own pace. And so it requires an enormous amount of patience for him. One thing that we do see is that it really depends on which subject you're in. Yes, I feel like some of the pedantic attention to English writing and things like that can be a little bit too much. But I have to tell you, my first grader's math ability already surpasses where I was in fourth or fifth grade. Growing up in the Midwest in the United States, I don't think I was asked to memorize my times tables until I was nine or ten years old. And my six-year-old has got them down. All my kids can do multi-figure computations in their head. I mean, we had heard, you know, different stereotypes about the East Asian model of education. But at least from our own anecdotal experience, that aspect of it has been true: it has done wonders for their mathematical ability.

**Chi-Ming Lam:** I think one of the most important things about the local schools is that classroom teachers think of themselves as teaching not just knowledge and skills, but also values like diligence, heart, the ability to self-correct, discipline, and so on. These values are not so emphasized in the Western world, where they emphasize freedom in learning. In local schools, teachers do not treasure freedom so much when compared with discipline. But it doesn't mean that international schools do not pay attention to discipline. That's why I said that there's just a difference in degree rather than in kind. Like Emma mentioned, we can use the concept to help our students to establish their cultural identity as a Hong Konger or Chinese. But it's not just the responsibility of the schools. Parents also have a very important role to play in shaping the identity of their kids. My daughter went through the local schooling system in Hong Kong, but she also got an international mindset, because the students had the chance to explore different things internationally, not just the issues localized in Hong Kong. I think it's related to the school mission in individual schools and whether the local schools have a global perspective. I don't believe that it is only the international schools that can help students develop a multicultural or global mindset.

**Jan Gube:** What's interesting is the meaning that we attach to the practices or the choices of parents. I grew up in a local setting, where there were very few Filipino students. There weren't really multicultural environments back then. Some of the issues I experienced are related to what Eric mentioned about the preparedness of teachers to teach non-Chinese kids effectively. And I say this, because one of my dad's struggles back then was when he tried to send me to the local primary school. He actually had to argue with the Education Bureau because the school didn't want to accept me. They were telling my dad, "oh, he's going to struggle here because this is a Chinese-speaking environment." But my dad said, "well, he's going to grow up here, he's going to be part of the society, I want him to pick up the language." He had to ring the EDB [Hong Kong Education Bureau] and take me there. After some kind of discussion, I think he had to ring the school, and I was eventually accepted. I struggled at first, but it worked out fine. My parents managed it by sending me to tutorial centers where I could get support in terms of my language. That was the practical stuff, but I totally agree there were values attached to these. I guess in that case, my dad's value was being pragmatic about wanting me to be able to find jobs here and to be able to compete with other applicants.

**Liz Jackson:** Quite a blending of material and practical considerations and motivations, and deep value judgments and identity judgments. Do you think that parents should have a choice over what kind of school environment their kids experience?

**Chi-Ming Lam:** This is exactly why I think there is a real dilemma here. In the text, I find two alternatives. One is talking about universal choice. What is the best answer about school choice that is relevant to all parents? The other one is the opposite: the individual choice of the parents. For me, this is a real dilemma, because you can't have both, and they are incompatible with each other. For example, we're talking about a universal choice of parents, what I can imagine could be the twenty-first-century skills and knowledge you want the kids to demonstrate and use in their future, universal to all parents because all parents would like their kids to survive in the twenty-first century by developing these kind of skills and knowledge and so on. But individual parents' choices are focused mainly on the individual needs of their kids. And those may not be the same as the twenty-first-century skills and knowledge. Maybe they would like to develop talents in sports or music to the fullest. Universal parents' choice is trying to meet the educational needs of the society. But individual parents' choice is trying to meet the specific educational needs of the kids, and you can't have both at the same time.

**Eric Layman:** I'm definitely hoping to guide my children in some important ways, but we're definitely consulting with them about what they feel comfortable with. Our two older children were experiencing some difficulties in the local system this past year, and they've been saying that they would want to go back to the US or they've really been missing Taiwan a lot. And we've been talking through that and talking about some different options. We're definitely keeping them in the loop and letting them voice their opinions as they get older. But I think that there's different reasons why we aren't comfortable with going back to the US, and part of that is the identity discussion, especially with all of the anti-Asian sentiment that's come about as a result of Covid in the US. And maybe if my children, once they're 18, want to potentially subject themselves to an environment where they could face, you know, racial epithets [they could move to the US]. But I don't feel comfortable intentionally putting my children in that environment.

And then in Taiwan, my two boys can sort of pass off as being fully Asian, but my daughter looks much more ethnically ambiguous and sticks out. And she got a lot of attention in Taiwan, mostly positive attention, people complimenting her on her big eyes or things like that, but she would just feel horribly uncomfortable and she wouldn't want to stick out at all. So as far as identity is concerned, one reason that we did feel so comfortable in Hong Kong is not necessarily that we would want our children to think that they were from Hong Kong, I don't know if that would be a realistic expectation, but just that my children's inherent sort of cosmopolitanism is not a rarity. You know, there's mixed kids all over, everyone you talk to has two or three nationalities. That's something that was important to my wife and I, thinking about the environment that we wanted our kids to be in, that they realize that there isn't only one way to be. There's not a lot of places in the world that offer that level of diversity.

**Emma Buchtel:** It's very weird to me to think that my children would be allowed to choose schools because I know that they would not choose the local schools. It's not fun. The homework in particular is not fun. Their impression is that the international schools are more fun. At least there's no homework. They always say either, "Why don't you take me back to the USA?" or "Why don't you send me to the international school? Why am I in this school? Why do I have to take exams? Why do I have to do the homework?" And so I actually have to be constantly trying to figure out, why is it so important to me to keep on sending them to the local school? What are the benefits? I do think fit has something to do with it. For example, my son has been really not thriving and getting bad feelings about himself and his abilities and not creating very good relationships with his peers. He hasn't adjusted. Maybe it's my fault, I haven't taught him well enough. But I know that children would choose candy all the time if they could. And they think international schools are candy.

**Chi-Ming Lam:** I think there's not only one choice, Emma. Maybe this local school doesn't fit your son's personality, but maybe another local school could. If you stick to your mindset, trying to help your kids to become more Chinese or to learn Chinese culture, to establish another kind of identity here in Hong Kong, you could also choose another local school. According to my experience, there are many different kinds of local schools. And maybe this is just about this fit between your kid and this particular school. Of course, it takes some work to study that school's mission and vision. This is a kind of a struggle among local parents. But at the same time it's a hard job to convince your kids which option is the best, especially when we know that it is actually not an easy choice.

**Liz Jackson:** Jan, what do you think about parents' choice? If your dad gave you the option, would you have gone to the international school?

**Jan Gube:** So far, what I've been hearing is that parents here have a lot of choices; in fact, parents are quite spoilt for choices. But based on my experience, not all parents have that kind of choice. I don't come from a very privileged family. So, to some extent, I think that the dilemmas that some parents have here come from the fact that they just have too many options! In my case, my parents' decision back then was relatively simplistic. They just wanted me to immerse in the local culture, they didn't care about whether the school was a "Band 1" school or "Band 2" school or "Band 3" or 4 or 5; back then it didn't matter to them, they just wanted me to fit in the local culture. And that's it. I struggled a lot in my Chinese as a kid, it sort of was a sink-or-swim kind of thing in school, so I may have switched to an international school if my dad gave me the option. But in hindsight, I've come to embrace what I went through in local schools as I now enjoy living here with virtually no language and cultural barrier. I guess what's really interesting is that if we try to look at the socioeconomic dimension here, I dare to say that not all parents have the same kind of mindset or choices. For example, twenty-first-century skills—my parents back then didn't think of these things. And other Filipino families that I know, they just wanted their kids to be part of the local culture. They just let it be and saw how the kids managed, how they survived in the local school. I think this is what makes Hong Kong so interesting. We have different education systems and different examination systems. That is really a choice to some parents, but it's not necessarily a choice to all parents.

**Liz Jackson:** I wanted to give each of you a chance to say how you would answer the dilemma if you were the parents in the case study. How is your decision influenced by who you are or your values?

**Chi-Ming Lam:** Nobody knows what the future needs or wants for our kids. We can only try our best to strike a balance between these two alternatives: universal parental choice and individual parental choice. As a father, I still think it is difficult to say what is the best choice, even if I discussed all the things with my wife together and tried to be more objective, not just based on my own values. Sometimes we need to listen to our kids. Our kid's future is his or her future, we need to talk with them, when they have the ability to show or express their ideas. We need to know what they think, before we can make the best choice for them.

**Jan Gube:** I think the short answer is that it's a choice that needs to be negotiated, because just looking at what my parents did, my dad wanted me to fit into the local culture. But he didn't tell me to be an academic. And to make things more complicated, I actually came from a Band 4 school and I didn't study very well in school. I guess it also illustrates Chi-Ming's point that you can never predict the future. I think as parents, for me as a future parent, it's just a matter of having that dialogue with them, analyzing the different choices. Asking them, is this your interest? What would that afford you in the future? What kind of opportunities would this give you?

**Emma Buchtel:** If you could identify your primary values—like I really want diligence but I also want creativity–then maybe you'll find an international school or a local school that would fit those. I guess I would still make the same choice of having them do local primary, and some form of international school for secondary. And, maybe the struggle is good for them, but it's just a reality that our cultural identities are not going to be simple. There will always be the struggle of trying to figure out: am I English? Am I a Hong Konger? Am I Chinese? Am I American? Maybe the very fact that we parents struggle with it, and then our children struggle with it, is something that cannot be avoided and shouldn't be avoided. It will always be there, and we can't solve it for our children. But they might find some interesting solutions to it themselves.

**Liz Jackson:** Thanks so much to all of you for your time. It was great to see you all and I have learned a lot from this conversation.

***Chi-Ming Lam*** *is Associate Professor of the Department of International Education at The Education University of Hong Kong. His research interests include the philosophy of Karl Popper, critical thinking, Confucianism, and philosophy for children. His books include* Childhood, Philosophy and Open Society: Implications for Education in Confucian Heritage Cultures *(2013),* Sociological and Philosophical Perspectives on Education in the Asia-Pacific Region *(co-edited with Jae Park, 2016), and* Philosophy for Children in Confucian Societies: In Theory and Practice *(edited, 2020).*

***Eric W. Layman*** *(PhD) is originally from the United States but has lived in East Asia for most of his adult life—more than twenty years in total. His dissertation investigates Indigenous education reform in Taiwan.*

***Jan Gube*** *is Assistant Professor at the Department of Curriculum and Instruction, The Education University of Hong Kong. He takes an interest in understanding and supporting how schools and civil society might leverage cultural differences in fostering equitable and caring learning environments. Jan's research engages with issues of diversity, race and ethnicity, particularly how their interrelations shape curriculum and pedagogy.*

***Dr. Emma E. Buchtel*** *is Associate Professor in the Department of Psychology at The Education University of Hong Kong. Prior to receiving her PhD, Dr. Buchtel spent four years in Changsha and Beijing, teaching English at the high school and* *university levels and learning Mandarin Chinese. In her research, she seeks to explore and deepen our understanding of Chinese cultural influences on psychology, including moral concepts, motivation and reasoning styles, and cultivate positive attitudes towards diversity among her students.*

## Character Guide

| Setting |
|---|
| A food market in Hong Kong |
| **Primary Characters** |

| | |
|---|---|
| **Cindy:** expectant parent, fluent Cantonese speaker | **William:** Cindy's colleague, Cantonese speaker |
| **Benny:** expectant parent, non-fluent Cantonese speaker | **Iris:** William's wife, non-fluent Cantonese speaker |
| **Puja:** Cindy's colleague, non-fluent Cantonese speaker | **Kenneth:** Iris and William's son |
| **Mark:** Puja's husband, English speaker | **Dev:** Mark and Puja's son |

## Discussion Questions

1 Not all parents in Hong Kong enjoy the wealth of options debated by the characters in this case. To what extent should parental choice about schooling be viewed as a privilege—or a right?
2 How much should parents consider the well-being of other children when making decisions about their own children?
3 Parents are called upon to make many choices for their children that drastically shape the opportunities and relationships available to those children in the future. How should parents understand their responsibilities to their children? At what point, if ever, should children themselves have a role in making decisions like those discussed in the case?
4 The parents in the case weigh the various benefits and costs of different educational approaches they perceive in the schools: a "traditional" approach that emphasizes memorization and a heavy workload and a "Western" approach, "where children have more freedom to just be children." What values inform these different approaches to education?

5 Cindy and Benny wonder whether they should make a choice that prioritizes their child's sense of belonging in Hong Kong or their readiness for opportunities outside Hong Kong. What values or principles should guide their thinking? Do the interests of their child recommend one approach over the other?
6 Language fluency plays a big role in the case. For instance, Puja worries that without fluent Cantonese, her son will never be "100% a Hong Kong person." How does language fluency shape identity and opportunities in your national setting?
7 What do the parents in this case seem to believe about the purposes of schooling? How do these beliefs compare to your own, or to the purposes of schooling that you see raised in other cases in this volume?

## Notes

1. Local schools include those fully organized and supported by the Hong Kong government, as well as "aided" or "grant" schools, which were originally founded by religious or charitable organizations, but also follow government curricula. Most local schools teach in Chinese, but some have options for English medium of instruction. Local schools charge tuition and have an admissions system. Some are elite and competitive, while others have poorer reputations and are relatively easy to join.
2. For more information on the challenges ethnic minorities face related to school choice, language learning, and social mobility, see Loh, E. K. Y. and Tam, L. C. W. (2016). "Struggling to Thrive: The Impact of Chinese Language Assessments on Social Mobility of Hong Kong Ethnic Minority Youth," *The Asia-Pacific Education Researcher* 25: 763–70; and Castle, J.-L. (2015). "Hong Kong Minorities "Marginalized" in School," *BBC News*. https://www.bbc.com/news/business-34444284. Views of ethnic minority and international parents in Hong Kong discussed here are taken from Groves, J. M., and O'Connor, P. (2018). "Negotiating Global Citizenship, Protecting Privilege: Western Expatriates Choosing Local Schools in Hong Kong," *British Journal of Sociology of Education* 39:3: 381–295.
3. International schools may teach in a variety of languages, including English, Japanese, and Korean. Non-local children can only apply to international schools; they are not eligible for local or DSS schools. Like all schools in Hong Kong, international schools charge tuition and have

competitive admissions. For more, see Ng, V. (2012). "The Decision to Send Local Children to International Schools in Hong Kong: Local Parents' Perspectives," *Asia Pacific Education Review* 13: 121–36.
4. The "stuffed Peking duck" approach refers to the notion of local education that is rigidly fixed with a teacher-centered orientation and a focus on memorization of content. More generally, some views of local people about local versus international schools which are discussed here come from Ng (2012). See also Ngan, M.-Y., and Chung, C. (2004). "Parental Choice of Primary Schools in Hong Kong," *Journal of Basic Education* 13:2: 79–105.
5. Dialogue that compares education from Eastern versus Western perspectives is informed by Layman, E. (2018). "Mixed: Educational Perspectives from Families of Mixed East and West Educational Background," *Global Education Review* 5:1: 52–72.
6. In recent years, less than half of students taking the Hong Kong Diploma of Secondary Education met the criteria for university admission, so most had to seek alternative pathways to higher education, such as less desirable self-financed post-secondary programs or study abroad. Meanwhile, Hong Kong universities also accept a variety of university entrance qualifications from students attending international schools in Hong Kong and schools around the world. See Pavlova, M. (2017). "Aspirations of and Realities for Hong Kong Students: Is the 'Formal' Transition System Effective?," *Educational Research for Policy and Practice* 16:1: 77–93.
7. 150,000 Hong Kong Dollars equals 19,250 USD. See: https://www.esf.edu.hk/school-fees/.
8. This example is taken from Groves and O'Connor, "Negotiating Global Citizenship, Protecting Privilege."
9. DSS schools generally follow the local curricula, with classes taught in Chinese, but they are more independent than local schools in terms of curricula, staffing, and admissions. Like all schools in Hong Kong, DSS schools charge tuition and have competitive admissions.
10. In 2021/22, fees for DSS schools ranged from HK$1,000 to HK$130,000 per year (USD130–16,700). https://www.edb.gov.hk/attachment/en/edu-system/primary-secondary/applicable-to-primary-secondary/direct-subsidy-scheme/schlist(fees)_e_c.pdf.
11. For more on corporal punishment in Hong Kong schools, See Kuen, K. S. M. (2021). "Child Abuse: How Hong Kong Can Ensure Educational Institutions Are Safe Havens," *South China Morning Post*. https://www.scmp.com/comment/letters/article/3149902/child-abuse-how-hong-kong-can-ensure-educational-institutions-are.

12. While technically "expatriate" or "expat" refers to a person who moves abroad to work temporarily for their national government or a nationally based corporation, as Groves and O'Connor describe, in Hong Kong they describe "'privileged migrants' from the Global North" rather than "unskilled migrants from poorer countries," although "expatriates are, technically, migrants too" (p. 386). See Groves and O'Connor, "Negotiating Global Citizenship, Protecting Privilege," for more analysis of the complicated treatment of the terms in Hong Kong.

# 9

# A Uniform Decision: Commemoration and Community in Public School

*Daniella J. Forster, Samuel Douglas, and Scott Imig*

---

*This case study takes place at a fictional Australian school receiving a high concentration of students with refugee backgrounds. Students with refugee backgrounds in New South Wales schools make up about 1.4 percent of the student population. Arriving in Australia mainly from war-ravaged countries and often learning English as an Additional Language or dialect (EAL/D), they are usually allocated to a few schools situated in economically disadvantaged areas.[1] While the term "students with refugee backgrounds" refers to a range of students entering Australia on various visas and those born in transit countries or recently after their family's arrival in Australia, many arrive directly from refugee camps having scant school-based experiences.[2] Schools hire additional EAL/D teachers, Arabic translators or refugee coordinators to liaise with families to support their acclimatization to Australian culture. Students who are involved in both their home culture and their new culture experience greater sociocultural and psychological adaptation. A significant aspect of Australian culture is the Anzac Spirit.[3] Anzac Day is a public holiday honoring the April 25, 1915, battle of Gallipoli, Turkiye, when the Australian and New Zealand Army Corps (the Anzacs) fought with the British Empire in the First World War. During the*

First World War, Australia lost ten times more lives as a percentage of the population, than the United States. Historians dispute whether Australian nationhood was "born" at Gallipoli.[4] Over 93 percent of Australians believe it should be commemorated each year,[5] with growing numbers attending dawn services around the country and expressing sympathy for military personnel's sacrifices.[6] All public schools hold some version of Anzac Day service on site and it is compulsory learning in the Australian Curriculum (v8.4).[7] In 2015, a report on the centenary celebrations of Anzac Day by the Department of Veteran Affairs considered multiculturalism to be a divisive risk to the holiday, but a later survey found minimal risk because culturally and linguistically diverse communities were "disengaged … and unlikely to participate" in Anzac Day commemorations.[8]

--

Robbie Jones kicked the floor with the toes of his runners, his small form gathered into the corner of the couch in Principal Greg Sefton's office. Greg watched the boy sympathetically—it wasn't easy coming back from a suspension. But after Robbie had hit a classmate on the playground, Greg had been left with little choice. Though Robbie had reported the classmate had first called him "povo,"[9] the rules were clear when it came to fighting.

"I'm so glad you're back with us today, Robbie," Greg smiled. "I know it's going to be a good day."

"Yes, sir," Robbie muttered, his eyes on the floor.

Greg hoped that it would indeed be a good day. When dropping Robbie off, his mother had let Greg know how difficult having the boy at home had been. Robbie's parents were divorced. His mother was struggling to pay the rent on her single income, and taking time off to care for him hadn't helped her situation. Meanwhile, after the divorce Robbie's father had been in and out of shelters for two months. The playground fight earlier in the week was just one sign that Robbie was struggling with the upheaval in his home life.

"What's one thing you can do to help make this a good day, Robbie?" Greg asked gently.

"I can stay with my mates and stay away from bludgers,"[10] Robbie said. "My dad's coming for Anzac, and I don't want to get in trouble again."

Greg nodded, but inwardly he flinched. He wasn't sure that Mr. Jones actually would be coming to campus to commemorate Anzac Day, but Robbie didn't need to know that, especially not today.

"Best get to class," Greg said, standing and opening his door. "I'll come and check later to see how you're getting on."

Left alone, Greg sighed. It was now time to prepare for his next meeting with a Year Five boy—a boy facing struggles of his own.

During this school year, Burnsley Public School had seen a steady in-flow of refugee families. The past few months had been a whirlwind of finding and developing new programs to support the refugee children, while maintaining learning and behavior support for struggling Australian-born students in this high poverty area—students like Robbie. Some of the changes Greg had made, like bringing on Mohammad Kahn to liaise and translate for Arabic-speaking families, had been an immediate success, with his caring affect and his knowledgeable linguistic and cultural translation. It was a coup having someone with Mohammad's background, an Afghan translator who risked everything to help the armed forces against the Taliban, end up in Burnsley repatriated under asylum.[11] This morning, Uncle Mo would join Greg to meet with Kawa and his father, Mr. Al Ahmad, newly arrived from Syria.

Despite Uncle Mo's success, there was still a lot of work to do to develop a truly welcoming and safe school culture. Greg was uncertain how his staff might receive some of the more extensive suggestions he was considering, such as intensive professional retraining in trauma-informed pedagogies and rearranging the school schedule to prioritize well-being over some curriculum reporting mandates. It was hard to know where to even begin.

And then there was Burnsley's Anzac Day commemoration. Since the 1970s, Burnsley had invited volunteers from the Returned and Services League (RSL) of Australia, led by a representative of the Defence Force. Current representative Lieutenant Parkes arrived in uniform to a school assembly where they flew the flag at half-mast and sounded the evocative lone bugle for the Last Post.[12] This event was especially important, sacred even, as Burnsley was located in a community of veterans, with a long Honours Board[13] in the school hall listing former students who went to war. But this year, Greg had been stalling on inviting the RSL members, including Robbie's ex-serviceman father. Greg was increasingly uncertain about exposing the refugee-background students, who had experienced so much trauma, to reminders of war.[14] Today he would raise the matter with the staff and make a decision about how to approach this important Australian holiday.

Opening the door to the Year Five classroom at his mid-morning break, Greg barely avoided colliding with a gaggle of students. "Whoa there you lot, get an early mark?"

"Miss Green said we could go to lunch early if we finished everything," said Robbie defensively.

"And you did finish everything, Robbie? Good job."

Robbie looked anxiously after the other boys—they had already started their wargame, playing soldiers among trees in the playground.

Greg nodded his head, "Go on then." Robbie raced out after his classmates.

Inside the classroom, Mrs. Lynn Green sat at her desk tidying her notes. She pushed a wisp of greying hair back into place.

"Hi Lynn, just wanted to see how the new kids were settling in, where are the rest of them?"

"They're with Uncle Mo—just me and the Aussie kids for the past hour, doing actual lessons."

"They're all Aussie kids, Lynn," he chided gently.

"Well, some are still trying for Protection Visas," Lynn corrected him. "And you can't expect the new kids to follow much of what's going on. The special English class is helpful, but I worry they aren't understanding, so I focus on hands-on learning when they do join us. And when they're away I get to spend a lot more time with the others, like dear Robbie, and even if English is not their second language, they need the extra attention."

Greg nodded.

"Honestly," Lynn sighed. "In all my time teaching, I don't think I've ever had student learning differences so pronounced. Some of these new kids, like Kawa, had only bits and pieces at the refugee camp. He's so quiet! And that other group"—she motioned out the door—"they have a lot of energy. Though Robbie seems more withdrawn lately, even before the suspension. I thought he needed a new friend, so I paired him with Kawa this morning in science; I hoped it might help them both."

Greg raised his eyebrows, encouragingly.

"Actually the kids thought it was a fun lesson!" Lynn continued. "We were using coloured balloons and testing out how temperature affected them, heating up the inside with a tea candle. But when the balloon popped—Gosh! You should've seen poor Kawa dive on the ground! That was unexpected! I'm trying but, hmmm, how do I structure my classroom so that each child's needs are met?"

"Science is a great choice for Kawa to get involved," Greg affirmed. "And Robbie's been OK with Kawa, he hasn't been acting out?"

"Oh no, he's been good—when poor Kawa went under the table Robbie crawled in too. And then they sat together for a story. I thought with Robbie's dad having been injured in Afghanistan and Kawa's experience they might form a bond. They are both such brave boys."

"Yes they are. And that's why I wonder whether we need to rethink next month's Anzac service," Greg mused. "Last year's speech by Lieutenant Parkes talked about the sacrifice of heroes with exceptional courage and the spirit of mateship. But I think we should remind our school that war has lasting effects on all people, not just the soldiers and their families. What do you think we should do to be more inclusive?"

Lynn thought for a moment. "I'm all for being inclusive. Anzac Day is more important to Aussies than Australia Day![15] The sacrifices made by people like my Grandad are at its heart, and kids are the future custodians of the Anzac spirit—kids like Robbie whose families are part of the story. Traditions need to be maintained. When the RSL representatives arrive at the school assembly, the school captains should recite the Prayer for Peace first and then the poems—like "A Hundred Years from Now"[16] and "Flanders Fields."[17] The Department[18] released this year's Anzac Day package recently, so I'll choose some pictures for quiet reflection while Lieutenant Parkes makes his comments and then you each lay the wreaths beside the memorial plaque. The catafalque party will be in formation while we listen to the Last Post and have a minute's silence with the flag at half-mast. For class activities afterwards, I always bring in my Granddad's war medals and encourage kids like Robbie to tell the class about their family's military service. Anzac Day is not just about Gallipoli anymore, it's about Australians' fight for freedom and democracy everywhere. I don't think we need to make changes to the way we've always commemorated their sacrifices."

"Thanks Lynn, you are very knowledgeable," Greg smiled, though his concerns that the traditional approach would glorify war still lingered. How would children like Kawa, who had lost so much to war, experience this event? "Could you speak to your ideas at this afternoon's staff meeting?"

At the end of the day, Greg made his way through the busy concrete path to the front of the school. "Khoda hafess Razia, see you tomorrow!"

A Grade Six girl wearing long sleeves adjusted her school-issued hijab over her hair. She playfully chided him, "It's *khodahafez*, Mr. Sefton!" She turned, hurrying her two younger sisters along while carrying their school bags on her shoulders. Greg's smile slipped knowing the school-wide Anzac event would be unlikely to entice Razia's mother or her grandmother from the family's cramped apartment. Why would they leave their complex when just walking down the street in their traditional clothing made them a target? He had reached out to the local Mosque to organize an Iftar at school, the breaking of bread after sunset during this season's Ramadan to make the school a more welcoming place for Muslim-refugee families like Kawa and Razia to visit. He called it a "sausage sizzle fundraiser" to encourage the whole community to come in.

Greg turned to watch the bustling throng. One parent, a deeply tanned man in dusty hi-vis construction clothes, stood apart from the other parents. He had a slight limp as he approached the principal—a visible reminder of the injuries he acquired in Afghanistan, though it was the hollowness of his eyes that Greg noticed most. Sometimes he saw that hollowness in his son, Robbie, too.

Greg caught his eye and approached. "Mr. Jones, this is a surprise. I'm sure Robert was picked up by his mother earlier, is everything OK?"

"Yeah, he's with her this week, that's fine. I, well, we—the RSL local members—had a question for you. At our monthly meeting last week, we were wondering why you hadn't made contact about Anzac day proceedings. The six of us have our uniforms pressed for the occasion, ready to form the catafalque[19] around the school's war memorial stone. We can be there at 9:45 for a 10am start?"

"That's quite a few people in uniform," Greg stalled, recalling Kawa's trauma response in Lynn's classroom.

Mr. Jones' pointed to the plaque embedded on the schoolgate, "These families are part of the school's history. My grandfather went to Burnsley as a boy and his name is engraved right here—he fought at Gallipoli. Like most of us who served, I wouldn't volunteer for the parade. But Robert needs to feel proud of his family, and he should know there is no more important day for the RSL than Anzac Day."[20]

Mr. Jones hesitated, and then continued. "You know these past couple of years have been hard on us. Anzac Day shows Robbie what we fought for, what I fought for, and what … who … we lost. And maybe he'll understand why I wasn't around when he needed me." Mr. Jones stopped abruptly.

Greg lifted the mood: "Robbie worked so hard in class this morning. You should be proud of him, he finished his work early. He's even been helping one of the new students in science. "

Mr. Jones looked pleasantly surprised.

Greg continued, "Maybe you can see it for yourself. Any chance you'd have time to help us with the Refugee fundraiser sausage sizzle? Actually, here comes Uncle Mo now—he can tell us more about it. "

Mohammad approached the two men from across the school path with a broad smile after a welcoming hand gesture. Greg turned to introduce him to Mr. Jones. "Meet Mohammad Kahn. Mo, meet Robbie's father, Mr. Jones.

Did you know that you share something in common—you were both with the Australian forces in Afghanistan?"

"Good to meet you," Mo said, gently.

Mr. Jones stuttered, visibly lost to some memory, before composing himself, "G'day, Mo."

His awkward response reminded Greg how much he needed Anzac Day to bring the community together. Greg wished he knew how he was going to offer something that supported kids like Robbie without disturbing kids like Kawa at the same time.

The staff enjoyed their special afternoon tea prepared in the local Mosque kitchen. Greg reached for a sticky sweet to go with his coffee.

"Mmm ... 'taj al malek', one of my favourites," grinned Uncle Mo, as the two bumped elbows and chuckled. Suddenly serious, Mo pulled Greg aside. "Listen, I wanted to talk to you before this Anzac Day discussion. I'm concerned that the school community doesn't appreciate how difficult it could be for our refugee families. Greg—you must encourage them to all stay home that day. Just look at Kawa's reaction today—that balloon wasn't a threat, yet he acted as though he was being shelled. How do you think he will feel when the soldiers come?"

"But they're part of our community," Greg began. "Did you ask them who will share their stories of—"

"Listen," Mohammad interrupted, lowering his voice, "Mr. Al Ahmad didn't tell you this morning, but Kawa lost his mother and his brother to horrific circumstances in Syria. His brother was critically injured on his way to school and the local hospital was non-operational; they couldn't save him. It was only after his mother disappeared from the terrible camp at Al Hol that they managed to reunite Kawa with his father and get here, somehow, together.[21] He is not the only one, they all have trauma and stories of war—their war, not some British war over a hundred years ago. I spoke with the families yesterday. They do not want to share those stories for Anzac Day."

Greg swallowed uncomfortably. Greg had known a bit of Kawa's story but not these details. "What should we ... ?" his voice trailed off. He lifted his eyes to Mohammad and felt the weight he carried, just for a second. "I'm thinking hard about it, Mo, I promise. Let's start the meeting—lots to cover." He motioned Mo to a chair and sat down.

Greg looked at the drawn faces around the table. His team needed to build solidarity quickly, among the faculty as well as the students and families. He had hoped that Anzac Day's commemoration would be that opportunity, but now he worried more than ever that next month's event would divide, rather than unite, the community. There was no time to waste. What shape should Anzac Day take and to whom should the Anzac Spirit belong?

# Conversation

**Daniella Forster:** Our key question here is: what shape should Anzac Day take, and to whom should it belong? Maryam, would you like to start with some of the dilemmas that really stood out to you?

**Maryam Zahid:** When considering the question, I can't help but become emotional with sadness, given my own personal journey and experiences. I arrived in Australia twenty-four years ago, forced by war and trauma to become a refugee from Afghanistan. I was only twenty years old and faced numerous challenges. I had no prior education, limited English language skills, and no work experience and struggled to integrate into society. During my time in school, I often felt self-conscious about my age and language barrier, trying to hide my insecurities from others.

Reflecting on the case study, particularly the concern about addressing war and trauma for refugee students, I strongly believe that discussing a community's history with war is essential because it reminds us that we are not alone in our struggles. Refugee communities often feel isolated and think their experiences are unique, but sharing our feelings and stories can help break down those barriers and foster understanding among others. Anzac Day could be an opportunity for healing and connecting with others who have also experienced the impact of war.

I strongly believe the question of what Anzac Day should encompass and who should be involved is crucial, and my perspective, shaped by my own journey, emphasizes the significance of acknowledging and supporting those who have suffered trauma due to war. By sharing our stories, once you communicate your feelings then others open up.

**Daniella Forster:** Thank you, Maryam. Maura, can I ask you to add on from Maryam's insight? What were the dilemmas you saw in the case?

**Maura Sellars:** I think one of the biggest dilemmas here is what we prioritize. For me, the priority is always the children. So while there's mandatory documentation about what should be included in education around Anzac Day, it seems to me that a deeper understanding of the process of integration and the process of mediating the impact is needed. Both the cognitive and the emotional impacts of trauma need to be addressed. This is a matter of equity. The lack of readiness jumped out at me in the case: Kawa's response to the balloon bursting, the public's response to traditional dress for Islamic women when they walk down the street. These communities are not ready. You can't make someone belong. They have to feel it. And these communities are saying, through their representative Uncle Mo who was walking this fine line, that they're not ready. And so in equity terms, that's the dilemma for me.

**Heather Sharp:** It's not necessarily my opinion that I'm expressing here, but I want to share an oppositional perspective to your response, Maura. One part of the student body might need some bringing on board, but the other part of the student community has actually been involved in Anzac Day for generations. The school has the honor board of past students who have fought in a series of wars. The community is, in fact, ready, so it's difficult when I hear you say that they're not. Is there a way that we can then bring on board those students that you think are not yet ready?

**Maura Sellars:** I'm looking from a cognitive and emotional perspective. The refugee parents are expressing that they don't want their children exposed to anything to do with war because everything is still raw. I'm not saying all children shouldn't participate. For example, I've taught in religious schools, and if people don't want their children to attend particular types of religious instruction, they are allowed to exempt their children. This is a much more critical point because it goes to the cognitive capacities to understand tradition. Children at this pre-puberty age are developing higher-order thinking skills, and we know now that cortisol actually inhibits a lot of these higher-order thinking skills and development. So, this aspect of the case shouted loudly at me that this part of that school community is not ready. When you prioritize children, you have to look at their individual circumstances and their home circumstances.

**Heather Sharp:** Thank you, Maura, for your response. I do appreciate it. I just wanted to have a really quick, oppositional point of view expressed for the sake of a debate or a complexity of thinking. To me, Anzac Day is unlike almost any day in any other nation in the world because it actually celebrates a military defeat. April 25, 1915, was the day that the Australian-New Zealand Army Corps fought in Turkey to open up the seas so that Russia, who was our ally, could transport their goods. It was an absolute colossal failure, and we withdrew 8 months later in defeat. Yet it's something that we Australians celebrate and seem to hold so dear.

So what shape should Anzac Day take and to whom should it belong? Here in Newcastle, the public schools, the Catholic schools, and the independent schools have gotten together for the past 50 years to do what they call "combined Anzac Day service." Representatives from all of the schools hear about different perspectives on Anzac Day to understand the history from different stakeholders, together. They have two parts to this ceremony. The first is like a meta ceremony because, as they introduce the catafalque party, the poem, and so forth, they actually explain why they're doing it. The second part is a play that the students dream up, script, participate in, and rehearse, ultimately showing it in the Civic Theatre in Newcastle. The play has a different theme each year that the students really embrace. This year's theme was the impact on families, and it was quite moving. I'm actually someone who's usually unmovable and highly skeptical when it comes to events that try to move people. But this was a very moving event, because you could see a lot of different voices coming to play.

You don't have to do Anzac Day in the way that you've always done it. We have this historical event, but the way we interpret it has changed throughout history, so let's forget any preconceived ideas. If I can say it, Maura has a preconceived idea about what the students and their families can handle. Lynn in the case has her preconceived ideas because of her grandfather, but she doesn't actually know what her grandfather's opinion is. So I would say, let's take it to the students and see what they would like to have happen for this important day.

**Maura Sellars:** I don't think I've got preconceived ideas, Heather. I think that I took what was in the case study about there being a lot of uniforms in what Lynn was proposing. Twenty years ago, I taught in a school very close to the Singleton Army barracks, so I have been in ceremonies for years where we were surrounded by soldiers in uniform. I can't say that any of the children were distressed, but none of them in those days were children with refugee and asylum seeker backgrounds.

**Heather Sharp:** Sorry, I didn't mean to cause offense by that.

**Maura Sellars:** No, no, I'm not offended at all. I'm just saying I took what was in that case study and put myself there after many years of teaching and saw red flags.

**Matthew Bradley:** Maura, I'll challenge you as well in terms of whether any of those students 20 years ago might have had refugee or asylum seeker background.

**Maura Sellars:** Oh yes, I've made a mistake, I know. I put my hands up.

**Daniella Forster:** So Matthew, what dilemmas were really jumping out at you?

**Matthew Bradley:** I actually don't see a dilemma.

**Daniella Forster:** Why don't you see a dilemma?

**Matthew Bradley:** Because the case is about the way that you make sure that all the people involved are seen and honored and that they can maintain their status and their values and their beliefs. So there's not a dilemma here—just a navigation of seeing and honoring people. How do I ensure that as soon as students step through that magic gate at the front fence of the school, they know, regardless of anything, that they are seen and that they are safe and that they're not going to, as much as I can manage, experience anything that is triggering or that makes them feel less than or othered? That includes Robbie, whose father is an army veteran, and that includes Uncle Mo and the students and families who are culturally and linguistically diverse and from a background with more trauma as well. You're looking at all of them with some degree of historical trauma associated with war. So I don't see any dilemma. It's just a navigation of how to honor everyone.

**Daniella Forster:** In educational ethics, when we talk about dilemmas, we are talking about the tensions between sometimes incommensurable values and resources. We use terms like triaging, for example. So when those needs are actually quite heightened, and you only have a certain amount of time or resources, there might be capacity for you to only do some of that. I'm going to press you then, Matthew: what values and principles are you drawing on to do that navigation work that you're talking about?

**Matthew Bradley:** I use the SCARF framework, which is a neurobiological framework for leadership developed by David Rock. It stands for Status, Certainty, Autonomy, Relatedness, and Fairness. You use those core values to make decisions and to reflect upon your interactions, particularly the way that you communicate with people, even finer aspects of communication like body language. It's just a matter of choice, because choice is power. And we're talking about bravery on Anzac Day. In my experience, families from refugee and asylum seeker backgrounds have taken some of the bravest actions without any certainty of being able to navigate to where they are. There's a commonality there. But the other part to this commonality is their grief over losing those they have loved and honored who have died in war. That's common across all of it.

**Maryam Zahid:** Matthew said that if you have a choice, you have power. I agree and as a refugee and a mother, I understand the importance of having choices and the power that comes with them. Unfortunately, many refugees don't have choice or power over their life and decisions, and families face systematic expectations in various aspects of their lives in Australia, including in schools. There's a lack of a comprehensive educational system within the community that could help them better understand Anzac Day and its significance.

I also understand that there are certain misconceptions and stereotypes surrounding individuals and families like me, who are women of colour and refugees. I've faced these challenges. People sometimes assume that we should only possess limited knowledge about Anzac Day. The language barrier further complicates matters, making it difficult for families to comprehend why their children are expected to participate in Anzac Day events, such as parades or church services. There are genuine concerns among families that their children might be influenced or pressured to adopt a different faith if they engage in such activities. Refugee families often face criticism for seemingly not allowing their kids to explore or embrace differences. However, this overlooks the fact that refugees often arrive with very little and might not have had access to extensive education about Australian customs and traditions. The absence of a systematic approach to educating these families and involving them in school decisions exacerbates the challenges they face. If we fail to work closely with these families, even though it requires time and effort, we won't achieve tangible results in making them feel safe and welcomed within the broader community.

**Matthew Bradley:** There are increasing numbers of department schools that run forums for parents. Many years ago, one of the initiatives that I ran was called a parent café. We had 5 or 6 language groups, with interpreters for each language group, talking about what was coming up in schools, focused on what everyone wanted for their children and the shared commonality of experience. It helped families understand their rights in terms of advocacy and choice. On the topic of choice, for Anzac Day students had a choice whether to attend the combined high school ceremony that Heather mentioned, which is not on the school site, which preserves that school site, in terms of its safety, for all students. This gives parents that choice as well, although the dramatic element probably makes it a little more confronting in many ways. And we also engaged with the local Gallipoli Club, as opposed to an RSL [Returned and Services League] club as in the case, and we also had students who could elect to be part of a delegation from the school that would actually go to the public Gallipoli ceremony and represent the school and their families. So there are options there for Greg to honor Robbie and his dad, who can actually form a delegation if they want to. It's the choice. If they want to engage then they can.

**Maryam Zahid:** But if I may add one more thing. If we always give these communities a choice, there may be many barriers to them participating, like the language barrier and the cultural barrier. They may not know the history and diplomacy around an event like Anzac Day. And the guilt trip that has been pushed on them culturally and religiously makes them so vulnerable and deprived of the right information. So when schools give them a choice to come, it's easiest for them to say no. Or they might let their kids participate, but it happens in a gender-unbalanced way. If they have to travel some distance, they send the boy and not the girl because families worry, "What if she gets upset? And what if it's not culturally appropriate?" So sometimes we have to push people to come for the sake of equity and inclusivity. We also can't assume that all kids who look Black and Brown are new arrivals. My daughter always says, "I'm not a new arrival!" But that's the assumption. And that's really dangerous.

**Matthew Bradley:** Maryam, I can tell you that I do work to encourage families to participate in our events, but I do so in an inclusive way. Recently, there was an excursion for our students, and I actually spoke with a reluctant family. I explained that these excursions are really important, but I acknowledged that they're really expensive. I said to the family, "How about I take care of the excursion fees for you?" Because if it's only about money, we can help them. However, I insisted that both the boy and the girl be able to go. Fortunately, her excursion was first, and her family let her go, too. In short, while educators should give families choice, they should do so with a degree of encouragement. That's another value within Australia, gender balance and equity. Maybe there should have been a female student included in the case study.

**Daniella Forster:** There is Razia, but she only has a very small part. We're concerned about how she's taking that co-parenting role with her siblings and with her mother coming into the environment of the school and feeling safe.

**Maura Sellars:** I was looking for a female.

**Daniella Forster:** There are lots of moving parts in this case. It is quite complex. And you all have just really unfolded so many different layers to the case. So what do you think Greg, the principal, should do in this case?

**Matthew Bradley:** I'm again reflecting on the SCARF framework: Status, Certainty, Autonomy, Relatedness and Fairness. I'd like to think that Greg's going to send his students to one of those combined events off-site that Heather referenced. If the school has a delegation that attends, Greg could go, as a leader, to support his families and students who want to attend the public holiday ceremony. I think that could honor and provide an expression of interest in the families' concerns. And in the school, they might do something like we did this year. I set up a craft activity to make flowers, and then each of the students as a class put their poppies into the garden, had a moment of silence to remember, and headed off back to class with some educational activities, but not everything to do with all the uniforms. I think that having those three blocks honors all the parties, and makes sure that they're seen.

**Heather Sharp:** I agree. And I think the event should be compulsory because I take Maryam's point that when you don't make things compulsory, people can opt out. Why should families then miss out on experiences and lose the richness of the culture of the nation that they're now part of? I like the idea of poppies because you can have so many colors, which opens up conversation about what we're commemorating. The red poppy commemorates dead soldiers. The purple poppy refers to animals in war. The yellow poppy refers to sick or injured veterans. The white poppy refers to peace. And another poppy has a black center with red and yellow on the outside, and it represents Aboriginal servicemen and women who participated in Australian conflicts. That brings in that nuanced aspect of Anzac Day commemoration and remembrance.

**Maura Sellars:** I think, again, it's about the children. The more formal things can happen wherever they like, but school must be a safe spot. You can't make people belong. You can make activities at school for your children—one in, all in—so long as they're safe and not to do with their perceptions of what it is to be at war or subjected to the consequences of war and loss and trauma. I think probably the best solution is for everybody to come together: my focus on the children, Matt's focus as a school leader, Heather's focus on history, and Maryam's focus on making sure people have new experiences and are included, including the girls.

**Maryam Zahid:** I want to emphasize how crucial it is to foster an inclusive society. Schools can play a significant role in this by reaching out to places of worship, such as mosques, synagogues, and churches, as well as community leaders. When these religious leaders and community figures are aware of what's happening at the school, it can make a huge difference in shaping parents' mindsets and attitudes. In my experience, I have collaborated with synagogues, mosques, and temples on projects related to preventing domestic violence. By starting with them and involving the community, we were able to address the issues effectively. Sometimes, in our efforts to be culturally sensitive, we might miss opportunities to push a little further and achieve even better and more significant results. When schools establish connections with influential figures within their concerned communities, the impact becomes much more significant. This outreach can create a sense of unity and understanding, fostering a more inclusive environment for everyone involved.

**Daniella Forster:** Matt, I have a question for you. In the past Anzac Day has been color-washed. We've talked a little bit about Aboriginal and Torres Strait Islander soldiers, but we haven't spoken about the Chinese-Australian soldiers yet, for example, and the complexity of their engagement and how the Australian community saw them. So how could schools make this event more genuinely inclusive of these diverse peoples and perspectives?

**Matthew Bradley:** I think that there's an entire generation of young people that take Anzac Day as a public holiday and not in the traditional spirit with which it was celebrated when I was young. I think that this is a larger picture to do with the multitude of views that you have both on school staff and in the community about why and how we celebrate Anzac Day and even Australia Day. When students come through that magic school gate, they don't see color. They don't see history. You can see it in the interaction of those two little Year Five boys who paired up for science. They actually have the capacity to transcend all of those things. Ultimately, the question you're asking me is, what is Australia now? And what will Australia be in the future? We have to tell a broader truth and honor a greater diversity of voices in order for it to be everyone's history.

**Daniella Forster:** My next question is for Heather. We're talking about Anzac Day as an important instrument to build a sense of patriotism and pride. But learning about history is really difficult, as we see in the case study. What principles or values should the school use to help figure out how to adapt older approaches to teaching national history, maintaining a sense of pride in Australia's defense forces conduct while not sanitizing history?

**Heather Sharp:** I'm not sure the purpose of schooling is to preserve a sense of pride in defense force conduct. So I reject the premise of the question in that respect. And while it is mentioned in the Junior High School syllabus to protect the Anzac legend, it's not in the syllabus to actually teach about Anzac Day in either primary or high school. But because it's such a cultural phenomenon, and celebrated publicly, it's about much more than the invasion of Anzac Cove. It's about what it means to be Australian. Most schools in Australia do have something about it, whether their celebration takes place on the school grounds or not.

I guess it should be taught as a cultural event because the students are bombarded with public messaging about it: from government messaging, private company advertisements and news media. Leading up to Anzac Day, we'll always have anti-war films showing, but then commercial companies have lots of gung-ho messaging about how great war is and how great Australian soldiers are. Speaking from a secondary teacher perspective, we should be critiquing the Anzac legend in school. It's difficult to do in primary school because things do need to be simplified to suit the cognitive and developmental level the child is at. There are many topics you wouldn't put into a Year Two classroom. But in a Year 11 or 12 classroom, to give an example you referenced, Daniella, you might discuss Australian Chinese soldiers, who enlisted even though they weren't officially allowed to until about 1917. They still did participate, because some recruiters turned an eye, and of course the most famous Australian Chinese person is Billy Sing, world-famous sniper. We can teach this history to children in a way that makes it interesting and accessible, and one way that is done is through picture books, which present to children complex ideas in a cognitively safe and emotionally safe way. These books can even be used in high schools for young people whose written literacy isn't stage appropriate.

One more note: a recent study found that approximately 90 percent of picture books actually reflect the dominant culture, which right now in Australia is a patriotic sense of being really proud to be Australian. So you must carefully select what messages you want to tell the students. But even though Anzac Day is a nationalistic event, I actually believe that one of the reasons it has not only survived 100+ years, but actually gotten bigger and bigger, is because it's able to embrace all different cultures and bring them in. Aboriginal and Torres Strait Islanders participate in Anzac Day because it means something to them. And even though Turkey was our enemy in the First World War, Turkish soldiers actually were allowed to march in Australia's Anzac Day parades. That's the only example I know, in any nation, of an enemy being allowed to participate in a celebrational parade.

**Matthew Bradley:** I won't challenge anything that's been said, but on the topic of military pride, I just wanted to point out that quite a number of my family remain serving members of the Air Force. My father-in-law actually runs a military museum. But my beliefs about the military don't impact my work as a school principal. Anything to do with my own personal beliefs should be set aside because of the professional nature of my work. My job is to educate kids, and that's it. We're here thinking about, "What are the ethical bits in this case?" But it's not my job to bring any of those beliefs into my professional role. My job is to see people, to create supportive environments, and to educate kids. That's it.

**Daniella Forster:** Maura, I have a question for you now. How do you think schools like Burnsley should prioritize the direct and indirect generational differences of trauma within their practices?

**Maura Sellars:** I think that there are a whole lot of things that could be done a lot better, like having all staff well educated about trauma-informed pedagogies and also about protecting themselves against vicarious trauma. We need a balanced, careful approach, not so much to helping children forget, but to actually mediating damage and developing good, positive relationships. When everybody is on the same page, you can work wonders with the right sort of professional development, the right sort of pedagogical approach, and the right sort of perspective on the job that you do. And for me it's always been about a child-centered approach with differentiation because there's a huge gap often between the lived experience of different members of the school community. Teachers need compassion, not just for refugee children but for all the children who suffer complex childhood trauma on a daily basis at home.

**Matthew Bradley:** To add to what Maura said, it's also about high expectations. I've never met a family that comes from a refugee or asylum seeker background that had more hope than when they enrolled their child in school, knowing that their kids would be in that school, that they would be appreciated, and that we expected them to succeed as much as their own parents expected them to succeed. And that there wouldn't be any excuses, even as we acknowledge that trauma can drive certain behaviors at different times, and we wrap a little bit of support around them.

**Daniella Forster:** Maryam, my question for you is that there's a real need for newly arrived students of refugee backgrounds to get their footings and to build trust and safety in their new surroundings. On the one hand, they need to keep a strong sense of their heritage and their traditions, their language and identity. On the other hand, there's a need to demonstrate that they want to belong, and some Australian citizens assume this group needs to assimilate, if you like. How can schools support students with this balance?

**Maryam Zahid:** As we all know, education is super important for a society where everyone feels included and well-informed. We can connect not only with kids but also with their parents through fun classroom activities and events we organize. By acknowledging families' traditional events, we make sure everyone feels welcome. You won't believe how much our relationships matter in all of this. Whether it's the principal, teachers, helpers, or cleaners, everyone on the school staff just wants to help their students. I remember back when I was a student, the school principal was the only one who truly understood me. That trust we had made a huge difference in my life. Now, with my own kids, if I notice something wrong, I tell them, "Go talk to the school principal." Because I know school staff can really make a big difference for both students and parents. Creating a friendly and supportive environment in schools can be so empowering for the students and their families. It's all about building strong connections and understanding each other.

**Matthew Bradley:** Daniella. I'm really sorry, but I've got to challenge your use of the word assimilation. I think we should talk about that some more.

**Maura Sellars:** I also picked up on the word assimilation. For a long time that word was part of policy, and it was part of what people have tried to do, to make little Aussies of refugee children in the hope that they will blend in. Why does anybody need to blend in? I think that this whole notion of assimilation downplays our kids' capacities to do what they can do well.

**Maryam Zahid:** On the topic of assimilation, it's important to address the way the community sector still uses this term solely for funding purposes. Even though we strive for something else, when we engage with policymakers and funding bodies, we find ourselves talking about wanting the community to assimilate with the rest of society. The project-based approach often prioritizes those who are easier to reach or the surface-level aspects of the community members. Not many are willing to dive into the deeper, more complex, and slower parts of the community because it requires a lot of hard work and effort.

To truly define what an inclusive society means, and what diversity entails, we must challenge these policymakers and funding bodies. We can't accept their insistence on using words like "assimilate." Thankfully, there are amazing researchers and principals who are putting in tremendous effort to challenge these perceptions. They assert that an inclusive society means working collaboratively with communities, making people feel comfortable, safe, and genuinely belonging where they are.

I strongly believe and we must to stand up for a more progressive and inclusive approach and ensure that policies and funding support the notion of genuine inclusion and diversity within our society.

**Daniella Forster:** Thank you all very much for this conversation!

***Maura Sellars (PhD)*** *is a Honorary Lecturer at the University of Newcastle, Australia. She has a particular interest in inclusive classroom practices, working with students' strengths and developing the students' cognitive capacities within diverse social and cultural communities. Her recent research publications include several articles and books strategies for including students with refugee and asylum seeker backgrounds.*

***Heather Sharp (PhD)*** *is an Associate Professor at the University of Newcastle, Australia. She has over twenty years' experience in education in school and tertiary contexts. Her research focuses on representations of histories in school and public contexts.*

***Maryam Popal Zahid*** *is an award-winning Afghan-Australian champion who has dedicated herself to empowering women through her organization Afghan Women on the Move (www.afghanwomenonthemove.org.au). Maryam's commitment to fostering positive change extends beyond her organization, as she also runs a consultancy agency, Women Empowerment Pty Ltd, guiding mainstream organizations on cultural diversity and women-related matters. Her journey of knowledge and growth continues at Oxford University, where she is currently studying Values and Public Policy: Political Philosophy in Practice.*

***Matthew Bradley*** *is Principal at Mayfield West Demonstration School in New South Wales, Australia. His work aims to offer equitable educational opportunities for students and support staff and enhance the sense of belonging, hope, and purpose in his community. Mayfield West Demonstration School was recently honored for its decades-long commitment as a partner with the University of Newcastle's teacher preparation program.*

# Character Guide

| Setting |
|---|
| Burnsley Public School in New South Wales, Australia, serving students ages 5–12. |
| **Primary Characters** |

| | |
|---|---|
| **Greg Sefton:** Australian-born principal | **Mohammad "Uncle Mo" Kahn:** Afghan-born family liaison |
| **Robbie Jones:** Australian-born Year Five student | **Lynn Green:** Australian-born Year Five teacher |
| **Kawa Al Ahmad:** Syrian-born Year Five student | **Mr. Jones:** Robbie's Australian-born father, a veteran |

# Discussion Questions

1. How do different characters in the case view the importance of Anzac Day? How do these views influence their thoughts on how it should be commemorated?
2. The origins of Anzac Day and its meaning historically stand in some tension with the realities of modern-day Australia. How do you see this tension influencing the dilemmas that the characters face?
3. Different characters have had very different experiences of war—as soldiers, as noncombatants forced from their homes, as the children of veterans, as citizens commemorating significant battles. How do these experiences influence the dilemmas they face?
4. Greg wants the Anzac Day celebration to be "inclusive." What do you think he means by "inclusion" here? How do other characters in the case understand inclusion?
5. The case opens with a scene centered on Robbie Jones, not Kawa, Uncle Mo, or any of the other characters. How does this opening frame the dilemmas that surface in the case?
6. At the end of the case, Greg feels for a moment "the weight [Mohammad] carried." What dilemmas does Uncle Mo face in the case? What values does he seem to prioritize as the school community plans the Anzac Day celebration?

7 Australia is not the only country thinking deeply about how to celebrate long-standing national holidays as an increasingly diverse nation. How does this case help you think about celebrating national holidays in your own country?

# Notes

1. In some of the most economically disadvantaged areas of Sydney are found the highest numbers of refugees on bridging visas, e.g., Merrylands, Fairfield, Bankstown, and Granville. "Statistics on People Seeking Asylum in the Community." Refugee Council of Australia. July 7, 2024. https://www.refugeecouncil.org.au/asylum-community/7/
2. Watkins, M., Noble, G., and Wong, A. (2019). *It's Complex! Working with Students of Refugee Backgrounds and Their Families in New South Wales Public Schools*. Retrieved from https://www.westernsydney.edu.au/__data/assets/pdf_file/0004/1504588/Its_Complex_Working_with_Students_of_Refugee_Backgrounds_and_their_Families_in_NSW_Public_Schools.pd
3. "The Spirit of ANZAC is an intangible thing. It is unseen, unpredictable, an unquenchable thirst for justice, freedom and peace. However, despite being intangible, the Spirit of ANZAC is a cornerstone which underpins our Australian image, way of life and indeed is an integral part of our heritage." Anzac Day Commemoration Committee (2024). "The Spirit of Anzac Day," Retrieved August 19, 2024 from https://anzacday.org.au/the-spirit-of-anzac
4. Lake, M., Reynolds, H., McKenna, M., and Damousi, J. (2010). *What's Wrong with Anzac: The militarisation of Australian History*. NewSouth Publishing.
5. McPhedran, Ian (2015). "Survey Finds 93 Per Cent of Australians Believe It Is Important to Commemorate Anzac Day." *News Australia Network*, April 7, 2015. https://www.news.com.au/national/anzac-day/survey-finds-93-per-cent-of-australians-believe-it-is-important-to-commemorate-anzac-day/news-story/e7564aa663bbe2adcdb2e876d1dbdc3c
6. Australia's military personnel have higher rates of PTSD than the wider community but are not adequately supported. See Twomey, Christina (2019). "Returned Soldiers and PTSD: When the War's Over but Battles Remain." *Monash University Lens*, April 24, 2019. https://lens.monash.edu/@politics-society/2019/04/24/1374433/returned-soldiers-and-ptsd and https://theconversation.com/veterans-have-poorer-mental-health-than-australians-overall-we-could-be-serving-them-better-119525

7. Bedford, A., and Barnes, N. (2022). "The Truth: What Our Students Really Learn about Anzac Day," *EduResearch Matters*, AARE. https://www.aare.edu.au/blog/?p=12645
8. Brunton, Colman (2011). *Department of Veterans' Affairs "A Centenary of Service" Community Research Phase II.* Sydney.
Department of Veterans' Affairs (2011). *How Australia May Commemorate the Anzac Centenary.* Canberra: Commonwealth Government Australia.
Drozdzewski, D. (2016). "Does Anzac Sit Comfortably within Australia's Multiculturalism?," *Thinking Space, Australian Geographer*, 47:1: 3–10.
9. A slang term for "dirt poor."
10. A slang term for "a lazy good-for-nothing."
11. Newcastle received a number of Afghan interpreters into the community, but some of their family members left behind are still in danger. Fowler, Gabriel (2021). "Former Afghan Interpreters Living in Newcastle Continue Their Pleas for Support." *Newcastle Herald*, August 24, 2021. https://www.newcastleherald.com.au/story/7399776/afghans-left-behind-being-taken-or-killed/
12. For example, this high socioeconomic public primary school in Westmead, an area in outer Sydney where more than 90 percent of students have a language background other than English. Westmead Public Schools (2019). "Anzac Ceremony." April 12, 2019. https://westmead-p.schools.nsw.gov.au/news/2019/4/anzac-ceremony.html
13. See image and symbolism of school Honour rolls: https://anzacportal.dva.gov.au/commemoration/symbols-commemoration/honour-rolls
14. Imig, S., Sellars, M., and Fischetti, J. (2022). *Creating Spaces of Wellbeing and Belonging for Refugee and Asylum-Seeker Students: Skills and Strategies for School Leaders.* London and New York: Routledge.
15. Lake, M., Reynolds, H., McKenna, M., and Damousi, J. (2010). (pp.112–20).
16. McCall, Rupert (2022). One Hundred Years from Now.
17. Field, A. E., and McCrae, J. (1919). In Flanders Fields.
18. Australian Government Department of Veterans' Affairs (2022). "New Resources to Help Educate ahead of Anzac Day." March 10, 2022. https://www.dva.gov.au/newsroom/latest-news-veterans/new-resources-help-educate-ahead-anzac-day
19. Catafalque parties are mounted around coffins as a sign of respect and around memorials on occasions of remembrance such as Anzac Day. The catafalque party consists of four members of an armed guard who stand, their heads bowed and their arms (weapon) reversed, facing outward approximately one meter from the catafalque as a symbolic form of respect for those who have fallen.

20. RSL New South Wales (2022). "RSL and Schools Remember Anzac Commemoration 2022." April 7, 2022. https://www.rslnsw.org.au/news/rsl-and-schools-remember-anzac-commemoration-2022/
21. Fears grow for Syria amid rising violence, deepening humanitarian crisis, UN News: Global perspective Human stories, United Nations, 9/3/22, https://news.un.org/en/story/2022/03/1113592

# 10

# Conclusion: Structuring Equitable Discussion

*Sara O'Brien, Meira Levinson, Tatiana Geron, and Ellis Reid*

---

The cases and conversations in this volume all explore the concept of equity as a complex concept and practice. While there is widespread agreement in the field of education that equity is an important value at the classroom, school, and policy levels, there is little agreement about the meaning of the term "equity," nor what it looks like to carry out this value in educational decision-making. In order to realize this value in any meaningful way, educators, families, communities, and policymakers must engage in conversation about their visions for equitable education. Normative case studies are powerful tools for these discussions. Grounded in both realistic problems of practice and philosophical principles, normative case studies can spark conversations that examine both the conceptual and practical dimensions of equity.

Given the many disparate—and sometimes competing—conceptions of equity that exist, the concept of "equitable discussion" might well mean something different to each reader of this volume. However, this chapter largely conceives of equitable discussion spaces as accessible and inclusive and offers ideas for facilitating conversations that center these two values.

# Equitable Conversations about Educational Equity

The cases and conversations in this volume are purposefully designed to provoke discussion of educational equity, and, ideally, conversation about them will take place in fair and equitable discussion spaces. Facilitators play an important role in shaping these spaces. Case conversations take place in a variety of settings: in conference rooms and lecture halls, academic classrooms and professional development settings, private offices and community spaces. We have run case discussions in all of these settings, generally using the standard discussion protocol presented on page 188.

As noted in Chapter 1, the discussion protocol postpones talk of actual decision-making about the dilemmas presented in the cases until the end of the conversation. This timing is quite deliberate. Educators make hundreds of decisions each day (if not more) and thus rarely have the luxury of time to sit with the dilemmas that they face. The protocol presented here gives educators time to reflect deeply on the challenges that these cases present, which allows for nuanced thinking and opportunity to explore multiple potential solutions. Facilitators play an important role in offering their participants the time and space for that reflection, encouraging the group to delay suggestions on possible courses of action in order to focus on the values, principles, and practical and policy considerations that make the dilemmas so thorny. Because the need to solve problems quickly is so deeply embedded in education, facilitators should be prepared to redirect conversation when groups begin to introduce solutions too early in the conversation.

## Creating Accessible Discussion Spaces

When preparing for case discussions, we find that the following strategies help us think through how to make our conversations accessible for many different people:

- *Be mindful of time constraints.* The protocol presented here assumes ninety-minute case discussions because fully unpacking the dilemmas raised in these cases requires a substantial amount of time—indeed, even ninety minutes is not enough to discuss them all in depth! That being said, time is a luxury that's too rarely available in schools, and it would hardly be equitable to preclude those short on time from discussing the cases. Therefore, the discussion protocol includes modifications that allow facilitators to run discussions in far less time, including within the standard 40- to 50-minute time blocks that often form school schedules.

- *Consider participants' availability to prepare.* When we know that participants will have little time to look at the case in advance, we generally have participants read the case during the actual discussion session, either silently and individually or together using a reader's theater script (see *Case Adaptations*). Especially when participants have varying amounts of time to prepare for the discussion, this option can support equity. In addition to the case study itself, some facilitators provide additional materials for their students or participants to read or view before the case discussion; this is particularly common in academic settings. These materials might include philosophical readings, empirical research, news articles, academic talks, or the accompanying conversations included in this volume. Again, be mindful of participants' availability to prepare additional materials beyond the case.
- *Provide supporting materials as needed.* Each of the cases presented here is designed to be easily read by a native English speaker in about ten minutes. You can also find versions of the cases written in the language of their context ("Private Equity" in Spanish, or "Caught in the Web" in German, for example) at justiceinschools.org. For users reading a case written in a language they don't speak fluently, consider whether they'll need any additional glossaries or vocabulary supports. Instructors and facilitators should also consider whether their groups will need any additional background information, particularly when reading a case from a different national setting. While the context paragraphs accompanying the cases do provide some framing, different groups may need more information to fully engage with the case.
- *Create opportunities for small group discussion.* We have run case discussions with groups as small as three and as large as three hundred (broken into twenty smaller groups). In general, it's helpful to have groups that are large enough to provide diverse viewpoints but small enough that everyone has ample opportunity to share their views—ideally, around 6–12 participants per case discussion group. Instructors and facilitators may create opportunities for larger groups (e.g. 15–25 people) to discuss some questions in pairs or trios even as they discuss other parts of the protocol as a whole group. Very large groups can be broken into smaller,

self-facilitating groups of 6–12 participants using the protocol as a guide; the instructor or chief facilitator may wish to circulate among them and share ideas and instructions periodically with the group as a whole.

## Establishing Norms to Support Inclusivity

A key function of the normative case study is to help people converse across lines of difference, but this kind of conversation is often challenging. In order to encourage participants to bring diverse viewpoints to a case conversation and engage with others' viewpoints as well, it's important to set community agreements before the discussion begins. Normative case studies are designed to present many reasonable and contrasting points of view about challenging topics that often engage readers' deeply held values and beliefs. Case conversations ask participants to not only examine and share these beliefs but also confront—with empathy and an open mind—potentially opposing beliefs held by others. In order to build a discussion space that allows for that empathy and engagement from all participants, facilitators can open the conversation with norms and expectations, to which the group may return if conversation becomes difficult. For groups that work together over longer periods of time, these expectations may be co-constructed. Even in groups that meet only once, facilitators can encourage group ownership of expectations by presenting a list of norms and leading a short conversation about them, asking participants to comment on or add to the list. Below is a list of norms that we commonly use in normative case discussions.[1]

---

**Discussion Norms**

- Respect Yourself and Others
    - (E.g., Actively listen; maintain confidentiality; and challenge ideas, not people)
- Acknowledge the Different Backgrounds and Experiences of Others
    - (E.g., Consider the role of your identities and power dynamics)
- Accept Challenge and Anticipate Discomfort
    - (E.g., Push your thinking; hold yourself and others accountable; and contribute to the conversation)
- Keep an Open Mind
    - (E.g., Allow for growth; listen before responding; and stay engaged)
- Embrace Uncertainty and Non-Closure

Another way to set the conditions for equitable discussion is by considering the multiple ways that participants enter case study conversations. While normative case studies provide a level of distance for groups to talk about challenging ethical topics, enabling them to focus on characters' experiences rather than participants' own, readers do often respond to cases emotionally. After all, ideally all readers will find some characters or stakeholders within the world of the case with whom to identify or empathize. Thus, while some participants enter into case discussions with a more analytical lens, eager to analyze the values and motivations of others, their fellow participants may enter with a more personal lens, recognizing their own experiences in the world of the case. Indeed, Maryam Zahid opens the conversation about "A Uniform Decision" (Ch. 9) by naming the emotional response she had to the case: "When considering the question of what shape Anzac Day should take and to whom it should belong, I can't help but become emotional with sadness, given my own personal journey and experiences." Hester Burn opens the discussion of "A Qualified Disaster" (Ch. 4) by asking her participants to consider their feelings as they read the case: "Did reading the case study and returning to that period [the start of the Covid-19 pandemic] bring back any uncomfortable emotional memories for you?" While not all participants in Burn's conversation pick up this emotional thread, her question demonstrates to the group that their professional experiences are not the only expertise that they bring to the table. In asking it, Burn highlights that an equitable discussion space allows for many pathways into the conversation.

With this goal in mind, in place of or in addition to the norms above, facilitators might begin case discussions with the Courageous Conversations Compass, created by Glenn Singleton (Figure 1).[2]

While the compass was designed to help people think about the ways they enter challenging conversations about race, we have found it useful for orienting people to the different ways that participants enter normative case discussions, whether or not the cases explicitly tackle race. Singleton identifies the four orientations as Believing (entering on the moral level, with deeply held beliefs about what's right that may be challenging to articulate), Thinking (entering on the intellectual level, eager to examine evidence, data, and concepts), Feeling (entering on the emotional level, bringing strong feelings raised by the issues), and Acting (entering on the relational level, eager to take action on the issues). Facilitators can use the compass, with its four points, to affirm the validity and value of different approaches to challenging conversations and help participants empathize with each other's

**Figure 1** Glenn Singleton's Courageous Conversations Compass.

stances. Each of the orientations has both strengths and limitations as a lens for viewing challenging topics, so when the group makes space for all four stances, more productive dialogue becomes possible. The compass can be particularly helpful for opening conversations about case studies that may be quite personal for the case readers, or conversations that seem likely to become contentious. If conversation does become heated, facilitators might pause the discussion and ask participants to reflect on the orientation with which they are approaching the conversation and work to understand how others' orientations might be different. They could also ask participants to intentionally try out a different stance, to imagine how someone using that orientation might view the dilemmas in the case.

## Facilitating Inclusive Discussions

Once we have set the expectations for the group, we find the following strategies helpful for facilitating inclusive discussions:

- *Frame the conversation.* Case studies serve many purposes in the field of education, and discussion participants may bring preconceived notions about case discussions from previous academic or professional experiences. Therefore, we let participants know that our goal is exploring dilemmas, and we open case conversations by defining a dilemma as "a situation where there is no one right answer and it is hard (even impossible) to realize all important values and principles at once." This definition helps set the conditions for a conversation that explores a variety of values, viewpoints, and potential solutions, rather than a conversation that attempts to build consensus on "one right answer." It also helps to set the conditions for inclusive conversation by emphasizing that while these many valid and important values sometimes conflict with one another, none should be discounted.

- *Individually invite participants in.* Ideally, once you have set the conditions for discussion, all participants will feel comfortable sharing their thoughts. But we don't live in an ideal world! One particularly warm way to invite participants into the conversation is by drawing on your knowledge of their professional or academic expertise. As an example, both Janine Bempechat (Ch. 5) and Douglas Yacek (Ch. 6) specifically invite the classroom teachers in their discussions into the conversation when the topic turns to how new programs might impact classroom-level decisions.
- *Bring in perspectives that might be missing.* Even in diverse discussion groups, there are inevitably beliefs and experiences that won't be represented. As facilitators, we often ask our discussion participants to consider which stakeholders might face dilemmas beyond the main actor(s) in the case study, as well as which potential stakeholders might be missing from the case entirely. Instructors and facilitators working with relatively homogenous groups might consider handing out supporting materials by authors with different expertise and experiences in order to provide more perspectives that groups can bring into the conversation. The case conversations (or excerpts from them) can serve as valuable resources in this respect.

## Further Facilitation Ideas

While we generally use standard discussion protocol to lead conversations about normative case studies, there are many ways to engage with these cases.

- *Reader's theater.* Rather than asking participants to read a narrative version of a fictional case before the conversation, facilitators can instead provide a "reader's theater" script of the case, which participants use to act out the case together before they enter the discussion. The scripts are shortened versions of the cases and spread dialogue among the characters and a narrator; ideally, they can be read aloud in 10–12 minutes. Facilitators ask for volunteers, who then read the script aloud to the group. Reader's theater works particularly well with large groups to provide a shared experience of the case before the large group breaks into smaller ones. Justiceinschools.org has a number of reader's theater scripts that facilitators can either download for use with their groups or use as models to adapt a case themselves.

- *"Four corners" discussions.* This variation works well when one facilitator is leading discussion with a large group (more than 20). Each of the four corners of the room should have a clearly posted sign: Strongly Agree, Somewhat Agree, Somewhat Disagree, and Strongly Disagree. The facilitator presents participants with different statements inspired by the case. Using "Remote Control" (Ch. 7), for example, a facilitator might give this statement: "The fourth grade teachers should require all of their students to keep their cameras on during virtual Fridays." The statements could also refer to the case more obliquely, with participants using the case as one point of reference for grounding their ideas. In this case, the statement might be: "Educators should enforce consistent expectations for their students." For each statement, participants choose a corner based on how strongly they agree or disagree. They generally begin by sharing their views with others in their same corner and then move to whole group conversation or to new groups made up of participants from different corners in order to hear a wide variety of perspectives.
- *Personal connections.* As noted above, readers often strongly identify with the characters and dilemmas presented in the cases. Facilitators can draw on these strong feelings by asking discussion participants to choose a character with whom they identify and to reflect on why they feel this identification. Users might do some writing about these connections on their own or might break into pairs or small groups based on which character they chose. Conversely, facilitators might ask participants to choose a character to whom they felt little or no connection and then to explore that character's perspective to better understand their values, beliefs, and motivations. Again, this exercise can be done individually, in pairs, or in small groups. Each variation helps participants dive into the core dilemmas of the case.

# Using the Conversations as Tools for Learning

While this chapter has thus far explored how to use the *cases* in this volume, the conversations that follow each case are also excellent tools for teaching and learning in academic, professional, and community spaces. This final section details some of the (many) ways that educators and facilitators might use these conversations.

## Conversations as Models of Facilitation

Normative case study facilitators often work singly, with few opportunities to see what moves their peers make in helping participants explore the complex challenges raised by these cases. This volume opens windows into colleagues' practices. Each conversation is facilitated by someone different and thus offers a peek at eight different facilitation styles. Readers may find many models to borrow from or even to emulate. For example, Ellis Reid frequently jumps into the conversation about "Basic Education for All" (Ch. 2) with questions that probe participants' thinking, returning to topics previously raised so that the group can explore them more fully. In contrast, Liz Block rarely intervenes in the conversation about "Private Equity" (Ch. 3), and when she does so it is to pull the conversation into previously unexplored areas. These include such complex and murky ethical waters as the diversity of the private education sector in Mexico, and how this diversity makes it difficult to create equitable policy impacting the whole sector. Daniella Forster takes a third approach in wrapping up discussion about "A Uniform Decision" (Ch. 9), as she poses preplanned, targeted questions to each of her four discussants based on their specific areas of expertise. Those using this volume to hone their facilitation skills might choose a favorite conversation and identify some facilitation moves they wish to try in their own conversations about the cases.

In addition to serving as models of facilitation, the conversations also serve as texts that instructors and facilitators can critique and analyze in the process of developing their own facilitation approaches. One might compare Reid's and Block's approaches as a means of considering: How active a role should facilitators take in case conversations? Under what conditions should they step in, and what form should their questions or comments take when they do? Instructors might also ask: when should facilitators play "devil's advocate" or offer a contrasting viewpoint, as Douglas Yacek does in "Caught in the Web" (Ch. 6) when he challenges Johannes Giesinger's assertion that technology can be a helpful tool when exploring the natural world? What facilitation moves are available to push on participants to justify their thinking, as Alysha Banerji does in the conversation about "Remote Control" (Ch. 7) when she asks Ivelisse Ramos Brannon, "What will more meetings help [the teachers in the case] do?" Alternatively, what are the signs that participants can be trusted to wend their own way toward complex exchanges or new ethical insights? The conversations in this volume can serve as rich texts to help individual instructors and facilitators, or groups studying normative case study discussion facilitation together, engage with these and similar questions and start to develop their own answers.

## Conversations as Insights into the Cases

Beyond their uses as models of facilitation, the conversations of course provide insights into the dilemmas raised in the cases, highlighting conceptions of educational equity that themselves spark reflection and conversation. For example, when discussing "Remote Control" (Ch. 7), Ben Paxton explores the relationship between equity and socioeconomic inequality as he thinks about the proposed camera policy for remote schooling: "One child is sitting at a kitchen table surrounded by their siblings in a smaller home, and one child has a home with a refurbished basement and a new foosball table. Is it the intention of schools to hide that from students? Are we protecting students from the effects of inequality in schools?" Paxton's reflections help prompt readers to consider whether it is more equitable to ignore the vast disparities in students' home lives or to bring them into the open to try to address them. Meanwhile, "Remaking the Grade" (Ch. 5) highlights the challenges that schools and districts can face when they *do* decide that equity requires addressing the disparities in students' home lives. When the district in the case introduced a new homework policy in an attempt to close the achievement gap, they faced criticism from a variety of stakeholders. In the conversation about the case, the discussants explore why so much conflict arose in a district where stakeholders on the whole conceptualized equity as equally high achievement for students regardless of different backgrounds and abilities. Their conversation highlights for readers that even when stakeholders hold similar conceptions of equity, deciding what to focus on in order to improve equity isn't straightforward. "It's seductive to pick the homework issue because it looks like it's a problem," Karen Mapp explains. "But when there's no process to do a root cause analysis and you don't involve any of the stakeholders, then you end up with this mess." From this conversation, readers better understand the deep work necessary to make equity a reality, even among well-intentioned people with similar visions of what equitable schools demand.

Read together, the conversations in this volume echo one another in interesting ways. Examining those echoes can help to deepen readers' understanding of equity. As an example, many conversations in this volume speak about the importance of choice, for students and families in particular. "School Choice in Hong Kong" (Ch. 8) is built on questions of choice, as the title indicates. The conversation explores the ways that parental choices about schooling impact not just individual children but the society more broadly, with Chi-Ming Lam arguing, "Universal parents' choice is trying to meet the educational needs of the society. But individual parents' choice is trying to meet the specific educational needs of the kids, and you can't have both at the same time." However, the conversation only briefly touches on the ways that choices are inequitably distributed in Hong Kong and around the world. In Chapter 9, Maryam Zahid explores this topic in the Australian context when she points out that many asylum-seeking families "don't have choice or power over their life and decisions" as the group considers whether refugee families in "A Uniform Decision" might be given a choice about whether to attend the school's Anzac Day celebration. Asyia Kazmi complicates the concept of choice even further in discussing "Basic Education for All" (Ch. 2). As the group discusses how students in Kenya might benefit from choosing their own pathway through secondary education, Kazmi points out that offering choices isn't enough: "It isn't just about choice. It's the ability to make an informed choice based on an understanding of where those choices will take you, and the benefits and costs of certain choices." While each of these three points offers significant insight into the individual cases and the contexts in which they are set, taken together they help readers develop a deeper understanding of educational equity, both the potential pathways and barriers to equitable education.

In another example, two conversations present distinctly different, even opposing, views on the role that individual teachers' beliefs and values should play in shaping equitable schools. When discussing "A Uniform Decision" (Ch. 9), Matthew Bradley argues strongly that educators and school leaders must set all personal beliefs aside when they enter school: "My job is to educate kids, and that's it." In contrast, Ben Paxton ends the conversation about "Remote Control" (Ch. 7) on an opposing note: "The individual teacher is going to have to make decisions at some point about whether or not the choices of their school administrator, their fellow teachers in their department, the school board, or their local community mesh with their own values and moral commitments. And if not, what are they going to do?" Taken together, these two arguments set up an interesting debate for readers: Should educators separate their personal values from their professional values? Is such a separation even possible? Facilitators and instructors can use both echoes and dissonance between the conversations presented here to open such discussions with their groups.

Here are possible ways that instructors and professional development providers might use the conversations to explore the cases further:

- *Create new pathways in the conversation.* By necessity, facilitators can only pick up so many threads in the complex tapestry of a discussion, particularly in a short session. There will always be possible avenues of conversation not taken. Facilitators or students studying these conversations might write their own follow-up questions to the participants and consider how following those new pathways might have reshaped where the conversation ultimately went. They might also consider ideas from the case itself that could have been explored more fully and craft questions to introduce those ideas into the conversation.
- *Find openings for new conversations.* Sometimes, case discussions include moments that could start not just a new pathway but an entirely new conversation. When discussing "Remaking the Grade" (Ch. 5), for example, Natasha Warikoo mentions that while the Arlington Public Schools eliminated *graded* homework, another district that she worked with faced challenges when they eliminated homework altogether for some grade levels. Her comment opens a new conversation about the ethics of homework itself, with a particular focus on the equity implications when some parents with means simply replace school-given homework with enrichment classes.
- *Consider which viewpoints are missing.* There are only so many areas of expertise and lived experiences that can be packed into one group of four or five people. Case users might discuss or write about whom they would invite to participate in a discussion about one of the cases in this book and why they would make those choices. Conversely, case users might examine the conversations here to try writing questions that they might have used as the facilitator in order to bring missing viewpoints into the conversation.

## Conversations as Tools for Surfacing Intuitions and Assumptions

In discussing "Basic Education for All" (Ch. 2), Pierre Germain Belinga points out, "Different societies will have different visions of what a good education means." Living in one society, immersed in its particular vision of what's "good," can make it hard to see those visions objectively and critique them. However, normative case studies can be a powerful tool for examining the assumptions we hold, collectively and individually, and the conversations in this volume help bring those assumptions to the surface. When discussing "Caught in the Web" (Ch. 6), for instance, Nicholas Burbules points out the characters in the case who fear the effects of bringing in more technology are making assumptions about in-person learning that may not be true: "I think it's important not to romanticize the traditional classroom. The traditional classroom also has equity issues and injustice issues." Attending to this case conversation can help readers question whether they themselves are overlooking any injustices in traditional educational models. Likewise, discussants in the conversation about "Basic Education for All" (Ch. 2) question whether framing presented in the case perpetuates misguided assumptions about what makes for a good education. "Maybe that's one of the weaker points of the case," Isaac Nyangolo argues, "the assumption that quality education is only measured in terms of whether you can read or write. There are other, wider goals like good citizenship and cultural awareness and understanding." Asyia Kazmi also points to "an assumption of the very traditional school model," with one teacher in front of a room of students. As they attempt to envision an equitable policy that would bring more students into secondary education, the discussants push past assumed models to consider alternative aims, structures, and conceptions of equity. Facilitators can use these conversations to help users examine assumptions about education and equity not only in the cases but also in their own contexts.

While most discussants in the conversations in this volume surfaced assumptions operating in their own countries, reading conversations about cases set in other countries can also help readers examine their own intuitions. As an example, the discussion about "School Choice in Hong Kong" (Ch. 8) deeply examines the many ways that language of instruction—and language of origin—impact students' identities and the opportunities available to both children and adults who live in Hong Kong. While the intricacies that the discussants explore are in some ways specific to Hong Kong, their conversation can also prompt readers to consider: What roles do schools in their own context play in shaping both individual identity and national identity, and how (if at all) is language central to that process? Are those the roles that they actually *hope* schools (and language) would play in shaping identity? Which of the three types of schools explored in the conversation appeals most to them personally—and why do they have that intuitive response? Diving into unfamiliar contexts—and analyzing their responses to the new ideas therein—provides readers the opportunity to reflect on the unconscious values and beliefs that shape their own ethical decision-making.

## Conclusion

The complex and often contrasting views of educational equity presented in the cases and conversations in this volume echo the multitude of conceptions that teachers, parents, students, school leaders, and policymakers hold around the globe. In these cases and conversations, those differing views are in dialogue with each other in a way that too rarely happens outside these pages. We hope that this volume makes it easier for groups looking to discuss educational equity—along with the other complex values and goals that encompass the field of education—to hold conversations across lines of difference in respectful, accessible, inclusive, and even equitable ways.

## Notes

1. This list is also published in the companion to this volume, *Civic Contestation in Global Education: Cases and Conversations in Educational Ethics*. Bloomsbury. The Norms are adapted from "Leveraging Norms for Challenging Conversations," Developed by Whitney Polk in collaboration with Dr. Aaliyah El-Amin. Harvard Graduate School of Education. 2016.
2. Singleton, G. E. (2015). *Courageous Conversations About Race: A Field Guide for Achieving Equity in Schools* (2nd edition). Thousand Oaks, CA: Corwin.

# Appendix

| Case Discussion Facilitation Guide (for 90 minutes, with notes for modification) ||
|---|---|
| **Before the Discussion** ||
| Consider the goals for your discussion.<br>• Who is your audience? How well do they know each other?<br>• Why is this group coming together?<br>Determine which materials you will need.<br>• Will you distribute the case before the discussion? (Is it reasonable to expect participants to read it before the event?)<br>• Will you devote time during the event for participants to read the case or perform the reader's theater script (see *Case adaptations*)?<br>• Are there any other materials that you wish to distribute alongside the case?<br>Determine group size(s). We recommend ideally 6–12 people per discussion group.<br>• Will you run one whole-group discussion yourself?<br>• Will you break a large group into smaller groups? Will those groups be self-facilitated or will you require a team of facilitators? | **Notes**: *When we run case discussions in undergraduate or graduate courses, we generally ask students to read the cases—and any accompanying academic sources—before the discussion. When running professional development with in-service educators, we sometimes ask our participants to read the case in advance, but we also often rely on reader's theater scripts, knowing how many demands teachers have on their time. Consider how you can maximize participation and learning for the group that you are working with.* |

| **Introductions (5-10 minutes)** | |
|---|---|
| Ask each member of the group to share their names and pronouns (if desired), along with any additional information that may be useful (professional role for educators, academic major for students, etc.). You may also include an icebreaker question for community building. | *Notes*: For virtual discussions, we often have discussion participants call on the next person to help the introductions run more smoothly.<br><br>*Modifications*: If all members of the group already know each other well, you can omit introductions. |
| **Discussion Norms (5 minutes)** | |
| Share a list of discussion norms for the conversation with participants. Once participants have had a chance to review the list, ask whether they wish to discuss or amend any norms or to add any new ones. | *Notes*: You can find a list of norms that we often use on page ____.<br><br>*Modifications*: If the group meets regularly, you can likely do a quick review of existing norms here. |
| **Case Recap (5 minutes)** | |
| Ask a volunteer to share key case details, using the character and setting chart at the beginning of the case. Other participants can chime in with ideas they feel have been missed. The goal of the recap is to remind participants about the "facts of the case" before they begin discussing the dilemmas. | *Notes*: While it's nice to have members of the group provide the recap, to save time you could present a short written recap or have the facilitator give a recap.<br><br>*Modifications*: If you are using a reader's theater script, you should omit the case recap. Be sure to budget 10-12 minutes for the group to perform the script. |
| **Discussion: What are the dilemmas? (15-20 minutes)** | |
| Before diving into the discussion, establish a common understanding of the term "dilemma." We share the following definition:<br>• Dilemma: A situation where there is no one right answer and it is hard (even impossible) to realize all important values and principles at once. | *Notes*: We often ask discussion participants to start by naming the most obvious dilemma, the one that's likely on most people's minds. Then we move to exploring dilemmas within that main dilemma and to looking at other dilemmas that might not be so obvious. |

| Begin the actual case discussion by asking participants to surface the dilemmas in the case, using the following questions:<br>• What are the dilemmas in this case? For whom are they dilemmas? | ***Modifications***: *If you are short on time, you can shorten this section to 10 minutes. But we recommend giving the group as close to 15–20 minutes as possible.* |
|---|---|
| **Discussion: Why are these dilemmas? (15–20 minutes)** ||
| • Before asking the next question in the protocol, give a short summary (2–3 minutes) of the dilemmas raised. Then, use the following questions:<br>   ○ Why are these dilemmas? What values or principles are at stake? Do people disagree about which values matter, which should take precedence, or how they apply in this case?<br>   ○ What practical and/or policy considerations are at stake? Do people disagree about which considerations are relevant, which should take precedence, or how they should be addressed in this case? | ***Notes***: *You may wish to provide discussion participants with a list of possible values that might be at stake in the case.*<br><br>***Modifications***: *If you are short on time, you can shorten this section to 10 minutes. But we recommend giving the group as close to 15–20 minutes as possible.* |
| **Discussion: What *might* be done in this case? (5-10 minutes)** ||
| Have discussion participants brainstorm possible courses of action that might be taken in the case. These can address any of the dilemmas raised and may be explored within the case or be totally novel. Use the following questions:<br>• What choices are available, and to whom?<br>   ○ How does each of these choices frame and address the issues at stake?<br>   ○ For each choice, what is gained? What is lost? | ***Notes***: *You may wish to give participants time to brainstorm or discuss in pairs before opening this question to the group, if time allows.*<br><br>***Modifications***: *If you are pressed for time, omit this section and instead move to the next question of what should be done.* |

| | |
|---|---|
| **Discussion: What *should* be done in this case? (5-10 minutes)** | |
| Ask participants to consider what should be done in the case, using the following question:<br>• What do you think should be done in this case, and by whom? Why? | *Notes*: Remember that there is no one best course of action in these cases (though some courses of action are definitely better than others, and some actions would be wrong to take). Participants should not be looking for the "right answer." Be sure to ask people to explain why they believe that the course of action they chose should be taken. |
| **Reflection (10–20 minutes)** | |
| Before ending the discussion, ask participants to reflect on the case and their experience discussing it. Use (some of) the following questions:<br>• What have you learned from talking about this case that might apply to other ethical dilemmas in education?<br>   ◦ What principles or values are you thinking about for the first time, or thinking about in a new way?<br>   ◦ What policies or practices are you thinking about for the first time or in a new way?<br>• What value is there, if any, to talking through a case like this with others?<br>   ◦ What did you learn about yourself?<br>   ◦ What did you learn about others?<br>   ◦ What did you learn about your institution, organization, or broader context?<br>   ◦ What did you learn about the process itself?<br>• What have you learned from this case and/or discussion that you'd like to take back to your own classroom/school/context?<br>• Is there anything else you want to bring up or discuss? | *Notes*: It's nearly impossible that you'd have time to ask all of the reflection questions listed here! Think about which questions will be most helpful for the group that you're facilitating and choose one or two accordingly.<br><br>**Modifications**: If this group is coming together for a specific purpose, you may want to tailor the reflection to that purpose. In the past, we have used this reflection time for discipline or grade-level teams to chat about implications for their classrooms, for example. We have also used this time for teachers across a district to reflect on the ways the case discussion helps them think about new policies being implemented. In our experience, discussion participants find this chance for reflection very meaningful—be sure to leave enough time for it in your discussion. |

# Index

academics 7, 19, 25, 36, 38, 46, 56 n.27, 59, 79–81, 85–7, 105, 128, 130, 149, 157, 186–7, 190–1
accountability 6, 51, 63, 80, 84, 95, 110, 112
achievement 66–7, 69–71, 81–2, 84–6, 96, 99 n.10, 149, 194
acting (Singleton orientation) 189–90
adequacy 2–3, 5, 49, 51, 67, 104
Advanced Level qualifications (A Level) examination 6, 57–9, 61, 63–70, 72, 73 n.1–73 n.2, 74 n.8
algorithms 6, 58–60, 70, 75 n.11, 109
All Lives Matter 123, 126, 132–3
Anzac Day 8, 163–5, 167–74, 176–8, 182 n.3, 183 n.19, 189, 195
apprenticeship 25, 68, 70
*Aprende en Casa* (Learning at Home) program 36–7, 42–3
aptitude test 66, 68–9
Arlington Public Schools 6, 80–1, 84, 86, 89, 91, 94, 196
assignments 6, 65, 79–80, 83–6, 88–9, 107–8, 129, 146
attainment gap 62, 76 n.25
Australia 1, 146, 151, 163–5, 167, 173–80

Back to School Index 40–1
believing (Singleton orientation) 189–90
Black Lives Matter 123
boarding schools 15, 19–20
Business and Technology Education Council vocational qualifications (BTECs) 68–9, 73 n.1

California 82, 96, 145, 148
camera policy 7, 124–5, 128, 131, 136, 194

Canada 29, 146
Cantonese 143–5, 147, 150–2
Chinese 143–52, 154, 156–9, 160 n.1, 161 n.9
citizenship 1, 24, 27–8, 30, 43, 116, 133, 179, 197
civic goods 114
class size 14, 32 n.1, 41
cohort of students 57–60, 62–4, 69, 74 n.6–74 n.7, 75 n.11
common good 27, 43
community 2, 7–9, 17, 19, 28–30, 36, 39–40, 42, 44, 46, 86, 90–6, 104, 109, 114, 118, 126, 129–31, 136–9, 165, 168–71, 173–4, 176, 178–80, 186, 188, 196
consistency 58–9, 61, 65, 67, 81–4, 88, 125–7, 131–3, 192
control 45–7, 85, 117, 126, 128, 138
cost 7, 17, 19–21, 26, 36, 41–3, 56 n.30, 95, 195
Courageous Conversations Compass (Singleton) 189–90
Covid-19 pandemic 5–6, 36–9, 42–3, 45–7, 49, 51, 57–72, 82, 104, 108, 123–4, 126, 134, 136, 155, 189
curriculum 25, 27, 47, 60, 67, 86, 104, 107, 113, 129, 150–1, 165
cyberbullying 104–6, 113

data 49, 59, 61, 64, 67, 81, 87, 89, 94, 96, 107
decision-making 6, 10, 62, 135, 185–6, 198
deliberation 9–10, 27–30, 126, 186
*Democratic Education* (Gutmann) 27
Department for Education 58–9, 63, 72

development/child development 4, 10, 46, 67, 85, 109, 111, 114–15, 124, 136, 154, 171, 177–8, 186, 196
digitalization 104–5, 108, 114, 117, 120 n.6
digital learning 7, 37, 41–2, 45, 103–18, 123–39
direct subsidy schemes schools (DSS) 143, 145, 147, 161 n.9
diversity 35, 42, 46, 156, 158–9, 177, 180, 193
Duncan-Andrade, Jeffrey 92

education/educational
　adequate 2–3
　civic 5, 121 n.13
　debt 81, 99 n.10
　equity 2–3, 186–92, 194–5
　formal 28–9, 58, 136, 176
　informal 29
　private 28, 39, 42, 45, 48–9, 51, 193
　public 39, 44, 46, 48, 50–2
　quality 20, 23–6, 28, 48, 80, 93, 197
　universal 5
elementary school 1, 36, 40, 49, 91
elite schools 43, 45, 47–8
embodiment 10, 116
employment 59, 67, 70
England 6, 57, 61–3, 74 n.7–74 n.8
English as an Additional Language/dialect (EAL/D) 163
English language 25, 66, 70, 86, 94, 139, 143–6, 149–54, 158–9, 160 n.1, 163, 166, 170
environment/environmentalism 2, 7, 40, 44, 68, 83, 104, 106, 108, 115, 131, 150–6, 158, 175–6, 178–9
equality 2–3, 7, 47–8, 59
equitable discussion 185–98
equity 1–10, 41, 47, 80–5, 88–90, 92–6, 110, 113–14, 117–18, 170–1, 185–98
ethics 3–7, 9–10, 30, 37, 39, 41–2, 46–8, 68, 113, 118, 131–2, 135, 138–9, 173, 178, 189, 193–4

facilitation model 193–4, 199–202
facilitators 186–94, 196–7
families 1, 5, 7, 24, 35–44, 72, 80, 83, 87, 89–94, 96, 105, 124–5, 128–9, 131–2, 135, 137–8, 143, 147–9, 153, 157, 161, 163, 165, 167–9, 172–5, 178–9, 195
feeling (Singleton orientation) 189–90
Feldman, Joe 79–80, 98 n.2
flexibility 28, 61, 90, 118, 128
flipped classroom 107–8, 113–15
food market 7, 143–4
"four corners" discussions 192
Free Day Secondary Schools policy 17
freedom 45, 48, 50, 104, 112–13, 146, 154, 167
Free Primary Education (2003) 13
free speech 132
fund/funding 1–2, 5, 17, 19–21, 30, 38, 42, 57, 103–4, 107, 111, 179–80

gender 1, 9, 21, 25, 174–5
General Certificates of Secondary Education (GCSE) examination 6, 57–9, 70–2, 73 n.1–73 n.2
general will 138
Germany 1, 103, 121 n.13–121 n.14
grades/grading 1, 6–7, 9, 25, 32 n.1, 57–70, 79–97, 98 n.1–98 n.2, 103, 124, 128, 132, 137, 146, 152, 154, 167, 192, 196
*Grading for Equity* (Feldman) 79–80, 98 n.2
Gunston Middle School 81
Gutmann, Amy 27
Gymnasium 103, 119–20 n.2

Hauptschule school 103
Heidegger, Martin 115
high-income countries 22–3
homework policy 6, 9, 36, 64, 79–97, 146, 151–3, 156, 194–6
Hong Kong 7, 143–61 n.3, 160 n.1–160 n.2, 161 n.6, 162 n.12, 195, 197–8

human rights framework 21, 26–8
hybrid learning 104–5, 107, 109–11, 123

Illinois 86
implicit bias 81
inclusivity 188–90
inequality 3, 18, 37, 41–4, 46–7, 50–1, 69, 88–9, 93, 129–30, 133, 194
injustice 60, 117, 135, 197
innovation 23, 25–6, 28, 30
integrity 67, 131–2
international school 143, 145, 147–54, 156–8, 160 n.3, 161 n.4, 161 n.6

justice 2, 5, 16, 21, 25–6, 28, 30, 35, 43, 52, 64, 69, 110, 123

Kenya 13–31, 195
knowledge 22, 24–5, 52, 85, 114, 117, 154–5, 165, 167, 173, 191
*Kultusministerium* (funding program) 103–4, 107, 120 n.3

Ladson-Billings, Gloria 81, 99 n.10
local schools 143, 145, 147–8, 150–4, 156–8, 160 n.1
Loft, Bridget 81, 83–5
López Obrador, Andrés Manuel 37
low-income countries 22
low-income students 81–3

Mandarin. *See* Chinese
Massachusetts 82
Matthews, Jay 80–1
media literacy 177
Meister-Eckhart-Gymnasium (MEG) 104, 107–8, 119 n.3
mental health 41
Mexico 1, 5–6, 35–45, 47–8, 50–2, 193
middle-class school 36, 39, 43–4, 48, 51, 62, 69, 76 n.23, 80, 83
migrants 1, 23
mock (practice) examinations 59, 64

Montessori schools 40
motivation 81, 85, 90, 109, 114, 150–2, 155, 189, 192

NAACP 81, 83, 87
national exams 18, 33 n.8, 57–8, 60
National Institute for the Evaluation of Education (INEE) 47
net enrollment 55 n.15, 55 n.18
Net Enrollment Rate (NER) 13
New South Wales schools 163, 180
normative case studies (NCS) 1, 3–10, 152, 185, 188–9, 191, 193–4, 197

OCR 61
OECD 19
Office of Qualifications and Examination Regulation (Ofqual) 59
online learning 6–7, 64, 103–18, 120 n.8, 134
opportunity 2, 6, 17, 22–3, 25–6, 29, 44, 46, 57–60, 66, 68, 70–1, 84, 89, 92, 94, 103, 124, 148, 158, 169–70, 176, 180, 186–7, 193, 197–8
*Opportunity to Return* 40–1

parents
    individual 155, 157, 195
    rights 126–8, 132, 135–7, 149, 174
    voice 83, 91, 95
pedagogy 8, 10, 40–1, 88, 112–14, 117, 151, 158, 165, 178
people with disabilities 1, 23, 81, 84, 154
personal connections 192
pluralism 35
policy 18, 23–4, 26–7, 29, 82–5, 92, 94, 124, 202. *See also* camera policy; homework policy
policymakers 1–2, 18, 22, 26, 30, 58, 60, 62–3, 83, 99 n.10, 179–80, 185, 198
population 8, 22–3, 29, 35, 37–40, 42, 46–7, 81, 151, 163–4
pornography 105, 111, 113
post-secondary education 84, 161 n.6

## Index

poverty 18, 20, 22, 165
preschool 1, 36, 38, 44–5, 49
primary school 1, 5, 7–8, 13–14, 16–17, 24, 28, 36, 49, 67, 149, 154, 177
privacy 7, 131–2, 135
private schools 5–6, 35–52
PROFECO (The Federal Consumer Attorney) 50
psychology 105, 111, 163
public education 39, 44, 48, 50–2
public policy 20, 27, 30, 47
Public Policy and Basic Education Act (2013) 13
public school 6, 8, 35, 38, 41–6, 48–51, 80, 96, 123, 134, 149, 163–80
public system 37–8, 40, 43, 48–51
pupil-teacher ratio 23–4

racism 8, 92, 94, 123, 132, 139, 156, 158, 189
Rawls, John 21, 51
reader's theater 187, 191–2
Realschule school 103
religious schools 42, 50, 171
remote learning. *See* digital learning
responsibility 6, 26, 28, 42, 65, 85, 110, 112, 133, 138, 154
restorative practices/justice 89
Returned and Services League (RSL) of Australia 165, 167–8, 174
rural students 22–4, 36–7, 41

safety codes 15
Salinas Pliego, Ricardo 41
SAT score 66, 68
school/schooling 2, 5, 7, 20, 22, 28, 38, 60–1, 148–9, 154, 177, 194–5
   administration 39, 72, 87, 103, 138
   closures 5, 39, 47, 50, 55 n.22, 60–2, 68, 124
   counseling 105, 111–12
   fees 17, 36–7, 39, 42, 44–5, 175
   finance 5, 28, 37, 39, 42, 50, 104, 148–9

   funding (*See* fund/funding)
   leadership 5, 8, 14, 29, 36, 58–9, 63, 65, 90, 118, 130, 134, 153, 173, 176, 195, 198
   reform 6–7, 111, 158
   structural improvements 104, 111–12
   systems 5, 7, 13, 21, 23, 87–8
secondary schools 5, 8, 13–19, 22–4, 36–8, 46, 48–9, 71, 149–50
Secretariat of Public Education (SEP) 46–7, 51
self-efficacy 105, 115
self-esteem 113
Singapore 29
Singleton, G. E. 189–90
small group discussion 187
smartphone 106–7, 114–17
SMV (*Schülermitverwaltung*) 108, 121 n.12
social capital 22
social class 94
   middle-class 36, 39, 43–4, 48, 51, 62, 69, 80, 83
   segregation 43–5
   upper-middle-class 48
   working-class students 62
social-emotional learning 41, 111
social inequality 18, 43
social justice 21, 25, 43, 52, 69, 139
social media 36, 105
South Korea 29
special education 81
stakeholders 3, 26, 28, 87, 91, 131, 135–6, 171, 189, 191, 194–5
standardized tests 98 n.1
standards-based grading 81, 83, 85
Status, Certainty, Autonomy, Relatedness, and Fairness (SCARF) framework 173, 175
student
   behavior 81–2, 85
   fairness 61–2
student-centered learning 90

students of color 6, 81, 84, 99 n.10
students with disabilities 1, 81, 84
supporting materials 187

Taiwan 151, 155–6, 158
taxes 37, 39–40, 42–5, 51, 104
teachers
    assessment 6, 59–60, 62, 70
    challenges for 64–8
    workload 89–90, 134
technology 23–4, 28, 30–1, 71, 103–5, 107–18, 197
testing (standardized tests) 62, 69, 72, 98 n.1, 103, 166
thinking (Singleton orientation) 189–90
time constraints 186–7
traditional classroom 7, 25, 117, 197
tuition 17, 20, 39, 42, 51, 143, 160–1 n.3, 160 n.1

the United States of America 1, 4, 6–7, 66–7, 79, 103, 123, 154, 158, 164
universal/compulsory education 5, 13, 17, 24, 38, 49, 164, 175

universities 5–6, 26, 57–60, 63–4, 66–9, 71–2, 74 n.8, 103, 106, 113–14, 145–7
upper-secondary education 36, 38–9

values 3–4, 29, 46–8, 67, 92, 94–5, 113, 131, 135–6, 138–9, 148–50, 154–5, 157–8, 173, 175, 177, 185–6, 188–9, 191–2, 196, 198, 201–2
Vietnam 29
Virginia 6, 80
Virtual Fridays 7, 124–5, 132–4, 192
virtual learning. *See* digital learning
vulnerability 8, 19, 37–40, 42, 46–7, 174

Waldorf school 46
Walker, Symone 81, 84, 87
Washington, D.C. 80
*The Washington Post* 80
women's education 22–3, 153, 171, 173, 176, 180
World Bank 18, 29–30

Zoom classroom 7, 124–5, 127–9, 132–4